TRAVELING *a* PILGRIM'S PATH

PREPARING YOUR CHILD TO NAVIGATE THE JOURNEY OF FAITH

FOCUS ON THE FAMILY®

TRAVELING *a* PILGRIM'S PATH

PREPARING YOUR CHILD TO NAVIGATE THE JOURNEY OF FAITH

TYNDALE

Tyndale House Publishers, Inc.
Wheaton, Illinois

CRAIG & JANET PARSHALL

A road map for parents drawn from John Bunyan's classic

PILGRIM'S PROGRESS

TRAVELING A PILGRIM'S PATH

Library of Congress Cataloging-in-Publication Data
Parshall, Craig, 1950-
Traveling a pilgrim's path: preparing your child to navigate the journey of faith /
Craig & Janet Parshall.
     p. cm.
At head of title: Focus on the Family.
Includes bibliographical references.
  ISBN 1-58997-048-9
1. Christian education of children. 2. Parenting—Religious aspects—Christianity.
3. Christian children—Religious life. I. Parshall, Janet, 1950- II. Title.
BV1475.3 .P37 2003
248.8'45—dc21   2003009992

A Focus on the Family book published by
Tyndale House Publishers, Wheaton, Illinois.

Editor: John Duckworth
Cover design: Kurt Birky
Cover photo: Photodisc

Printed in the United States of America

03 04 05 06 07 08 09/10 9 8 7 6 5 4 3 2 1

Table of Contents

Dedication

To our granddaughter, Madeline Parshall, and to all of those
other precious grandchildren that may also come along:
May their feet be quick to follow the pilgrim's path,
and may their hearts delight in the way of the Lord.

Acknowledgments

Many thanks are due to Kurt Bruner and Mark Maddox at Focus on the Family, for encouraging us in the vision that would finally become this book. We are ever thankful, also, to John Duckworth for his editorial contribution—particularly in helping us to make this book (we hope and pray) a practical guide for parents.

Marilyn Clifton, our administrative assistant, was, as always, instrumental in providing us with research; secretary Sharon Donehey's help was greatly appreciated in the manuscript preparation.

But it is our four children—Sarah, Rebekah, Samuel, and Joseph—who truly gave us the motivation to write this book. God appointed them to bring to the two of us both the blessing and the challenges that come with parenting. Through raising them, we saw God's Word proved reliable, His love shown incomprehensible, and the resource of prayer made invaluable!

Finally, we thank John Bunyan himself. Did he know, as he sat in that forlorn jail in Bedford, England, how his allegorical story of every Christian pilgrim's journey would convict, inspire, and encourage fellow travelers for hundreds of years hence?

We will have to keep that question for another day—when we look him up among the happy inhabitants of the Celestial City.

Chapter 1

INTRODUCTION

The Adventure Begins

This book will make a traveler of you,
If you'll agree that its advice is true;
It will direct you to your heavenly home,
If you can understand its prose and poem.
Yes, it will give the lazy energy;
And cause the blind delightful things to see.
—*John Bunyan*

Everyone loves a good journey. We all like to see new places and new things, and break from the patterns of our everyday lives.

When the Parshalls take a family trip, things usually go pretty much as planned. Sure, we may have a flat tire. Or we forget to bring along extra change for a tollbooth, or we leave behind a favorite pair of sneakers. By and large, though, family trips tend to be rather predictable and safe.

Imagine for a moment, however, taking your children on a trip through the war-torn mountains of Afghanistan. There's danger at every turn: The dusty roads are filled with land mines, and snipers fire at you from the hills.

Or think of having to sail your family across the ocean—not on an ocean liner, but on a homemade raft. Like Tom Hanks in the movie *Cast*

Away, you lash logs and beach debris together. You set sail, but storms batter your tiny craft and it slowly begins falling apart. Great whales rise from the deep; one flip of their tails could send you to the bottom.

Could you protect your child on that kind of journey?

Chances are you won't have to. But these hazardous scenarios are all too similar to a trip your children *will* have to take: the journey into the perilous world of the near future.

DANGEROUS JOURNEY

If anyone doubted that our world has grown more dangerous, the question was settled by the September 2001 terrorist attacks on the World Trade Center and Pentagon. Even before that, though, the news was filled with stories of school shootings and drive-by gang violence.

Other dangers have crept up more subtly. Movies, music videos, video games, and shock-rock have filled the minds of children and teenagers with violence, super-sexuality, and anarchy. In the U.S., society has steadily drifted away from the idea of "one nation under God," replacing it with official hostility toward expressions of Christian faith in the public arena. Children face titanic pressures to experiment sexually. And even in the church, a large percentage of teens and preteens don't know the core beliefs of Christianity—much less believe them.

If all this gives you a sinking feeling, join the club. It's that feeling you get when you realize that your child's journey is going to look less like a family trip to Aunt Tillie's, and more like that ride through a war zone in Afghanistan. What you thought would be a pleasant jaunt to the beach has suddenly turned into a harrowing ordeal on a crumbling raft in the middle of the Pacific.

That's the bad news about the quest our children are about to undertake.

But there's good news, too. We've discovered a resource that can help parents prepare their children for the challenges ahead. Parenting for the twenty-first century is a task that was modeled for us long ago in this resource. Using it, we can equip our sons and daughters to follow Jesus in the decades to come. That's because the dangers and challenges of the future, though they may come in new forms, are found along a well-worn path.

A SPIRITUAL TRAVEL GUIDE

What we Christian parents need is a paradigm—a pattern to show our children which way to go in the decades ahead. True, the Bible is the ultimate authority in raising our children—a God-inspired road map. But is there a "travel guide" to give us hints about pitfalls to avoid, great places to stay, and the route that will get us to our desired destination?

We discovered such a "travel guide" when our children were young. It happened when we began reading to them from a children's version of John Bunyan's classic, *The Pilgrim's Progress.*

The two of us had read the story as literature in college. We loved this thoroughly biblical, highly imaginative allegory. It appealed to our sense of drama and provided a practical view of the road each Christian must travel.

As parents, we were looking for a way to hold the attention of our young listeners while instructing them on the basics of the Christian life. *Pilgrim's Progress* did both, and quickly became a favorite in our house.

Now that our children are grown (Sarah, our oldest, is a married lawyer in the Baltimore area; Samuel is married, has a new baby, and is finishing up graduate school; Joseph is in college; daughter Rebekah has returned to graduate school after acting with a Shakespearean theater company), we're glad we made *Pilgrim's Progress* an important part of our family life.

A LOOK AT THE BOOK

We aren't the only ones who love *Pilgrim's Progress*, of course. Next to the Bible, it's been ranked as the most-read book in history. Though first published in 1678, it retains incredible relevance to modern believers.

Since *Pilgrim's Progress* was written in the prose of Bunyan's day, you and your family may want to use one of the contemporary versions available. The excerpts from *Pilgrim's Progress* in this book are adapted and abridged in modern English from an 1853 edition; you'll find them in italics.

Pilgrim's Progress reminds us that the Christian journey, from acceptance of Jesus Christ to arrival in heaven (the "Celestial City," Bunyan calls it), is a great adventure. It's easy to forget that as we view the traps and temptations surrounding our children in the twenty-first century, but with the help of this story we can approach parenting with less fear and trembling—and more faith and confidence.

That's not because Bunyan pulls his punches. Far from it! *Pilgrim's Progress* is a powerfully practical view of the trials and tribulations all of us encounter in our walk with the Lord. It's no glossy, "everything's rosy" view of the Christian life. It uncovers the warts-and-all truth about us "sheep" who struggle to follow the Good Shepherd.

In Bunyan's story you and your children will meet a host of characters—some good, some bad, some downright hideous. Each has a revealing name—Atheist, Faithful, Evangelist, Goodwill, Hypocrisy, and many more.

The hero of the story is named Christian. Married, with children, he lives in the city of Destruction at the start of the tale. When we first meet him, he's in tears—despondent over what he's read in a book (the Bible). It seems God's judgment is coming to his town.

But then he meets Evangelist, who gives him a scroll and instructions to head for the "narrow gate" not far away. There he'll receive directions on how to escape the impending judgment.

Christian tries to convince his wife and children to leave with him, but they refuse. (A few years later, in a sequel, they would change their minds and follow Christian's footsteps.) Sad but determined, Christian sets out alone on his pilgrimage.

Even in this there is a powerful message for us as parents. No matter how much we may support and direct our children's spiritual journeys, in the end they will have to travel the road by themselves—with God's help.

And what an adventure that journey is going to be!

BUNYAN'S PROGRESS

If *Pilgrim's Progress* is our travel guide, what about its author? What kind of tour leader does he make?

Of all those in seventeenth-century England, John Bunyan could have won the title "Least Likely to Write a Christian Masterpiece Influencing Millions Around the World." Yet that's exactly what he did.

Bunyan was born to a poor family near Bedford, England, in 1628. The nation was in the midst of a great religious and political struggle; the Parliamentarians, led by Oliver Cromwell and supported by the Puritans, sought democratic representation. The Crown resisted.

Civil war broke out in 1644. At age 16, John Bunyan was recruited into the army, on the side of the Parliamentarians. After spending most of his teen years in the military, he quickly married.

Bunyan was anything but the "religious" type as a young man. He gained a reputation in his hometown as a foul-mouthed troublemaker. One who knew him described him as "a very great, profane sinner, and an illiterate man."

But then Bunyan met John Gifford, a Bedford pastor who had persecuted Puritans before accepting Christ as Savior. When Gifford presented the gospel, Bunyan responded by embracing Jesus.

Still, Bunyan's spiritual journey would take several twists and turns. At first he was plagued by self-doubt, unable to believe that God's grace was enough to save a sinner like himself. Constant backsliding into old habits only made things worse.

When he finally understood the nature of grace, and the absolute sufficiency of Jesus' sacrifice on the cross, Bunyan became a changed man. He dove into Bible study, joined Gifford's church, and was a sold-out disciple of Jesus. Eventually he was convinced that God had called him to preach.

But that presented a problem. Preachers were required to register with the government—and to agree never to preach any doctrine at odds with the Church of England.

Bunyan, believing that preaching the truth must never be compromised or restricted, refused to follow the rule. He was in mid-sermon when two sheriffs from the king arrived with an arrest warrant and took him to jail.

Thus began the first of Bunyan's imprisonments. The first lasted 12 years; the second was shorter. He was separated from his impoverished family, languishing alone in the dark, filthy confines of his Bedford cell.

But something amazing happened during those years. As Bunyan pleaded with God in prayer and devoured the Scriptures daily, a vision of the Christian life formed in his fertile imagination. His doubts, struggles, sufferings, and victories took on an allegorical life of their own.

The seeds of *Pilgrim's Progress* had taken root.

Let's Go!

As Bunyan began scratching out the story that would touch generations, he was doing something for us as twenty-first-century Christian parents. He was telling a tale so biblical in its foundation, so universal in its application, that it can guide us as we direct and protect our families in the decade ahead.

It's time to head down the narrow path. Our children are already on their way.

We're headed in that direction too. Won't you join us as we begin the great adventure?

Do you seek something rare and profitable?
Can you uncover truth within a parable?
Are you forgetful? Need help to remember
From New Year's Day till ending of December?
Then read my musings; they will stick like burs,
And may be, to the helpless, comforters....
Would you then read, perhaps not knowing what,
Yet know for certain that you're blessed or not
By reading the same lines? Well, then, let's start,
And join my book together with your head and heart.

Chapter 2

THE NARROW GATE

Guiding Your Child to Spiritual Commitment

—◦

"Well, neighbor Obstinate," said Pliable, "I have reached a decision. I intend to go along to the Celestial City with this good man, and to cast my lot with him." He turned to Christian. "But, my good companion, do you know the way to this desired place?"

Christian nodded. "I was told by a man named Evangelist to go quickly to a little gate that is before us, where we shall receive instructions about the way."

"Come then, good neighbor," said Pliable. "Let us be going." Then they set off together.

Eventually Pliable encountered difficulty and turned back. But Christian reached the gate, a sturdy panel of stout, rough cedar boards. Over it, written in gold on a white-painted plank, was, "Knock and the door will be opened to you" (Matthew 7:7).

So he knocked.

There was no response.

He rapped again, but nothing happened.

A third knock produced the same result.

Finally he cleared his throat, and his voice was hesitant:

"May I now enter here? Will he inside
Open the door, and wide, though I
Do not deserve it? If so, I vow
To sing his lasting praises, starting now."

A Gate Worth Finding

A lot of travelers would have given up by now. Just getting to the gate has been a daunting challenge for Christian!

First, he had to conquer the dangers of the Slough of Despond. This fearful swamp drowned its victims in the muck and mire of guilt. Christian fell into the despicable bog—and because of the huge burden of sin on his back, began to sink deeper and deeper. In the nick of time, a man named Help arrived to haul Christian out.

Then Christian encountered Mr. Worldly-Wiseman—a self-assured fellow from the town of Carnal Policy. Warning of woes on the road ahead, Worldly-Wiseman convinced Christian to take a side route through the Village of Morality. It was a disastrous detour; Christian, tricked into passing by Mr. Legality's house, found himself under a high cliff with a dangerous overhang. Flashes of fire filled the sky as the terrified pilgrim froze in his steps, afraid that the cliff might fall on him, or that he would be burned to death.

Fortunately, Christian's mentor Evangelist reappeared—and declared that the pilgrim had gotten sidetracked. Evangelist explained that the path to the Village of Morality had been founded on moral law, but lacked the forgiveness found only in Jesus Christ. Reminded by Evangelist to head for the straight and narrow gate that leads to salvation, Christian finally reached that modest-looking entrance.

At last a grim-faced, gray-haired man named Goodwill came to the gate. "Who are you?" he asked. "Where do you come from, and what do you want?"

Christian looked down at the ground. "I ... I am a poor, burdened sinner," he said. "I come from the city of Destruction, but am going to Mount

Zion, so that I may be spared the punishment to come." He lifted his chin, but not his eyes. "I've been told that going through this gate is the way to get there. That's why I need to know whether you are willing to let me in."

A gentle smile slowly replaced Goodwill's somber expression. "I am willing with all my heart," he said. And with that he unlatched the gate.

LET ME IN!

Clearly, Bunyan wanted the gate Christian encountered to symbolize a truth Jesus had taught: "Enter through the narrow gate. For wide is the gate and broad is the road that leads to destruction, and many enter through it. But small is the gate and narrow the road that leads to life, and only a few find it" (Matthew 7:13-14).

Christian has entered the gate—and his life will never be the same.

Goodwill turned away, peering into the distance. "So," he asked, "who directed you to come this way?"

"Evangelist told me to come here and knock, as I did. And he said that you, Sir, would tell me what I must do."

Placing a hand on the gate, Goodwill looked Christian in the eye. "An open door is set before you," he declared, "and no man can shut it."

DON'T CLOSE THE DOOR!

Has your child entered through the narrow gate?

As Christian parents, we need to shepherd our children, tenderly but surely, to that same life-changing entrance.

It's easy to lose sight of that priority when we spend so much time providing a home, putting food on the table, nursing them when they're sick, playing with them, and supervising their education. But our number-one task is to teach and model the truth of the gospel. If we don't direct our children toward an eternal destiny as followers of Jesus Christ, we've neglected our highest privilege and most profound responsibility.

It's not an unpleasant duty—but it's a 24/7 effort. Note the *continuous* approach God told Israelite parents to use as they passed truths about the Lord to the next generation: "These commandments that I give you today are to be upon your hearts. Impress them on your children. Talk about them when you sit at home and when you walk along the road, when you lie down and when you get up" (Deuteronomy 6:6-7).

The toughest part of this assignment is not the "talk," but the "walk." Our own children watched us carefully, wanting to see if what we said aligned with what we did. In our family, as in yours, values have been more "caught" than "taught."

Families like ours—and yours—provide the best environment for leading children to Christ. Just as Evangelist led Christian to the narrow gate, we parents are called to instruct our young pilgrims about the reality of sin, the pitfalls of the world, and the need to head straight for the gate that leads to forgiveness and eternal life.

THE CONVERSION EXPERIENCE

Some parents wonder what it should look like when their children receive Christ as Savior. For Christian, it looked something like this:

The highway up which Christian was to go was fenced on either side with a wall. That wall was called Salvation. So up this way did the burdened Christian run—but not without great difficulty, because of the load on his back.

He kept running until he came to a small hill. On it was a cross; at the bottom was a tomb.

Just as Christian reached the cross, his burden loosened from his shoulders and fell from his back. It began to tumble down the hill. It rolled to the mouth of the tomb—where it fell in, and was gone.

Christian grinned. He looked as if he might float into the sky at any second. When he spoke, it was almost with a laugh: "He has given me rest through His sorrow, and life by His death!"

Then he stood still a while, staring. Why, he wondered, did the sight of the cross ease him of his burden? He looked, and looked again, even till the tears began to fall down his cheeks.

As he stood looking and weeping, three strangers approached. Their faces and clothes shone like glass in the sun. Christian's hand flew up instinctively to shield his eyes.

"Peace be to you," the Shining Ones saluted him.

"Your sins are forgiven," the first stranger announced.

The second stranger stripped Christian of the rags he was wearing, then helped him change into a crisp, clean outfit.

The third stranger pulled a stamp from his pocket and inked a mark on Christian's forehead. From the other pocket he produced a small book. "Read this as you travel," the man said, "and when you reach the celestial gate, turn it in."

Stunned, Christian could only nod. Then he watched as the three glowing figures continued down the road and finally disappeared.

Will your child's experience differ from this? Of course! And that's as it should be.

Looking back at our own four children, we're thrilled to remember how they invited Jesus Christ into their hearts in different ways and at different times. Most were at home; one was on a family vacation. Our two daughters responded directly to our own presentations of how to begin a relationship with God; our oldest son was led to the Lord by his sister.

Our youngest son, Joseph, had still another story. He seemed very interested in the gospel and listened carefully as the plan of salvation was explained to him at bedtime one night. Looking down into his big, brown eyes, we told him about God's unconditional love.

How we wanted this little one to know and experience God! We knew that what he was hearing could change his life forever, and his choice would have eternal ramifications. Pretty big stuff for a seven-year-old!

His response: "I want to think it over."

For us, it was an anguished moment. Somehow we resisted the temptation to coerce a confession of faith from this precious person, and respected his need to make an authentic decision for Christ.

The next morning our son walked into the kitchen—and promptly announced that he was ready to invite Jesus into his heart! God heard our silent hallelujahs, even if our son couldn't.

Each of our children's decisions for Christ was preceded by slow, consistent teaching about Jesus that occurred in a variety of settings—during car trips, at the dinner table, in Sunday school, at bedtime, and on nature hikes. We found that all of life is an opportunity to share the love of Christ with our children.

That's why kids need not just *quality* time, but *quantity* time. Introducing them to Jesus is a time-intensive, long-term project. They usually don't wait patiently for an "altar call" at family devotions. We can't predict when the soft soil of their hearts will be ready to receive the seed of a gospel invitation.

You've Only Just Begun

Challenging as it may be to lead our kids to the narrow gate, we need to remember that the journey only *begins* there.

When Christian began his sojourn, he decided to seek the benefit of the pilgrim's path that lay beyond the gate. He became *spiritually committed* to follow God's way.

As parents, we want our children to commit themselves to continuing—not just starting—the journey. Such dedication has never been easy, but it's harder than ever today. Apathy and cynicism about spiritual truth are likely to increase in the coming decade, especially among young people. We need to understand the forces that are working against us.

Today's kids are enticed into passivity—the opposite of commitment. Affluence and a commercial culture encourage self-indulgence and self-gratification. The idea of recognizing personal sin seems quaint. Committing to a spiritually disciplined life is seen as a pointless and loathsome chore.

These trends are not only present in the "secular" world; they're also prevalent in the church. According to a study by the Barna Research Group, the majority of believing Christians admitted that they were more influenced by financial self-interest than by spiritual values. Barna found that fewer than half of "born-again" teenagers claimed an absolute commitment to their Christian faith.[1] Only 43 percent of Christian teens said they were likely to be personally active in a Christian church after they leave their families.[2]

While there is talk of "spirituality" among teens, there is a decreasing number of Bible-believing, born-again evangelicals in that category—dropping from 10 percent in 1991 to 4 percent in 2000.[3]

With God's help we can reverse this trend, starting with our own children. We can point them toward the straight and narrow way that begins at the gate of salvation.

The earlier we start this process, the better. Research by Barna also shows that children ages 5 to 13 are about 5 times more likely to accept Christ as Savior than when they reach the age of 19.[4] As the primary "Evangelists" to our young pilgrims, we must bring the message of Christ to them as early as possible—and continue to teach them at every opportunity.

TAKING ACTION

How can we accomplish those lofty goals? What strategies can help you lead your children toward genuine commitment to Christ?

To answer that question, consider how Hopeful, Christian's fellow pilgrim, became convinced that Jesus deserved his belief and loyalty:

As Christian and Hopeful hiked down the road, their conversation turned to the manner in which Hopeful had begun his journey. "And how was the Lord revealed to you?" Christian asked.

Hopeful hesitated. "I did not see Him with my bodily eyes," he said at last, "but with the eyes of my understanding. One day I was very sad—I think sadder than at any other time in my life. It was because I'd gained a fresh sight of the greatness and vileness of my sins." He looked down at the dirt, as if remembering. "I could think of nothing but hell, and the everlasting damnation of my soul. But suddenly I seemed to see the Lord Jesus looking down from heaven on me, and saying, 'Believe on the Lord Jesus Christ, and you will be saved.'"

Hopeful shook his head. "I told the Lord I was a very great sinner. He answered, 'My grace is sufficient for you.'

"Tears came to my eyes," Hopeful said, his voice husky. "I asked further, 'But, Lord, can such a terrible sinner as I really be accepted and saved by You?'

"It was as if Jesus Himself answered, 'He who comes to Me, I will not cast out.'"

His pace slowing, Hopeful scratched his chin thoughtfully. "From all of this I gathered that I must look for righteousness in Jesus, and for payment for my sins by His blood. I saw that He died in obedience to His Father—not for Himself, but for anyone who will accept that gift and be thankful for that sacrifice."

Hopeful halted in the middle of the road and threw his arms skyward. "My heart was full of joy, my eyes full of tears. My love for the name, people, and ways of Jesus Christ was running over!"

Christian smiled. "This was indeed a revelation of Christ to your soul. But tell me what effect it had on your spirit."

Hopeful folded his arms across his chest, thinking. "It made me see that all the world is in a state of condemnation. It made me see that God the Father, though He is just, can justly justify the sinner who comes to Him. It made me greatly ashamed of my former life, and angry over how ignorant I had been. After all, I'd never had a thought that so clearly showed me the beauty of Jesus Christ. It made me love a holy life, and long to do something for the honor and glory of the name of the Lord Jesus."

He fixed Christian with an earnest look. "I thought that if I had a thousand gallons of blood in my body, I could spill it all for the sake of the Lord Jesus."

❧ ❧

GETTING THROUGH THE GATE:
PRACTICAL PROGRESS FOR PARENTS AND KIDS

Hopeful's trip through the narrow gate revolutionized his priorities, his view of God, even his view of himself. Why? Because that process followed three principles every Evangelist—parental or otherwise—needs to know.

Principle #1: Open the Eyes of Their Understanding

"I did not see Him with my bodily eyes," Hopeful said, "but with the eyes of my understanding." In order to choose Christ, our kids must *understand* what they're doing. True, no human can completely fathom the mysteries of why and how God redeems people. But pressing unprepared children to make a decision for Christ, or marching them through the "motions" of conversion, is counterproductive. It yields "converts" whose "faith" is confused and feeble, often based on fear or a desire for parental approval. Children who are rushed through the gate, not knowing where they've been or where they're going, are likely to leave the straight and narrow path sooner or later.

Parental Action: Build a Foundation

To ensure that your child has enough background to make an informed choice about belonging to Jesus, try the following.

Reveal your relationship. As Rick Osborne and Marnie Wooding write in *God's Great News for Children*:

> Many parents wonder how to help their children build a lasting relationship with Jesus. The first step in any relationship is an introduction. Children learn about relationships by watching their parents interact with others. Including your children in your relationship with Jesus is the first step.... Sharing your relationship with God demonstrates that God is an important part of your life.[5]

Toward that end, let your child watch you relate to God. Here's how:

- Show your son or daughter a list of things and people you've been praying about.
- Invite him or her to listen with you to a favorite praise song; talk about how it helps you worship.
- Share a problem-solving insight you've gained through reading the Bible.
- If a special spot—perhaps a park bench, beach, or forest trail—helps you meditate on God's greatness, bring your child next time you go there and explain its significance.

What if your relationship with God isn't perfect? Join the club! Your child needs to understand that his or her journey with Jesus will have its ups and downs too. Instead of faking piety, let your kids see your struggles with unanswered prayer and lingering questions. When you fail, admit it—and use the opportunity to express thanks for God's grace and forgiveness.

Unfurl an overview. Many children in Christian families collect scraps of biblical truth over the years, but never quite stitch them together into the "big picture." Does your child understand the why and how of deciding to follow Jesus, or has she merely picked up bits and pieces about Philistines, Pharisees, and Philippians? To help her grasp the basics, explain briefly who

Jesus is, why He had to die for us, and how to receive God's forgiveness. Depending on the age of your child, you might want to share a summary like the following, adapted from "The Gospel in a Nutshell" (*Focus on the Family Parents' Guide to the Spiritual Growth of Children*):

1. Everyone has sinned (done things that are wrong).
2. The penalty for sin is death.
3. Jesus never sinned, so He didn't deserve death.
4. Jesus willingly paid the death penalty for everyone else.
5. Because of that, all who accept Jesus' death as payment for their sins can be forgiven and have a wonderful relationship with God as His children.[6]

These Bible verses may be helpful too:

- "For all have sinned and fall short of the glory of God" (Romans 3:23).
- "The wages of sin is death" (Romans 6:23).
- "Without the shedding of blood there is no forgiveness" (Hebrews 9:22).
- "For God so loved the world that he gave his one and only Son, that whoever believes in him shall not perish but have eternal life" (John 3:16).
- "The gift of God is eternal life in Christ Jesus our Lord" (Romans 6:23).
- "If you confess with your mouth, 'Jesus is Lord,' and believe in your heart that God raised him from the dead, you will be saved. For it is with your heart that you believe and are justified, and it is with your mouth that you confess and are saved" (Romans 10:9-10).
- See also Romans 3:21-26; Colossians 2:13-15; Hebrews 9:23-28.

For more help in sharing the "big picture" with young children, see *God's Great News for Children*. And keep in mind this reassuring thought from the authors: "There are no textbook answers to sharing the Gospel with your child. God will provide you those moments to share because He wants your child to come to Him even more than you do. Relax, God is on your side."[7]

Parental Action: Connect Facts and Feelings

Hopeful's encounter with the gospel wasn't just a matter of theology. It was intensely emotional. "One day I was very sad—I think sadder than at any other time in my life," he recalled. "It was because I'd gained a fresh sight of the greatness and vileness of my sins."

Our children need to see the emotional side of salvation, too—not to shame or scare them through the gate, but to make sure the message reaches their hearts as well as their heads. Not every child will cry when pondering how his or her sins led to Christ's painful death, but it's only natural to feel pangs of regret. Not every child will jump for joy when God's forgiveness lifts the burden of guilt, but it makes perfect sense to feel like celebrating.

As one child exclaimed after praying to receive Christ as Savior, "I feel so light, I feel like I could fly!" Our kids need the chance to experience and express the emotions that come with such a life-changing decision.

To help your child do that, try the following:

Consider God's feelings. Encourage your child to see things from God's point of view. Ask, "How do you think God felt when Adam and Eve disobeyed? How do you think He feels when you do something wrong?" Don't stop with negative emotions, however; help your child sense the love the Father must have felt for us in order to send His only Son.

Take your time. Let each concept sink in before moving on. If you quote Romans 3:23, for example, ask how your child feels about the fact that everyone has sinned. Is he embarrassed? Worried? Confident that there's "safety in numbers"? Your young pilgrim's reactions may not match Hopeful's—or yours. Instead of assuming that your child feels repentant and wants forgiveness, find out.

Throw a party. As Hopeful told Christian, once he had entered the gate of salvation, "My heart was full of joy, my eyes full of tears. My love for the name, people, and ways of Jesus Christ was running over!" Your child may not be quite so excited, but chances are that he or she will at least feel relieved and perhaps enthused about the adventure ahead. Mark the event with a "second birthday party" or a homemade "second birth certificate."

Principle #2: Be Equally Clear About the Bad and Good News

The word *gospel* means "good news," but a child who doesn't understand the bad news that precedes it may not see what all the fuss is about. After all, who needs "saving" if you're not about to drown?

There was no doubt in Hopeful's mind that his straits were dire. "I could think of nothing but hell, and the everlasting damnation of my soul," he said. Fortunately, the story didn't end there. "But suddenly I seemed to see the Lord Jesus looking down from heaven on me, and saying, 'Believe on the Lord Jesus Christ, and you will be saved.'"

Our kids need both sides of the story—the threat and the promise. Here's how to make sure they aren't shortchanged.

Parental Action: Talk Straight About Sin

Admit the problem. In John Bunyan's day, few Christians flinched at mentioning sin and eternal punishment. Today, however, many believing parents hesitate to bring up such "dark" subjects; their children are more likely to hear about the earthly benefits of belonging to Jesus, like inner peace and meaning. While kids can be confused by information for which they're not ready, offering them a cure without acknowledging the disease can be even more perplexing. Very young children may not grasp the concept of death, eternal or otherwise, but most understand what disobedience is—and that wrongdoing deserves a penalty.

You can explain the idea of sin and separation from God without frightening or puzzling your child. Here's how *God's Great News for Children*, designed for ages 5-9, presents the story of the Fall and its consequences for us:

> Adam and Eve had put their own will before God's and now everything changed. Their actions had built a wall of sin between them and their heavenly Father. God had to send them out of His wonderful garden.
>
> God still loved them very much, but because Adam and Eve had sinned, sin became part of them. It was like sin had put a hurt or scar on their spirit that would never go away. Even Adam and Eve's children would carry that scar and be born apart from God. And so would their children and so on, all the way to us today.[8]

Be sure to make the problem personal, too. Say to your child, "I've done some wrong things in my life. How about you?"

Parental Action: Offer Hope in God's Love

Tell the rest of the story. After giving your child a chance to mull over the "bad news," ask him or her, "If you were God, what would you do about this?"

Note the child's answer, which may tell you whether he or she sees God as loving, harsh, or indifferent. Then relate the "good news," perhaps along these lines from *God's Great News for Children*:

So is that it? The end of the story? Are people always going to be separated from God? No! Even though God hates sin, He loves us! He had a plan to help people get free of sin and come back to Him again. God the Father would send His Son, Jesus, into the world to wipe away the damage that Satan had done.[9]

Avoid jargon. It's easy for adults to use terms like "salvation"—and easy for kids to be mystified by them. Children may not understand what it means to be "saved," for instance, unless you speak first about being "rescued." Point out examples in the newspaper and on TV of people being rescued from fires, floods, and other dangers. Demonstrate "rescuing" your child from an imaginary alligator or earthquake. Then explain that Jesus came to rescue us.

Once they're in "rescue" mode, most kids can easily grasp the idea of being "saved"—as in saved from a mudslide, monster, or motorcycle crash.

Principle #3: Point Them to Christ Himself

"Follow Me!" Jesus called to those who would become His disciples. They did—drawn by His love, His miracles, His integrity, His courage. All too often, however, we parents call our children to follow us, or a church's doctrine, or a set of rules; Jesus ends up playing only a cameo role on the cross.

Hopeful, on the other hand, was attracted directly to Christ. "After all," he said, "I'd never had a thought that so clearly showed me the beauty of Jesus Christ. It made me love a holy life, and long to do something for the honor and glory of the name of the Lord Jesus."

Only Jesus inspires that kind of loyalty—or deserves it. Let's point our children in His direction and say, "Follow Him!"

Parental Action: Show Them His Beauty

Read all about it. Want a fresh look at Jesus? Read an eyewitness account of His life in Matthew, Mark, Luke, or John with your child. Rediscover the qualities that drew *you* to Him. Keep a running list of details you might not have noticed before, especially those that reveal Jesus as the kind of Person you and your child would like to follow. Some examples:

- The generous way Jesus called Judas "Friend," even when the latter came to betray Him (Matthew 26:50).
- The warmhearted way He not only allowed children to come to Him, but called them over (Luke 18:16).
- The straight-talking way He confronted a man He'd healed, saying, "See, you are well again. Stop sinning or something worse may happen to you" (John 5:14).

Watch Him at work. Rent a movie depicting the life of Christ and discuss it with your child. The *Jesus* film provides a straightforward retelling; *Jesus of Nazareth* uses more poetic license. For an older child, especially one who's "heard it all before" in Sunday school, you might want to try the energetic, thought-provoking (but much less literal) film version of the musical *Godspell.*

Parental Action: Ask for a Response

Hopeful, it seems, couldn't help but respond to Christ's offer of forgiveness. Does your child also understand the need to respond?

As the authors of *God's Great News for Children* advise kids,

> If you do something wrong and your parents are upset, you know they will forgive you. But remember, you still need to ask. It's the same with becoming God's child. Jesus already died for you and God will forgive you right away. But, you still need to ask. Nobody else can do it for you. God loves YOU![10]

When it appears that your child understands the basics of what Jesus has done for him or her, it's time to ask—not press—for a decision. You might say, "Do you want to pray now to ask God to forgive you and to let you start a relationship with Him?" Using the word *now* makes it easier for your boy or girl to pray alone, or for you to ask again later if needed.

GATEWAY TO ADVENTURE

When your young pilgrim chooses to enter the gate of salvation, both of you will have reason to rejoice. Pray for your child, and be patient. By God's grace, the day will come—if it hasn't already—when the two of you will share the joy Christian felt when his sins were forgiven:

At last he shook himself and smiled. Then he laughed. He jumped three times for joy, then set off down the path, singing:

"I came this far weighed down with all my sin;
No one could ease the grief that I was in,
Till I came here—and what a place is this!
It seems the beginning of my bliss.
It's where the burden fell down from my back,
And where the strings that bound it to me cracked.
Great cross! Great tomb! Or, should I say, praise be
To Him who there was put to shame for me!"

Chapter 3

A STEEP CLIMB

*Helping Your Child Deal with Difficulty
in a Culture of Comfort*

※⊙

*Christian came to the foot of the hill called Difficulty, at the bottom of which
was a spring. There was also a fork in the road; one way went to the left, the
other to the right, while the narrow way went straight up the hill.*

*Christian paused, drinking from the spring to refresh himself. Then he
began to scale the hill, saying,*

> *"I'll climb this mountain, even though it's steep;*
> *I'll make it even if I have to creep;*
> *For I can tell the way to life lies here:*
> *Come, pluck up, heart, let's neither faint nor fear.*
> *No matter if it's tough, the right way's best;*
> *The wrong way isn't worth it, even if it means a rest."*

*Two other men, Formalist and Hypocrisy, also came to the foot of the hill.
They saw that the hill was steep and high, and that there were two other ways
to go. "Surely these two ways will meet again with the one in the middle, on
the other side of the hill," they said. "Let's take them."*

One of these paths was named Danger; the other was Destruction. The man who took Danger ended up lost in a great forest; the one who followed Destruction found himself in a wide field, full of dark mountains, where he stumbled and fell, and rose no more.

~◉

WHEN THE GOING GETS TOUGH

Formalist and Hypocrisy picked routes that seemed easier than the path of Difficulty that lay straight before them—and paid an awful price. Christian, on the other hand, wisely took the way marked for followers of Jesus. But he quickly learned what all pilgrims learn—that the straight and narrow road is not always on level ground.

If you've done much bike riding, you know a little about the hill of Difficulty. When you begin riding at the bottom, the incline doesn't look too bad. But halfway up your heart pounds, your muscles quiver, you start to sweat, and your resolve to get to the top begins to waver.

Spiritually speaking, that hill might look like this:

- You resolve on New Year's Eve to get up early every morning and read your Bible, but by Valentine's Day you can't seem to drag yourself out of bed.
- You've always worked hard to be ethical at the office, but now the boss wants you to "cook the books" to make the company look more profitable—and you really need this job.
- You've prayed for 20 years that your aunt will become a Christian, but she's still hostile to "religion"—and you don't see the point of praying anymore.
- You've always trusted God to protect you and your family, but when your daughter loses a leg in a car accident, your faith seems to hit a brick wall.

Vince Lombardi, famed coach of the champion Green Bay Packers, said, "When the going gets tough, the tough get going!" That saying conveyed a powerful fact: The true test of our character comes on the steep roads, not the downhill stretches.

When our children pass through the gate of salvation, we need to tell them the truth: The Christian life is full of blessings, but it also takes effort. Choosing to obey the Lord Jesus means going against the ebb and flow of the world; taking the "easy way out," meanwhile, can mean heading for danger and destruction.

"It's Too Hard!"

Our children live in an era that's more conscious than ever of the need for physical exercise. But when it comes to spirituality and moral values, laziness is encouraged.

In our computer-driven digital age of technological convenience and instant gratification, the goal of life for many is to seek comfort, entertainment, leisure, and the path of least resistance. Spirituality is fine as long as it makes you feel good. But if it threatens your comfort, or requires that you break a sweat to help someone else, it's less popular than pedaling uphill.

Our son-in-law Matthew, a member of his church's youth ministry team, says that one of his most frustrating experiences is dealing with teens who are addicted to the easy road. He's worked with promising young men who seem serious about their relationship with God—but end up washing out. The problem? They don't have the discipline to stay on the right path. It's just too much work.

That's true of many kids, especially when it comes to entertainment choices. A disturbing number of young people—even those who consider themselves Christians—believe faith shouldn't be allowed to cramp their style when it comes to music, TV, movies, and the Internet. The book *Mind over Media* by Stan Campbell and Randy Southern quotes kids who think discernment would be too steep a slope to climb:

I just watch what is fun for me.... There's no limits.

—Rick L.

To be honest ... I pretty much watch whatever I want to....
I won't, like, walk out of a movie or anything like that.

—Khristen B.[1]

Many would-be pilgrims, it seems, are choosing not to climb anything higher than a molehill. That's no surprise in our comfort-first society, but it can be disastrous for our children.

One young man who grew up attending a church youth group discovered the truth of that statement. He was a kid who chose the easy way, as he recounted in the video version of *Mind over Media*:

> There was a night that a movie called *A Clockwork Orange* came on HBO and [I] had watched it with a friend of mine. And there are some really sick things that go on in that film. These are things that I should have been ashamed to be watching or to even, you know, agree to look at. And I just stayed for the whole movie as though there was nothing wrong with it. The film in combination with … other types of things … leaving God, looking for entertainment in the world—again, it desensitized me to what I would normally see as being wrong.… Mainly a lot of sexual things.[2]

The young man who spoke those words was Lucas Salmon. He was interviewed in prison—where he was serving a sentence after being convicted of rape and murder.

CAUTION: DANGER AHEAD

Will this tendency to avoid the "hard road" disappear in the near future? Not at all. As parents, we need to be alert to the social trends that will worsen this problem during the coming decade—trends that will woo our children toward what seems the easiest route, but ultimately leads to destruction.

According to the World Futurist Society, leisure-oriented commerce—vacations, entertainment, personal convenience—will be the dominant force in the world economy in less than 15 years. Already "virtual reality" entertainment is on the rise, letting us pay a fee to sit through fake jungle rides, cyberspace voyages, and simulated car races. Experts in outdoor and recreational activities say that most teens prefer their computers or video games to the inconveniences of actual travel, hiking, or camping.[3]

In such a world of virtual reality, there is no personal discomfort. In this, and in a million other little ways, our culture will keep urging us toward greater passivity and the avoidance of real-life challenges. It will beckon us to take the easy road.

Christian theologian Harold O. J. Brown, convinced of this drift toward self-indulgence, wrote a book titled *The Sensate Culture.* Professor Brown points out that a "sensate" society is one whose chief goal is to maximize pleasure and minimize difficulties. It's the modern version of the ancient Epicurean philosophy, "Eat, drink, and be merry, for tomorrow we die."

Growing up in such a culture, our young pilgrims will find it natural to ignore Christ's call: "If anyone would come after me, he must deny himself and take up his cross and follow me" (Matthew 16:24). Like Formalist and Hypocrisy, they'll be tempted by alternate routes that promise happiness without diligence, doubts, or deprivation.

Eventually, though, these shortcuts will bring only disaster: "There is a way that seems right to a man, but in the end it leads to death" (Proverbs 16:25).

CLIMBING THE HILL:
PRACTICAL PROGRESS FOR PARENTS AND KIDS

No parent wants a child to lose his way. How, then, do we help our kids to choose the right path, even if it leads uphill?

To answer that question, let's look at Christian's decision to take the difficult way—and to stay on it.

Principle #1: Love the Truth
Here's what happened as Bunyan's hero made his way up the incline:

The hill grew steeper. Christian slowed from running to walking. Finally he fell to his hands and knees, and it was all he could do to crawl.

About midway to the top of the hill was a pleasant grove of trees, made by the Lord of the hill for the refreshment of weary travelers. Christian stopped there to rest. He pulled the book—the one he'd been given by the Shining Ones at the cross—from the pocket of his coat, and it comforted him as he read. Then he looked down at the coat itself, also a gift from the Shining Ones, and admired its embroidery.

In time he began to nod, then nap. He fell into a deep sleep, and the book fell out of his hand.

It was almost dark when he felt a hand on his shoulder, shaking him. Christian's eyelids snapped open; dazed, he heard a voice say, "Be more like the ant, you lazybones; consider its hard-working ways, and be wise."

Blinking, Christian looked back and forth but saw no one. Slowly his head cleared, and he got up. Remembering the voice, he worked his way up the hill as quickly as he could, and finally reached the top.

Christian loved the truth. He couldn't get enough of it, whether from the book he kept in his coat or from the voice of an unseen counselor. The source of truth in both cases was Scripture; Christian valued it because he believed in absolute truth, and believed that the Bible was the place to find it. Our children need the same certainty. Here's how to help them develop it.

Parental Action: Honor the Bible

Your child needs to know that, on his or her journey to the Celestial City, God's Word is the map. It lays out the straight way and warns of dangerous detours. It really is "a lamp to my feet, and a light for my path" (Psalm 119:105).

Show that it's special. How can you demonstrate that the Bible is God's message? Some parents emphasize treating the physical book with reverence, discouraging children from putting it on the floor or from even setting other books on top of it. While the Bible shouldn't be tossed around carelessly, it's most important to show respect by reading and obeying it. When your family faces a major decision, call a meeting and work together to find and apply Scripture passages to your deliberations. Let your kids know how your own choices—to spend time with them, to send them to a particular school, to care for an ailing grandparent—are informed by God's Word. Cite specific verses when you can.

Send them to the statutes. When our children had questions about right, wrong, and the things they heard from sources outside our home, we used the "statute book" approach. It came from Craig's experience as a first-year lawyer. The senior partner in his firm was a brilliant, no-nonsense attorney who had a way of cutting to the bone of any legal issue. When Craig would come to him with a question, the partner's response was always the same: "Did you read what the statutes have to say on the subject?" When Craig admitted he hadn't pored over those thick volumes, the man would say, "Don't bring the question to me until you've hit the statutes. They are the law; I'm not."

Needless to say, Craig learned to read the statutes. So when our kids posed a question about evolution, for example, we would ask, "Have you read the Bible on that question? What does Genesis say?" That was our starting point—one that implied respect for God's Word.

Keep it handy. Christian made sure his beloved book was never far away (and was devastated when he misplaced it—but we'll have more to say about that in the next chapter). For younger pilgrims, try keeping a children's Bible on the kitchen table; share a few pages with your child at snack time. Encourage him or her to look at the pictures when the mood strikes. For older kids, beat the "I can't find my Bible" syndrome by slipping a pocket edition into a jacket or backpack, or placing a larger copy in a dresser drawer (after all, it works in hotel rooms).

Parental Action: Teach Absolutes

No matter how handy your Bibles are, however, they'll mean little to a child who doesn't believe they're the source of absolute truth. Christian understood that truth doesn't change just because circumstances do; remember these lines from the pep talk he gave himself?

> *"No matter if it's tough, the right way's best;*
> *The wrong way isn't worth it, even if it means a rest."*

Christian knew that facts are facts regardless of how hard they are to follow. That certainty gave him a compass—something our children desperately need.

Make up your mind. Do *you* believe truth is absolute? Or do you believe in situational ethics—standards that vary according to circumstances? Ask yourself those questions before trying to address the issue with your child. Sadly, pollster George Barna discovered that fewer than half of all born-again adults, and only 9 percent of born-again teens, are certain of the existence of absolute moral truth. If *we* don't get this right, what can we expect of our children?

Take a hike. Go for a walk with your child, preferably in an area that's unfamiliar to him or her (but not to you). As you start out, explain that a compass is a device that shows you where to go. Say that you've brought a compass with you—and produce a large arrow you've cut from cardboard. Point the arrow in a direction and say, "There! That's the way to go!" A few yards later, give the child a chance to do the same thing, pointing the arrow in any direction he or she pleases. Repeat this process several times until you're in "uncharted" territory. Then say, "Well, we may be lost, but at least we still have our compass!" Ask the child to get you back home using the arrow—which will, of course, be useless. Explain that a real compass helps us find our way because it points to something that doesn't change—magnetic north. The cardboard arrow simply points wherever we like. In the same way, we need the Bible's unchanging truth to keep us on the right road in life; our shifting feelings will get us off the track.

Parental Action: Tout Diligence over Laziness

Christian's unseen counselor, rousing him on the hill of Difficulty, paraphrased Proverbs 6:6: "Go to the ant, you sluggard; consider its ways and be wise!" We may have to use different words, but our kids need more than ever to hear the countercultural message that effort, not laziness, gets results.

Let them finish. Our children won't learn endurance if we keep completing tasks for them. Claire, a mom whose middle-school son Davis often falls behind in his homework, habitually bails him out—typing assignments on the computer, cutting articles from the newspaper, and doing research for science projects on the World Wide Web. No wonder Davis keeps leaving jobs undone. Next time your child runs out of enthusiasm before running out of work, resist the urge to step in and erase the consequences. It's better to lose points on a book report than to develop the bad habit of quitting halfway up the hill.

Encourage higher goals. Kids are sometimes willing to climb hills that would leave us gasping for breath. Dr. James Dobson, in his book *Parenting Isn't for Cowards*, tells the following story about his daughter:

> I remember calling home some years ago from a city in Georgia where I had traveled for a speaking engagement. Danae, who was then 13 years of age, picked up the phone and we had a warm father-daughter chat. Then she said, "Oh, by the way, Dad, I'm going to be running in a track meet next Saturday."

"Really?" I said. "What distance have you chosen?"

"The 880," she replied.

I gasped. "Danae, that is a very grueling race. Do you know how far 880 yards is?"

"Yes," she said. "It's a half-mile."

"Have you ever run that far before?" I asked.

She said that she hadn't, even in practice. I continued to probe for information and learned that nine schools would be competing in the meet, which was only three days away. My daughter intended to compete against a field of other runners who presumably had been training for weeks. I was concerned.

"Danae," I said, "you've made a big mistake. You're about to embarrass yourself and I want you to think it over. You should go to your coach and ask to run a shorter race. At that speed 880 yards will kill you!"

"No, Dad," she said with determination. "No one else signed up for the 880 and I want to run it."

"Okay," I replied, "but you're doing it against my better judgment."

I thought about that beloved kid the rest of the week and wondered what humiliation was in store for her. I called again on Saturday afternoon.

"Guess what, Dad!" Danae said cheerfully. "I won the race today!" She had indeed finished in first place, several yards ahead of her nearest competitor. The following year, also without training, she won the same race by 50 yards and set a school record that may still be standing.[4]

Just as Danae ran her "hill of Difficulty" despite her father's misgivings, your child may amaze you by giving up a vacation to go on a missions trip, helping a "scary" homeless person, or defending his faith to skeptical peers—if you don't discourage him.

Principle #2: Mold Realistic Expectations

People in John Bunyan's era didn't have to be told that life is difficult. Mothers died in childbirth; children toiled in the fields to survive; the disabled had to beg for bread. Bunyan himself was thrown into prison for preaching without a license. "Comfort" was only for a few, and had to be found without automobiles, pizza delivery, or home theater systems.

Today, though, most kids in our society grow up thinking ease is their birthright. Many parents reinforce this notion by shielding their children from the sight of suffering, not to mention inconvenience and disappointment, and by responding to every whim with the promptness of an ambulance service. The result: Kids assume life in general, and the Christian life in particular, are designed for their amusement. When they're not sufficiently entertained, they're ready to change the channel.

You can cultivate more realistic expectations in your child with methods like the following.

Parental Action: Lend Historical Perspective

Does your child know what life was like before he was born? Does she realize that people didn't always have cell phones, microwave ovens, and instant messaging? When it comes to the past, our culture's amnesia is notorious; many adults as well as children can't imagine life without modern conveniences.

Visit museums. Many museums of natural history feature dioramas and walk-through replicas of homes used by pioneers, native Americans, and others. Take your kids to these displays, pointing out similarities to and differences from your abode. Ask children to imagine what life was like in those days. If you visit an art museum, look at paintings for hints of daily life in other eras.

Read about the past. Historical novels for children, like those in Focus on the Family's KidWitness Tales and Christian Heritage Series, help kids understand the challenges faced by young people in earlier times. Depending on the maturity and reading ability of your child, you also may want to recommend classics like *David Copperfield, Little House on the Prairie,* and *The Diary of Anne Frank.*

Parental Action: Widen Their World

Kids also need to know that everyday struggle isn't just historical. Does your child realize how privileged she is, and that most of the world's people can only dream of the luxuries she takes for granted? Your goal is not to make your child feel guilty, but to help her remember others' discomfort when deciding whether something is "too hard" to endure.

Travel without tourism. If your church sponsors a cross-cultural service project—an evangelistic trip to Haiti, a house-raising in Mexico, an AIDS prevention campaign in Namibia—encourage your child to go if he's old enough. Kids are often shocked to see the deprivation in countries like these, and come back with a more realistic view of what it means to face difficulty. If you vacation in a country where poverty and affluence coexist, talk about the disparity you see instead of trying to ignore it. Closer to home, if you live in a relatively affluent locale, find out whether your church can partner with one in the inner city or an economically depressed rural area.

Help in a hospital. Is there a children's hospital within driving distance? If so, chances are that its playroom could use volunteers to boost the morale of young patients and their parents and distract them from the pain and anxiety of treatment. Find out whether your child can accompany you on a visit. The prospect of spending time with youngsters who are hurting, nauseated, or fighting for their lives is a frightening one for most people, but you and your child may be surprised to find friendships forming with those who know the hill of Difficulty only too well.

Principle #3: Provide Purpose

What kept Christian going when the going got tough? He shared his secret with a fellow believer along the way:

The young woman named Prudence asked Christian, "Do you ever find that the problems of this world lose their power to annoy you? How does that happen?"

Christian chuckled knowingly. "When I think of what I saw at the cross, that will do it. When I look at the beautiful new coat I was given, that will do it; when I read the book I carry in my pocket, that will do it; and when I think about the place I'm going, that will do it."

"What makes you want so much to get to Mount Zion?" Prudence asked.

Christian's voice took on a new zeal. "Why, I hope to see alive the One who hung dead on the cross! I hope to be rid of all those things that annoy me in this life—like death! To tell you the truth, I want to be with the One I love; I love Him because He eased my burden. And I'm weary of my inner sickness; I'd rather be where I won't die anymore, and with the crowd that will continually cry, 'Holy, holy, holy!' "

Christian was eager to move forward, knowing that each step took him closer to his final destination, his real home. We need to impart to our children a feeling of anticipation and excitement over the fact that one day they'll stand before the King of Kings—and He'll know them by name. Here are some ways to give your child that sense of purpose.

Parental Action: Raise Their Sights

If your kids know more about who designed the newest Nintendo game than they do about who designed the universe, it's time to lift their gaze from the trivial.

Change the rules. Find an old "Trivial Pursuit" board game—or any game featuring trivia questions. As you play, give extra points to anyone who can follow a question with one that has *eternal* significance. For instance, "How can a person store up treasures in heaven?" or "What do you hope people say about you 100 years from now?"

Ask, "WWJD?" Give this familiar abbreviation a twist. Instead of asking what Jesus *would* do in a situation, ask your child what Jesus *will* do when we meet Him face-to-face. What would your child *like* Him to do? How can he or she get ready for that incredible moment? Emphasize the joy of meeting Jesus personally, rather than the possibility that He won't be pleased by your child's earthly performance. There's a place for the latter, but forgetting the excitement of our ultimate homecoming could keep your child from looking forward to it.

Parental Action: Remind Them of Rewards

The Celestial City seems awfully distant, even irrelevant, to many kids. They need frequent reminders that sticking with the spiritual struggle has its benefits, both in this life and the next.

Get hyped about heaven. Most kids tend to see heaven in one of two ways—either as an everlastingly boring church service, or as a customized theme park in which everyone indulges in his or her favorite activities and foods. Help your child understand that heaven is the greatest place because God is there, not because we may be able to fly or eat all the chocolate we can hold. Explain that God will make sure life in His presence is perfect. Read Revelation 21 together; draw a mural on newsprint or butcher paper depicting the awesome sights described in that chapter.

Look down the road. Have lunch with your child and an older Christian relative or friend from church. Ask the older person how God has helped him or her on the road to the Celestial City. What have been the rewards of knowing and following Jesus? Why does this person look forward to heaven? What were the biggest "hills of Difficulty" on the way, and how did the person handle them? What has made the journey "worth it all"?

WINNING THE UPHILL BATTLE

The more your child falls in love with Jesus, the more she'll want to be with Him—even when the road gets rough. The Book of Hebrews tells us that the best way to stay on the pilgrim's path is to keep our gaze on Christ:

> Let us fix our eyes on Jesus, the author and perfecter of our faith,
> who for the joy set before him endured the cross, scorning its shame,
> and sat down at the right hand of the throne of God. Consider him
> who endured such opposition from sinful men, so that you will not
> grow weary and lose heart. (Hebrews 12:2-3)

The grade may grow steep, and your child may be tempted to shift into neutral—or even reverse. But with the right map and compass, realistic expectations, and a sense of purpose, he or she will be well prepared to keep on keeping on.

Chapter 4

THE LOST BOOK

Rediscovering God's Word with Your Child

‿❧

Just as Christian reached the crest of the hill, two frightened-looking men came running in the opposite direction—nearly bowling him over. Their names were Timorous and Mistrust.

"Sirs!" Christian cried. "What's the matter? You're going the wrong way!"

The two men paused, huffing and puffing. "We...were headed for the city of Zion," Timorous managed. "But the further we got...the more danger we found. So we...turned around...and are going back."

"We...even saw a couple of lions," Mistrust added. "Don't know whether they were awake or asleep, but...they could have pulled us to pieces."

Christian shivered. "You're scaring me," he said. "But going back won't help me. If I return to my own country, which is headed for fire and brimstone, I'll certainly perish there. But if I can get to the Celestial City, I'm sure to be safe. I have to try! To go back is death; to go forward is fear of death, then eternal life. I'm going forward!"

Mistrust and Timorous, unconvinced, continued to flee. As they ran away, Christian turned toward the Celestial City. The further he walked, however, the more he thought of the dangers the men had described.

"I'll read from the book and be comforted," he told himself. But when he felt the chest pocket of his coat, there was nothing there. He gasped. "W-where is it?" he whispered. "I must have the book! It's my pass into the Celestial City! What am I going to do?"

Suddenly he remembered how he'd slept in the grove of trees on the side of the hill called Difficulty. "Lord," he prayed, falling to his knees, "forgive my foolishness." Getting to his feet, he went back to look for his book.

His eyes searched every foot along both sides of the road; he found himself sighing, then weeping. If only he could find the book that had been his comfort so many times on this journey!

Finally he reached the grove, and the sight of it made him feel even worse. If only he had not slept there!

REST AND RECKLESSNESS

Remember the nap Christian took halfway up the hill of Difficulty, as mentioned in the previous chapter?

He stopped at a place of rest provided by God. He enjoyed reading the book he'd been given, which represented God's Word. Eventually he nodded off, letting the Bible slip from his hands. When he awoke he forgot the book, and left it behind as he continued his journey.

Christian didn't intend to forget God's Book, but he was careless. One of the surest ways to "lose" God's Word is to simply neglect it—a problem still faced by families today.

SLEEP ATTACKS

In general, our boys and girls are good at understanding the theological importance of the Bible. According to researcher George Barna, some 60 percent of teens can articulate the fact that the Bible is accurate in everything it teaches.[1] In a survey by Josh McDowell, which was limited to evangelical, churched youth, 71 percent said they believed that the Bible was absolutely true.[2]

Yet McDowell asked the key follow-up question: "How often do you read the Bible?" The results were disheartening. Over half the respondents indicated that they didn't read the Bible at least once each week. Some 38 percent said they consulted Scripture "rarely" or "never."

We parents need to communicate to the next generation the importance of God's Word. Our kids, meanwhile, need to experience the joy of having their lives changed by the power of inspired Scripture.

Psalm 119 makes it clear how vital it is to have personal time in God's Word. Verses 9-11 in that chapter are among our personal favorites:

How can a young man keep his way pure? By living according to your word. I seek you with all my heart; do not let me stray from your commands. I have hidden your word in my heart that I might not sin against you.

How practical the Bible is! Spending time in it can keep our "way pure." Hiding it in our hearts and obeying it can keep us from sin.

But the power of God's written truth will do our children no good if it stays on the bookshelf. This means taking the time to study it diligently—and apply it personally. And *that* means learning to maintain a disciplined routine of individual Bible study.

If you think it will be easy to teach your child to establish this habit, though, you may be in for a surprise. Children come up with some of the most creative excuses imaginable for not reading the Bible. Here are some we've heard within the ranks of our own tribe:

- "I can't do my Bible study first thing in the morning; I'm just not a morning person!"
- "I can't do my Bible study during the day because I've got school—and then after school I've got _____ (sports, science club, part-time job, homework, student council meeting, baby-sitting, etc.)."
- "Study the Bible just before bedtime? Oh, that doesn't work. I just fall asleep and wake up the next morning with my face in the book of Romans!"
- "I can't do my devotions at the same time as my sister—she's copying me!"
- "I do all my studying better with my headphones on."
- "God won't grade me—but my math teacher will!"

No question about it—carving out time for personal meditation on God's love letter is not an option, it's a must. But how do we help our children do that?

One of the best ways is to lead by example. Do you have your own time of regular Bible study? Do you share with your child some of the exciting things the Lord shows you in His Word?

When our children were young, Janet was an at-home mom who started her day with devotions and a cup of coffee at the kitchen table. She let our kids know how wonderful it was to sit down with God's special Book and see what He wanted to teach her.

One day, our elementary-age daughter Sarah walked into the kitchen and saw Janet reading the Bible. "Why do you read the Bible in the morning?" Sarah asked.

"Well," Janet replied, "I read it because it tells me what God wants me to know. And I read it in the morning because I want His teaching to be the very first thing of the day."

Sarah took a minute to think. Then she sat down next to Janet and asked question after question about God. Soon she was praying to receive Jesus Christ as her Savior.

We realize now how important it was for Janet to show that God's Word was part of her daily life. It not only made a statement about the Bible, but also helped to bring our daughter into God's kingdom.

Regular times of family worship and Bible teaching can also bring the point home in an exhilarating—albeit occasionally challenging—way. This works best if you teach one truth at a time. We've learned that it's much more important for our children to absorb and apply a few concepts than it is to master the intricacies of systematic theology or spell the word *eschatology*.

We need to lead our young ones to the revolutionary idea that the power of God's Word comes not just in reading and understanding it, but in *applying* it—to their friendships, to that mean student who picks on them, to that teacher who always seems suspicious of them. Then, and only then, will they see that God's Word is not only true, but also potent and relevant.

SHARK ATTACKS

Not everyone agrees with that assessment of the Bible, of course. Take Obstinate, a critic encountered earlier by Christian on the road to the Celestial City:

Obstinate and Pliable walked at Christian's elbows, one on each side. Raising a skeptical eyebrow, Obstinate turned to Christian. "What are the things you

seek," Obstinate asked, "since you leave all the world to find them?"

"I seek an inheritance that doesn't rot or rust," Christian replied. "It's kept safely in heaven, to be given at the right time to those who faithfully pursue it." He patted the chest pocket of his coat. "You can read all about it in here if you like—in my book."

Obstinate snorted. "Away with your book," he said with a sneer. "Will you go back with us or not?"

Christian shook his head. "Not I," he answered. "I have laid my hand to the plow; there's no turning back."

"Come then, neighbor Pliable," said Obstinate, stopping on the path. "Let's turn around and go home without him."

Pliable quit walking, but looked uncertain. Christian halted a few paces ahead and sighed.

"I've seen plenty of these crazies," said Obstinate, rolling his eyes. "When they get an idea in their heads, they think they're smarter than seven sane men."

Pliable bit his lip nervously. "N-now, don't make fun of Christian," he said. "If what he says is true, his goals are higher than ours. I'm inclined to go along with him."

Obstinate smacked himself on the forehead with his palm. "What, another fool? Listen to reason, and go back! Who knows where a lunatic like this will lead you? Go back, and be wise!"

"Obstinate," said Christian, "it's you who should come with Pliable. The things I spoke of are real, and many more glories besides. If you don't believe me, read this book. The truth of it is confirmed by the blood of the One who made it."

The legacy of Obstinate continues today. There are forces at work in our culture that make it easier than ever to devalue the Word of God. In fact, our children are growing up in an environment where the Bible is under attack as never before.

A television program illustrates this heightened assault on the Bible. In the year 2000, ABC's Peter Jennings hosted a two-hour special titled "The Search for Jesus." It was a prime-time, full-scale offensive against the veracity of the New Testament record about Christ.

What many viewers didn't realize was that four Bible "scholars" featured prominently on the program were actually fellows in a project called The Jesus Seminar. This group, which conspicuously omits any orthodox Bible scholars, has reached the astonishing conclusion that only 18 percent of the words of Jesus that appear in the New Testament are worthy of belief. The group also declares that a mere 16 percent of the events in the life of Jesus, as recounted in the New Testament, actually happened. To put it another way, according to these "experts," some 80 percent of the Gospels of Matthew, Mark, Luke, and John could be cut out and thrown away without losing anything credible.

The battle over the Bible, which used to be fought primarily in college religion departments and the cloistered halls of theological schools, has reached the mass media. In the coming decade our children will be exposed to more harsh attacks on Scripture's accuracy. We need to teach them principles of Christian apologetics—the basics of what the Bible says and why it should be believed.

A good place to start is with this statement by Dr. Norman Geisler and Ron Brooks in their book *When Skeptics Ask: A Handbook of Christian Evidences* (Baker Book House, 1995):

> The Bible is the Word of God. This teaching stands on no lesser authority than Jesus Christ Himself, who confirmed the inspiration of the Old Testament and promised the New Testament. The testimony of Jesus and the apostles is that the Bible is inerrant in that it teaches about all matters, down to the tenses of verbs, and the very last letters of words. Also, we have a great deal of evidence to show that the Bibles we have in our hands represent the original manuscripts with a very high degree of accuracy, like no other book from the ancient world. The Bible in your hand is God speaking to you.[3]

BACK TO THE BOOK:
PRACTICAL PROGRESS FOR PARENTS AND KIDS

With the forces of disbelief and inertia working against you, how can you get your children to trust and study Scripture? Here are three principles that can help.

Principle #1: Give Yourself a Second Chance

Christian deeply regretted losing his book, but didn't go on without it. He backtracked, found it, and moved ahead. Many of us have tried to study the Bible regularly and urged our families to do so, but with less than stellar results. It's time we stopped berating ourselves for those lapses, rediscovered Scripture, and made it a natural part of our lives.

Parental Action: Chill Out

Alex is a father who believes Bible reading must be a daily event, preferably at the crack of dawn. Unfortunately, he's never been able to live up to this expectation. Daily Bible study has always seemed to him an unpleasant but mandatory chore, one he'd better complete if he wants God's approval. Failing to meet that standard, he finds himself mired guiltily in the Slough of Despond—hardly ever reading the Bible himself, much less inspiring his kids to do so.

Alex needs to relax. Instead of being a legalistic bundle of nerves when it comes to Scripture reading, he can begin to see it as one important but nonthreatening way to cultivate his relationship with God. He can start where he is, reading as much and as often as he can while still enjoying and absorbing what he reads. He can work up to daily study, expecting plenty of misses along the way—and giving up his assumption that God has an arsenal of lightning bolts aimed at him. Once Alex lightens up, his children will be more likely to see Bible reading as a boon, not a ball-and-chain— and maybe even try it themselves.

Parental Action: Explore New Approaches

"We tried Bible study," some parents say. "It didn't work." All too often what they tried was sitting on the couch or at the dinner table, droning through verse after verse as the kids' eyes glazed over. Coming up with more creative ways to interact with God's Word isn't just for youth group leaders and curriculum writers; you *can* try this at home! Here are a few ideas:

- Act out a Bible passage, either with a narrator reading and others pantomiming, or with assigned characters speaking dialogue from the text. Younger children can help out with sound effects.
- Let each person study the verses silently and create a song, comic strip, or greeting card that summarizes what he or she just read.

- Read responsively, or from different versions, or over a two-way radio, or from a Bible CD-ROM.
- Go outside to read a passage about creation; sit in the car while reading about Paul's travels; eat a meal as you read about the Last Supper.
- Give each family member a lump of clay, scraps of felt, or a box of toothpicks; encourage each person to make a shape or pattern that expresses his or her feelings about a Bible passage.

Principle #2: Connect Bible and Life

Christian didn't have to be coaxed to read his book. Why not? Because he knew it contained solace and guidance he couldn't get anywhere else. He would have been puzzled by the claim that the Bible is irrelevant to everyday life.

When today's kids want to be soothed or directed, they're more likely to consult peers, the Internet, or MTV; the Bible barely makes the list. You can help your child understand that the Bible isn't just one option for consolation and advice—it's the *best* option.

Parental Action: Sell the Benefits

What have your kids learned so far about the Bible? Perhaps they've been told about its *features*—that it contains a certain number of books, was written during a particular period, was inspired by God, and contains history, poetry, epistles, and prophecy. But advertising experts know it's most effective to promote a product's *benefits*, not its features. People want to know what a toothbrush or umbrella will *do* for them, not just that it has nylon bristles or a wooden handle.

Christian knew the benefits of his book, and promoted them to others along his journey. You can do the same with your child.

Respond to felt needs. A glass of water doesn't seem valuable unless you're thirsty. In the same way, when your child is filled with confidence, verses about God's ever-present help may not mean much. But when he or she feels sad after losing a Little League game, it's an opportunity to share a passage about the Lord's compassion and His trustworthy plans for each of us. When your child is anxious about a social studies test or getting a vaccination, try working a Bible story about God's provision into your conversation. When he or she is lonely after moving to a new town, look at verses about God's companionship and His understanding of our need for friends. In time your child will come to see that the Bible offers not only admonition, but assistance.

Stage a sword drill. Many children don't seem to realize they can "search the Scriptures" when they need help. For Web-savvy kids, explain that the process is like using an Internet search engine. Practice searching by staging an old-fashioned "sword drill," but with a difference. Instead of looking up Bible passages by book, chapter, and verse, have a contest in which you call out a "real-life" topic like happiness, fear, winning, or the future. See how speedily your child can find a verse that addresses the subject. If she can't, check a concordance together.

Parental Action: Make Application Specific

"So what?" It's a question your child may feel like asking after hearing a Bible story or passage, even if he doesn't ask it out loud. If we fail to answer that question, our kids may grow up agreeing with those who say the Bible is irrelevant.

Here are some "application" statements that only vaguely connect Scripture passages to contemporary concerns:

• "So we need to ask God to show us His will."
• "Jesus healed the sick, so we know He cares about people."
• "We don't know when Jesus will return, but we can be sure He will."

Here, on the other hand, are questions that could spur your child to make specific, personal applications:

• "Since you're trying to decide where to go to school next year, how should we ask God to help you?"
• "If Jesus cared enough to heal the blind man, how do you think He feels about your broken wrist?"
• "If you knew Jesus was coming back in 48 hours, what would you do to get ready?"

Principle #3: Respond to Objections

When Obstinate ridiculed Christian's belief in the book, Christian could have been cowed into silence. Or he could have retorted, "The book says it, I believe it, that settles it!" Instead, he chose to calmly defend the book and give a reason for his trust in it:

"Obstinate," said Christian, "it's you who should come with Pliable. The things I spoke of are real, and many more glories besides. If you don't believe me, read this book. The truth of it is confirmed by the blood of the One who made it."

We owe our children a calm, reasonable defense of God's Word—and the tools to help them do the same with others.

Parental Action: Don't Fear Doubt

Some parents panic when their kids ask tough questions, especially about faith. But when children express doubts, we can be thankful that they're starting to think for themselves, and that they're testing their ideas on *us*. Doubts give us the chance to prepare our kids for even harder questions that may come later—when they're beyond our sphere of influence.

Congratulate thinkers. It might be more convenient if your child never questioned your views, but then she would "own" *your* faith, not hers. Affirm your child's God-given intelligence, and thank her for coming to you with questions. This isn't a stalling tactic; it's recognizing the start of a lifelong process in which each of us can make an increasingly personal, genuine commitment to God and His Word.

Let them hear the other side. After playing with a friend, 10-year-old Ben asks, "Mom, how come we believe what the Bible says about hell? Matt says his church doesn't." Mom's first thought is to keep Ben away from Matt's "bad influence." But should she?

That may depend on Ben's maturity level and Matt's interest in convincing Ben of his position. The sure thing is that Mom should stay calm, gather some facts, and explain *both sides* of the issue in terms Ben can understand. She'll want to make the best case she can for relying on the Bible—without misrepresenting its critics. Someday Ben will hear more thoroughly and forcefully from the opposition; when that day comes, he'll remember his mother's honesty instead of feeling misled.

Parental Action: Find Answers Together

While it's important to reply to our children's questions about the Bible, we don't have to do so immediately. There's almost always time to say, "I don't know, but we can find out."

Consult the experts. When it comes to apologetics, you don't have to reinvent the wheel. Check your church library or local Christian bookstore for the many resources available. Children ages 9-12, for example, will enjoy *It Couldn't Just Happen* by Lawrence O. Richards (Word, 1994). This colorful volume is packed with amazing facts about God's creation, reinforcing the Genesis account. Teens will find solid evidence for Scripture in two books by Lee Strobel with Jane Vogel—*The Case for Christ: Student Edition* (Zondervan, 2001) and *The Case for Faith: Student Edition* (Zondervan, 2002).

Make it a team effort. Depending on your child's age, she may be able to help you locate answers—and will be more likely to remember them if she does the digging. Check the resources just listed, as well as the Internet. You might also arrange for your child to bring her question to a Sunday school teacher, a Bible study leader, your pastor, an appropriate call-in radio show, or an instructor at a nearby Christian school or college.

I FOUND IT!

If the Bible has been a "lost book" at your house lately, don't despair. Past neglect doesn't have to keep your children from a future of exploring, trusting, and profiting by God's Word. You can experience the joy of rediscovering this treasure, even as Christian did:

At length Christian reached the grove. Sitting down on a bench, he began to cry again. But then, as Providence would have it, he glanced sorrowfully under the bench. There was his book!

Trembling, he snatched it from the ground and slid it into his coat pocket. With a sigh of relief he leaned back against the bench. His joy over finding the book could not be put into words; those pages were the assurance of his life, his acceptance at the Celestial City.

Patting his chest pocket, he prayed, "Thank You, Lord, for directing my eye to the place where this book lay." After wiping away his tears, he rose from the bench and resumed his journey. And how nimbly he went up the rest of the hill!

Chapter 5

A ROOM CALLED PEACE

Teaching Your Child the Virtue of Virtue

～๑

Christian stood before the iron gate where the Porter was. "Sir," Christian called, "what house is this? May I lodge here tonight?"

The Porter, whose name was Watchful, was a towering, beefy man with a bushy, white mustache. Precision and dignity marked his manner, but his voice boomed like a foghorn. "This house was built by the Lord of the hill," he declared. "He built it for the relief and security of pilgrims." The Porter lifted his chin and frowned. "May I ask where you have come from, and where you are going?"

"I have come from the city of Destruction," Christian replied, "and am going to Mount Zion. Since the sun is now set, I would like, if I may, to stay here tonight."

The Porter asked his name, and how he had come to arrive so late in the day. Christian's replies seemed to satisfy him, and he drew himself up even taller and straighter. "Well," he said, "I will call out one of the virgins of this place. If she likes what you have to say, she will bring you in to the rest of the family. Those are the rules of the house."

So Watchful the Porter pulled a cord that hung at his side. A bell clanged, and a few moments later a beautiful but serious-looking young woman named Discretion emerged from the house.

"Why was I called?" she asked when she reached the gate.

The Porter cleared his throat. "This man is on a journey from the city of Destruction to Mount Zion. But being weary and with night falling, he asked me if he might lodge here tonight."

True to her name, Discretion asked Christian a series of cautious questions. When she had discerned his identity and purpose, she smiled—yet her eyes brimmed with tears. After pausing, she said, "I will call forth two or three more of the family."

Her skirts rustled as she ran to the door. "Prudence!" she called. "Piety! Charity! Come outside!"

Soon three more young women, equally lovely and sober, approached the gate. After a little more conversation, they agreed to invite Christian inside. The gate swung open with a squeak, and as they all reached the porch, other family members joined them. Bowing his head gratefully, Christian followed them into the house.

When he had come in and sat down, Piety, Prudence, and Charity talked with him until supper was ready. Their conversation lasted until late at night.

After they had committed themselves to their Lord for protection, they retired. The pilgrim was given a large upper room, whose window opened toward the sunrise. The name of the room was Peace, where he slept till daybreak. Then he awoke and sang:

> *"Where am I now? Is this the love and care*
> *Of Jesus, on the journey pilgrims share,*
> *Providing a way that I can be forgiven,*
> *And letting me move in next door to heaven?"*

A HOUSE THAT IS A HOME

John Bunyan calls it "The House Beautiful." It's a place especially designed for travelers on their way to the Celestial City. The architect is none other than the Lord.

The House Beautiful is one of the most delightful stops Christian makes on his long journey. There he meets four beautiful maidens—Discretion,

Prudence, Piety, and Charity. Those names may sound old-fashioned, but they express timeless values that followers of Jesus are to practice.

Discretion is the ability to make responsible, thoughtful decisions rather than being guided by impulsive, arbitrary desires.

Prudence is being self-governed by wisdom and reason rather than passion or emotion.

When Bunyan mentions *piety*, he's using a word misunderstood today. Often we think of someone who's "pious" as a stuffed shirt, a self-righteous, fun-preventing prude. But the term *pietism* was first attached to a seventeenth-century German Christian movement centering on personal Bible study, consistent Christian living, and missions—a marked departure from the cold, formal religion of that day. True piety is devotion to God.

Lastly, *charity* is the King James word for *love*.

In this house built for Christians, then, we find personal responsibility, wisdom, devotion to God, and love. But there's something else, too: peace.

At the end of the day, Christian is led to a special room that's quiet and secure, and which faces the beauty of the morning sunrise. This room is called "Peace."

It's no accident that Christian finds himself sleeping peacefully in a house occupied by virtue. Bunyan is telling us that the way we and our children live our lives will determine whether we achieve true inner peace—one that passes all understanding.

WHAT IS VIRTUE?

Virtue is another of those old-fashioned words. William Bennett, former U.S. Secretary of Education, helped bring the term back to public discourse with *The Children's Book of Virtues* (Simon & Schuster, 1995). His book reminds us how relevant the idea of virtue—of personal character quality—really is.

What are the virtues God wants us to practice? Scripture gives us several guidelines.

Philippians 4:8 instructs: "Finally, brothers, whatever is true, whatever is noble, whatever is right, whatever is pure, whatever is lovely, whatever is admirable—if anything is excellent or praiseworthy—think about such things."

Galatians 5:22-23 tells us that "the fruit of the Spirit is love, joy, peace, patience, kindness, goodness, faithfulness, gentleness and self-control."

Virtues like these are not a matter of human imagination or reasoning. They're the values God Himself says He wants us, and our children, to live out every day.

VIRTUE, VICE, AND VIOLENCE

America's founding fathers understood the importance of virtue. They considered moral character to be a matter of national survival. In 1796, retiring President George Washington spoke of the need for virtue in what became known as his "Farewell Address":

> Of all the dispositions and habits which lead to political prosperity, Religion and morality are indispensable supports. In vain would that man claim the tribute of Patriotism, who would labour to subvert these great Pillars of human happiness, these firmest props of the duties of Men and citizens.... Reason and experience both forbid us to expect that National morality can prevail in exclusion of religious principle.[1]

Today, though, the society Washington hoped for seems only a dream. Virtue is commonly derided. As a result, there is little peace.

All too often, for example, the news is filled with reports of yet another public school rampage. A troubled teenager fires shots at teachers and classmates. More death, more tragedy, more questions.

Should we blame the weapons? The parents? Pass more laws? Demand more security?

Or do we need more virtue—more personal responsibility, wisdom, devotion to God, and love?

Our children's world is caught in a titanic struggle between virtue and its opposite. More and more young people totter on the brink of destruction, providing evidence of character's collapse. More and more kids risk ruining their lives—and others'—with dangerous behavior. Youthful criminal conduct is increasingly violent.

Contrast that with the tranquil picture of Christian basking in the warmth and security of "The House Beautiful." The difference between the ugliness of evil and the beauty of virtue couldn't be more striking.

In a violent, desperate world, the virtuous character of our children can provide an eloquent argument for the reality of God. Our kids—empowered by the Spirit, shaped by godly parenting, and directed by Scripture—can make an eternal difference in what Bunyan called the "wilderness of this world."

CAN WE DEVELOP VIRTUE?

Seeing moral virtue as a noble goal is an ancient idea. The Greek philosophers pondered it thousands of years ago. Yet they were wrong about *how* true virtue could be achieved.

The Greeks thought that merely increasing their children's knowledge could lead the younger generation to enjoy more virtuous lives. Plato put the matter plainly: "Vice is ignorance. Virtue is knowledge."

Plato was a genius, but he was wrong. Virtue can't be produced by education alone, nor by reason. It's not a matter of intellect or knowledge.

If it were, Western society would be much different. America, for example, is one of the most educated nations on the planet. Yet that has not slashed its murder rate. Nor has its multibillion-dollar education system stopped teen pregnancy, drug abuse, or the disintegration of families.

Benjamin Franklin, believing virtue was the key to successful living, had another plan for developing it. He set down 13 qualities he wanted to attain: temperance, silence, order, resolution, frugality, industry, sincerity, justice, moderation, cleanliness, tranquility, chastity, and humility. Ever the innovator, he devised a weekly chart to measure his progress, calling it his "bold and arduous project of arriving at moral perfection." In the end, though, he had to admit his experiment was a failure.

Franklin's defeat wasn't due to a lack of role models. Under the category of "humility" he reminded himself to "imitate Jesus." But his inability to achieve moral perfection through self-effort echoed the experience of the apostle Paul, described in Romans 7:18-24:

I know that nothing good lives in me, that is, in my sinful nature. For I have the desire to do what is good, but I cannot carry it out.

For what I do is not the good I want to do; no, the evil I do not want to do—this I keep on doing. Now if I do what I do not want to do, it is no longer I who do it, but it is sin living in me that does it.

So I find this law at work: When I want to do good, evil is right there with me. For in my inner being I delight in God's law; but I see another law at work in the members of my body, waging war against the law of my mind and making me a prisoner of the law of sin at work within my members. What a wretched man I am! Who will rescue me from this body of death?

Paul gives us the answer: Only Jesus Christ has the power to free us from the grasp of sin. When we give our lives to Him, the Holy Spirit lives in us. When we obey the Word of God and yield to His will, we can "walk by the Spirit" rather than the "flesh."

We parents must teach our children that real virtue is possible only when God gives us His power to live good lives. The ability to be virtuous comes solely from our heavenly Father. It can never result merely from our own efforts, no matter how hard we try.

At the same time, we need to impress on our kids that while God gives the *power* to live virtuous lives, there's still a crucial part for *them* to play. They need to *practice* virtue as they walk with the King.

Here's how we explained that concept to our own children. As each of them arrived at car-driving age, we used this illustration: *Owning* a beautiful car with a powerful engine will not get you where you want to go. That requires the *practice* of driving safely. God gives the *power*; the Christian is to willingly submit to that power, and to practice daily virtue.

In addition, we need to let our kids know that practicing godly virtues brings a bonus: the harvest of inner peace.

We remember well how our daughter Sarah learned that lesson. One day, when she was about nine years old, we filled our minivan's tank with gas at a station near our home. Sarah looked around the store as we paid the bill. When we were on the road again, we noticed an outbreak of whispering in the backseat; Sarah was passing out pieces of a candy bar. We quickly deduced that she'd stolen it from the store.

Confronted, she confessed. We turned around and headed back to the gas station, even though there was a long line of customers and we were going to be late for our trip to the zoo. Sarah told the manager what had happened; we then went home to get 25 cents from Sarah's piggy bank, and she paid for the candy. That night, as she snuggled in her bed, she told us it felt good to do the right thing

Several years later, when Sarah was taking a pre-calculus course in high school, word got around that someone had gotten a copy of the final exam—answers and all. Sarah, who'd been struggling in the class, thought back to the candy incident—and decided not to join the group that had access to the stolen test.

She took the exam the honest way, and passed. Those who used the stolen test were caught, and flunked the course.

Sarah still recalls the sweet sleep she had the night after taking the exam. She was experiencing the peace that comes from pursuing virtue.

Cultivating Virtue:
Practical Progress for Parents and Kids

People used to say, "Virtue is its own reward." Today's cynics say, "Virtue is its own punishment." Parents who want to overcome this attitude have their work cut out for them, but the task isn't insurmountable. Here are some principles and practices to help.

Principle #1: Value Good over Glitter

Christian was grateful for the hospitality he found at The House Beautiful. The décor wasn't elegant, the food wasn't gourmet fare, and the conversation didn't feature the latest jokes. But Christian didn't complain. He knew character is more important than pizzazz.

Our culture doesn't seem to grasp that. Virtue just isn't hip. But you can give virtue an "image makeover" in your family—by using activities like the following that link old-sounding words and modern life.

Parental Action: Show Virtue Is Timeless
Catch it on camera. Give your child a list of half a dozen virtues and a digital camera, instant camera, or camcorder. Follow as he or she roams the

neighborhood or a nearby park or playground, looking for examples of the virtues in action. For instance, "patience" at the playground might be represented by children waiting their turn for a swing; "compassion" might look like a parent removing a splinter from a child's finger. If your child is too young to handle this alone, help out. If you have more than one child and can make the activity a contest, so much the better. Afterward, look together at the photos or video and talk about the virtues depicted.

Rap it up. With your child, write and perform a rap promoting one or more biblical virtues. Here's a sample verse:

> One fruit of the Spirit, they say it's gentle;
> The world says to do this you'd have to be mental;
> But God knows gentleness leads to peace;
> Without it, the fighting will never cease.

Create virtuous designs. If you have a son who's into superheroes, ask him to name and draw some new ones who have virtuous powers like "superfaith" and "discernment vision." If you have a daughter who likes fashion, ask her to design some outfits that embody the virtue of joy—yet also retain qualities like modesty and purity.

Parental Action: Reward Substance, Not Style

Post an "Honorable Roll." Many parents are happy to laud their children for getting on a school's academic honor roll. But who gets extra tokens at Chuck E. Cheese's for being virtuous? Each month or quarter, put an "Honorable Roll" on your refrigerator or bulletin board, listing righteous things you've noticed your child doing. If you have more than one child, be sure to come up with at least one item for each so that no one gets totally discouraged. If you offer further incentives, such as a small toy for each item that makes the list, you may even find kids competing to do the greatest number of noble deeds.

Sing unsung heroes. As a family, identify someone in your church or community who practices virtue without fanfare. For instance, one man might exhibit dependability by regularly mowing the church lawn, or show compassion by caring for injured animals he finds along the highway. Then do one of the following to honor that person:

- Make up a song about him and sing it for him, either in person or on tape.
- Feature him on a homemade "Person of the Year" magazine cover and present it to him.
- Make a "trading card" with the person's picture on it, listing virtuous "stats" on the back, and give it to him.

Be an invisible helper. Try this game with younger children. Explain that you're going to leave the room for five minutes. During that time, your child will have a chance to do something helpful. It could be small, like picking up a stray paper clip, or bigger, like dusting all the furniture. After five minutes, your job will be to guess what your child did. Follow this activity by identifying the virtue your child displayed (obedience, love, etc.) while you were gone. Explain that what a person does when no one's watching tells a lot about his or her character.

Principle #2: Spend Time with Virtuous Companions

Christian's stay with the occupants of The House Beautiful was a welcome respite on his long, arduous journey. He loved being with people who shared his values, and they were happy to encourage him. Our children may not realize it, but they need the companionship of fellow believers too. We can't create friendships for them, but we can make it easier for them to interact with those who reinforce—instead of ridicule—godly virtues.

Parental Action: Encourage Positive Friendships

When your child has virtuous friends, peer pressure can be healthy. He may be held accountable by Christian pals; he may want to pattern his life after the guy who memorizes Scripture or the girl who seems to know Jesus so well. Godly friends move kids toward a godly future.

Make church connections. Sunday school classes, youth groups, children's choirs, and other church programs can be great places to find good companions. If you have preschoolers, try arranging playdates with children of parents you meet at church; friendships formed early can last a lifetime. If possible, volunteer to help with the children's program so that you can see whether it allows your child to truly interact with others. When opportunities arise for your child to deepen Christian friendships at camp or on a retreat, take them. If the cost of such an activity makes you hesitate, find out whether your church offers financial assistance—as many do.

Invite them home. Get to know the kids who influence your child. Make your home a place where your child's friends are welcome; have snacks on hand, and try to keep your schedule loose enough to allow for casual conversations with (not interrogations of) your guests. When your child's friends are present, follow your family's usual procedures regarding prayer before meals, devotions, and other expressions of faith; the reactions of your child's friends may tell you something. If another child seems to be influencing yours negatively, you may need to limit contact—but if your family can be a positive influence on the friend, try not to miss that chance.

Parental Action: Find Better Media "Friends"

Not all companions are made of flesh and blood. Some arrive in your home on TV, CD, and DVD. Their influence on your child can be enormous. Do these "virtual" companions promote godly virtues? In addition to monitoring your youngster's entertainment intake, try taking these positive steps.

Discover CCM. Young pilgrims aren't helped by spending time with recording artists who promote "virtues" like hedonism, anarchy, and hopelessness. If your teen or preteen hasn't discovered contemporary Christian music (CCM), try introducing him to this collection of musicians who—though they certainly aren't perfect—generally attempt to advance Christ and biblical values. To get started, check the book *Chart Watch* by Bob Waliszewski and Bob Smithouser (Tyndale, 1998), which contains album reviews and hints about choosing Christian artists whose styles might appeal to your son or daughter. Keep up with current albums by subscribing to *Plugged In* magazine; teens can read about the spiritual commitments of CCM personalities in magazines like *Brio* (for girls) and *Breakaway* (for boys). All three of these periodicals are available from Focus on the Family (1-800-A-FAMILY).

Find the moral of the story. If you're already advocating virtue with younger children through video and audio series from your local Christian bookstore—series like VeggieTales, Adventures in Odyssey, Bibleman, and Ribbits—great. But are you helping your kids absorb the messages in these stories? While you don't want to turn fun into tedium, ask a few casual questions after your child watches or listens. For instance, after viewing the

VeggieTales video *Dave and the Giant Pickle*, ask, "Who do you think was the greatest hero in this story? Larry-Boy? Dave? Was there a hero you couldn't see? What do you think makes a person a hero? What kind of hero would you like to be?"

Have a movie night. Get the book *Movie Nights*, edited by Bob Smithouser (Tyndale, 2002). Designed to ease discussion between parents and teens, this guide features descriptions of selected movies you can rent on video and helps for talking about the moral values therein. You can take the same approach with younger children, watching their favorite TV shows and films and asking them which characters made good or bad decisions and what happened as a result.

Be a V-Chip. Explain to your child that some TV sets contain a "V-Chip" that helps parents block certain shows that are violent or otherwise unsuitable. If your family watches TV, assign each person to be a "V-Chip" for a week—with the "V" standing for virtue. Put a bell or battery-powered buzzer next to your television set. For a week, instead of just filtering out bad programs, your human V-Chips should ring the bell or buzz the buzzer when a show presents a biblical virtue in a good light—and share this information with at least one other family member.

SAFE AT HOME

Everyone wants peace. But the world can't give it—especially the world in which our children find themselves.

Jesus tells us that He alone brings true peace (John 14:27). When our kids learn to live virtuous lives in His power, they'll experience the peace of God.

Bunyan's pilgrim isn't the only one who can enjoy the tranquility of living amid personal responsibility, wisdom, devotion to God, and love. As you and your children learn to practice biblical virtues, your home can be a "House Beautiful" too.

Chapter 6

THE DEVIL
AT THE DOOR

Preparing Your Child for Spiritual Warfare

꠸

As Christian began to step through the gate of salvation, Goodwill suddenly grabbed his arm and yanked him to the other side.

Startled, Christian stumbled. "What was that all about?" he asked when he had regained his balance.

Goodwill's smile faded, and his voice dropped to a murmur. "A little distance from this gate," he explained, "there is a strong castle, of which Beelzebub is the captain. From there, he and his followers shoot arrows at those that come up to this gate. The goal is to kill the traveler before he can enter."

Christian's eyes widened. "Then I rejoice—and tremble."

꠸

Before Christian passed through the gate, he didn't realize that the lair of a sworn enemy lay nearby. Beelzebub—one of the names for Satan—loved to fire his deadly arrows at would-be pilgrims.

Christian had already learned the hard way that the pilgrim's journey is pocked with pitfalls. Now he has learned one of the most important lessons of all: Once we decide to enter God's doorway to salvation, we align ourselves against the forces of hell.

The Invisible Enemy

Goodwill, the gatekeeper, was aware of a danger that Christian hadn't even noticed. Before coming to Christ, we don't appreciate the spiritual warfare that's taking place all around us either. As the apostle Paul noted in 1 Corinthians 2:14, "The man without the Spirit does not accept the things that come from the Spirit of God, for they are foolishness to him, and he cannot understand them, because they are spiritually discerned."

Even many "born again" young people dismiss the idea of spiritual warfare. In fact, many don't believe Satan is a real being. A survey by Josh McDowell's ministry in the 1990s found that 51 percent of church-attending, evangelical youth believed Satan wasn't real—or weren't sure. In 2000, a Barna Research Group poll reported that 65 percent of teens thought Satan was only a symbol of evil, not an actual person.

These statistics are part of a larger battle. We are raising our children in a culture that talks about "spirituality" but shows less and less understanding that God and Satan are personal. The idea that Satan leads a spiritual army is even less acceptable to people today.

From a biblical perspective, however, there are two worlds: the observed, natural, physical world, and the unseen, spiritual world, which is understood only by those who have received Jesus Christ by faith. One of our most vital responsibilities as parents is to help our children understand that they have a powerful enemy who is real, and whose strategies are designed to foil their quest for the Celestial City:

> For our struggle is not against flesh and blood, but against the rulers, against the authorities, against the powers of this dark world and against the spiritual forces of evil in the heavenly realms. (Ephesians 6:12)

Our daughter Rebekah observed the reality of this spiritual struggle. As a teenager she had a friend we'll call Jerry, a young man who shared her love of theater and music. Over the course of several years Rebekah noticed a slow change in him; he began dressing in black and talking more and more about witchcraft, Satanism, and the occult. Rebekah tried to remind him that there was only one way to fulfillment—that God's power was the only power worth having. But Jerry had been captured. Eventually Rebekah learned that Jerry was into drug abuse and a homosexual lifestyle. His life was unraveling in self-destruction and despair, thanks to a very real foe.

PREPARING TO HIT THE BEACH

The next day Discretion, Piety, Prudence, and Charity led Christian into the armory. There they showed him all kinds of equipment which their Lord had provided for pilgrims—including sword, shield, helmet, breastplate, and shoes that would not wear out. There were enough arms to equip as many men for the service of their Lord as there are stars in the heavens.

Later they harnessed Christian from head to foot with armor, in case he should meet with assaults on his journey. Being thus outfitted, he walked out with his friends to the gate and was on his way.

What an impressive armory Christian was shown by his hosts in The House Beautiful!

Some of the equipment—sword, shield, helmet, etc.—is familiar to those who've read Ephesians 6:13-17:

> Therefore put on the full armor of God, so that when the day of evil comes, you may be able to stand your ground, and after you have done everything, to stand. Stand firm then, with the belt of truth buckled around your waist, with the breastplate of righteousness in place, and with your feet fitted with the readiness that comes from the gospel of peace. In addition to all this, take up the shield of faith, with which you can extinguish all the flaming arrows of the evil one. Take the helmet of salvation and the sword of the Spirit, which is the word of God.

But in addition to these tools of war, Bunyan's original text lists relics of biblical battles—the rod of Moses, pitchers and lamps and trumpets of Gideon, David's slingshot.

What do these artifacts of the Old Testament have in common? First, they were used by men and women of God to win great battles in His name.

Second, they were not the kind of weapons any skilled soldier would want to use in war; they were simple tools of everyday life. Yet with God leading the charge, these items became awesome armaments.

Christian was being taught a powerful lesson by the maidens of virtue: Spiritual warfare is God's battle, not ours, and it must be won God's way. Only then can the Lord amaze us by using our ordinary lives to vanquish the Prince of Darkness. In the words of Zechariah 4:6, " 'Not by might nor by power, but by my Spirit,' says the LORD Almighty."

Spiritual warfare is fought and won with the weapons of God, not man. Victory is assured for the soldier who follows orders, because the outcome of the battle is His—not ours.

Meeting Satan in the Ring

Now, in this valley of Humiliation, poor Christian would face the greatest danger yet. He hadn't been there long before he spotted a foul fiend coming over the field to meet him. The creature's name was Apollyon.

The monster was hideous to behold. His skin was scaly, like that of a fish; he had wings like a dragon and feet like a bear. Out of his belly came fire and smoke, and his mouth was like a lion's.

Christian froze. Should he go back? Should he stand his ground?

"I have no armor for my back," he told himself. "If I turn my back to this monster, he'll pierce me with arrows." His armor clanked as he stood taller. "I'll stand my ground," he murmured. "If nothing else, it may save my life."

He walked on, and soon he could see Apollyon's snakelike face. It held a scornful expression, and when the beast finally spoke, its guttural voice was equally filled with disdain.

"Where did you come from?" Apollyon snarled. "And where are you going?"

Christian tried not to tremble. "I am come from the city of Destruction, the place of all evil, and I am going to the city of Zion."

The beast snorted. "Then you are one of my subjects, for Destruction is mine. I am the prince and god of it! Why have you run away from your king? If I thought your service to me were ended, I would strike you to the ground with one blow!"

Christian's heart pounded. "I was, indeed, born in your territory. But your service was hard, and no one could live on your wages. After all, the pay for sin is death! So when I was grown, I set out to improve my lot."

The verbal parrying continued. Then something like a chuckle came from Apollyon's throat. He fixed Christian with a cold smile that bared most of his fangs. "You call yourself a servant, eh? You have already been unfaithful in your service to this Prince. What makes you think you'll receive wages from Him?"

Christian felt perspiration break out on his forehead. "In what way," he asked, "have I been unfaithful?"

"You practically fainted in the Slough of Despond," the creature cackled. "You tried all the wrong ways to get rid of your burden. You fell asleep and lost your book. You nearly turned back when you saw the lions. And deep down, when you tell others about your journey, you want them to think you're a hero!"

Christian sighed. "All this is true—and much more that you've left out. But the Prince I serve and honor is merciful, and ready to forgive. He has already pardoned me."

Apollyon's grin vanished, and he spat on the ground. "I am this Prince's enemy! I hate Him, His laws, and His people!" His hand went to his crossbow. "I am here with a purpose, Christian. I have come to stop you in your tracks."

Instinctively, Christian raised the shield in his hand a little higher. "Apollyon, be careful what you do. This is the King's highway, the way of holiness. Watch yourself!"

The beast spat again, and seemed to straddle the whole road. "You don't scare me, pilgrim. Prepare to die! I swear by my infernal den that you'll go no further. Here I will spill your soul!"

Apollyon's eyes seemed to glow red as he shot a flaming arrow at Christian's chest. Ptang! came the report as the arrow hit the shield and dropped to the ground.

Suddenly Apollyon's darts were coming Christian's way as thick as hail. Christian maneuvered his shield as quickly as he could, but was soon wounded in his head, hand, and foot.

Christian drew his own bow and let an arrow fly—then another, and another, all of them deflected by Apollyon's shield. Then it was the fiend's turn. Christian blocked the darts with his shield, but the pain of his wounds was like fire.

Christian resisted as manfully as he could. But as the combat raged for an hour, then half a day, he grew weaker and weaker.

Finally Apollyon, seeing his opportunity, rushed at Christian and began to wrestle with him. All at once Christian's feet slipped out from under him, and the sword flew from his hand.

"I have you now!" the beast said with a laugh, and raised his sword for a final blow.

With his last ounce of strength, Christian reached toward the spot where he thought his own weapon had fallen. Just as it seemed Apollyon would triumph, Christian's fingers closed around the handle of his sword.

"Don't rejoice over me, my enemy," he breathed. "When I fall, I shall arise." With that he thrust his sword at Apollyon's chest.

Roaring in pain, the creature fell back.

Christian scrambled to his feet. "In all these things we are more than conquerors through Him who loved us!" he cried, and brandished the sword once more.

With a hideous hiss, Apollyon spread forth his dragon wings. A moment later he was rising into the air, wings beating. In another moment he had sped away.

Weak and shaking, Christian managed a smile as he watched the creature flee. He would never see the beast again.

Christian's battle with the hideous Apollyon is the most fearsome challenge he's encountered so far. Bunyan gives us a bone-chilling picture of how ferocious our enemy is, and how deadly his blows can be.

Who is Apollyon? In Greek, his name means "the destroyer." He probably represents the Apollyon in Revelation 9:11, the fallen angel who has power over the abyss and unleashes a horrible attack against believers. Bible scholars disagree over whether Scripture's Apollyon is Satan himself, or a high-ranking demonic prince.

What is Christian's first response to this fire-breathing monster? Total fear! Yet in the end, the battered Christian drives off his enemy. How?

First, Christian ignores Apollyon's chest-thumping "tough guy" routine. Our pilgrim overcomes the blustering threats and accusations by citing the forgiveness he's received in Christ.

Next, Christian realizes that his spiritual armor can protect his front, but not his back. It dawns on him that his battle equipment was designed for plowing straight ahead by faith, leaving no option for retreat. He stands his ground.

Then, as Apollyon hurls flaming darts, Christian wards off most of them with the "shield of faith."

Finally, using his only offensive weapon, Christian vanquishes Apollyon. We—and our young pilgrims—can do the same today, courageously wielding the "sword of the Spirit, which is the word of God" (Ephesians 6:17).

SPIRITUAL ARMOR IN ACTION

A few years ago we saw how important it is to prepare our children to fight the spiritual battle. It happened when our college-age son, Samuel, was critically wounded in an accidental shooting.

A friend standing next to Samuel was holding a handgun his father had given him, and it went off. The bullet entered the back of our son's head, ricocheted off the membrane surrounding the brain, and exited through the other side of his skull. Miraculously, the bullet did not invade his brain—and he survived.

But he had suffered a serious head injury with devastating effects. We had to withdraw him from college and bring him home for recuperation and rehabilitation. At first he couldn't see out of one eye; his hearing, sense of smell, and taste were impaired. He couldn't walk straight or feed himself, and one side of his body was partially paralyzed. At night he would roll and moan in bed with excruciating, relentless head pain. We took turns sleeping on the floor of his bedroom with him.

One night he bolted upright from restless sleep and yelled for us.

"Is Jesus in the room?" he cried out.

"Yes," one of us answered. "He's here. And He will still be here with you when you wake up in the morning."

It was a spiritual battle as well as a physical one. During months of rehabilitation, as Samuel faced the possibility that he would never fully recover, it seemed Apollyon was bellowing at him, "You were once strong and healthy. Now look at you. Where is your God now? Where is He when you scream in pain at night?"

But Samuel held the shield of faith. He believed the Lord loved him. We would pray together, work together, and cry together through his slow recovery. We relied on the sword of the Spirit—including the scriptural promise that God does not test us beyond our ability to withstand.

Through God's mercy, Samuel made a complete recovery. He graduated from college—and recently married a wonderful Christian girl, Allison.

We echo Christian's last words before he drove off Apollyon, based on Romans 8:37: "In all these things we are more than conquerors through him who loved us."

DEFEATING THE DEVIL:
PRACTICAL PROGRESS FOR PARENTS AND KIDS

Christians don't always agree on the nature of spiritual warfare. It's clear, though, that our children won't be able to sit on the sidelines in a battle that's likely to heat up during the next decade. Here are some things you can do to help them get ready.

Principle #1: Take a Balanced Approach

How do we prepare our children for the prevailing climate of opinion, which will ridicule their Bible-based view of Satan, sin, and demonic warfare?

The first thing to understand is the need for balance. C. S. Lewis noted that there are two common mistakes Christians make when it comes to the devil. One is to deny that Satan exists; the other is to develop a morbid fascination with the subject. John Bunyan's protagonist managed to avoid both extremes. We must teach our children to do the same.

Parental Action: Tell Them the Devil Is Real

Find personal references. Using a concordance, locate as many Bible passages as possible that mention the devil (look under words like "Satan" and "Deceiver," too). Read some with your child. Here are a few examples:

- The Serpent in the Garden (Genesis 3)
- Satan and God discuss Job (Job 1)
- Jesus is tempted in the wilderness (Matthew 4)
- Satan is thrown into the lake of fire (Revelation 20)

After reading each passage, ask, "Does the devil seem like a real person here—or just a force, like gravity? How can you tell? Why do you suppose some people have such a hard time believing the devil is a real being?"

Emphasize villainy, not scariness. Parents who want to tell young children about the devil face a dilemma: How can you describe Satan without giving a little boy or girl nightmares? Try talking about the devil as the ultimate "bad guy," not the ultimate boogeyman. Portraying Satan as horned, hoofed, or hooded is more medieval than biblical. It's more accurate to call him a power-hungry liar who masquerades as an "angel of light" (2 Corinthians 11:14). Instead of stressing spookiness, explain that the devil refuses to obey God—a concept most children should be able to grasp.

Parental Action: Tell Them the Devil Is Doomed

The second part of a balanced approach is to assure our kids that there is victory in Christ. Satan has temporarily raised a rebel kingdom on earth, but it will not stand. Looking at the Book of Revelation will show young pilgrims that Satan's doom is certain. We also need to let them know that Satan has no hold over them now: "You, dear children, are from God and have overcome them, because the one who is in you is greater than the one who is in the world" (1 John 4:4).

Update "Fortress." With your older child, look up Martin Luther's classic "A Mighty Fortress Is Our God" in a hymnbook. Both the devil's wiles and his eventual downfall figure prominently in this song, especially in lines like these:

> For still our ancient foe
> Doth seek to work us woe;
> His craft and power are great,
> And armed with cruel hate,
> On earth is not his equal.
>
> Did we in our own strength confide,
> Our striving would be losing;
> Were not the right Man on our side,
> The Man of God's own choosing.

Dost ask who that may be?
Christ Jesus, it is He...

After reading (or singing) the lyrics, challenge your child to put them in modern language that still rhymes. Work together as needed. If one or both of you are musically inclined, you might even want to put your new lyrics to a fresh tune.

Write his epitaph. After talking about the devil's future defeat, ask your older child, "If the lake of fire had a tombstone for the devil, what do think would be written on it?" Encourage your youngster to use his imagination; come up with your own version, too. Here's an example to get you started:

Here lies Beelzebub,
Thought he was smart;
Took on the Lord
With hate in his heart;
Just couldn't stand
To be under God's thumb;
Here lies Beelzebub—
Boy, was he dumb.

Principle #2: Clarify What's at Stake

Just as Christian was surprised to find himself in Beelzebub's sights at the gate, our kids may be taken aback to learn that they're in the midst of a spiritual war. "I didn't sign up for that!" they may think. Others may simply be mystified by the idea of an unseen battle. Here are some ways to help children come to terms with a sometimes confusing concept.

Parental Action: Explain the Warfare Analogy

Use the news. When it comes to battle, your child's frame of reference may be the U.S. war on terrorism that followed September 11, 2001's airplane hijackings and attacks on the World Trade Center and Pentagon. If he or she watched news reports of this event and of U.S. planes bombing Afghanistan, you can use these images to help explain the idea of spiritual warfare. Observe that some of the devil's assaults will be open, obvious "air attacks"—perhaps in the form of withering ridicule by non-Christian kids.

But the devil is also fond of sneak attacks, tempting us at our weak spots. Like a spiritual terrorist, he hides and waits and strikes in unexpected ways. Resisting such an enemy requires being on the alert—and assuming he is always out there.

Allow battlegrounds and playgrounds. Children want to view the world as a playground, not a battlefield. Keep this in mind as you tell them about spiritual warfare, taking care not to overload them with "war talk." Young children can understand that Satan is real—but so is God, who loves them and will take care of them. Early elementary-age kids need to learn the details of Satan's fall and ours, and the part he plays in temptation. Preteens are ready for the "big picture" of end-times Bible prophecies, including God's victory over the devil. Whether your child is in first grade or twelfth, let her know that even though much of life is fun, the playgrounds are surrounded by the fields of battle.

Parental Action: Help Them to Stay Alert

Life has so many interesting distractions; who wants to be on spiritual alert all the time? We can almost hear our own foursome in their earlier years, shouting in unison, "What a bummer!" Yet Scripture delivers this mandate: "Be self-controlled and alert. Your enemy the devil prowls around like a roaring lion looking for someone to devour" (1 Peter 5:8).

Try color codes. In 2002, increased concern over terrorist threats led the U.S. Department of Homeland Security to adopt a color-coded system to indicate a threat's urgency—yellow being less worrisome than orange, and orange less alarming than red, for example. You can use the same idea to remind family members that spiritual attacks are always possible. Make a chart to post on the refrigerator or bulletin board, featuring colored circles (choose your own hues) that represent various states of alertness. Every so often, perhaps when you're all at the dinner table, ask, "What do you think our state of spiritual alertness should be this week? Why?" Put a magnet or pushpin on the chart to indicate the consensus or average. The point is not to literally assess the risk of spiritual onslaught on any given day—a difficult task at best—but to remind kids that the danger is always there, and to talk about why we may be more vulnerable at some times than at others.

Build an early warning system. Help your child to recognize early when he or she needs to resist the devil (James 4:7). Most kids, like adults, "play along" with temptation as long as they can, rather than drawing a line at the first sign that they might be a target. Read James 1:13-15 together, which notes the fact that temptation tends to occur in stages. Then talk about how a boy might be tempted to hit his sister. What would be the first hint of trouble? When the boy gets mad enough to hit? When the thought of hitting enters his mind? When he raises his hand to hit? Chances are that the two of you can identify an earlier point—the beginning of the argument, for instance—at which the boy could see a fight brewing, and back off until he and his sister can talk without arguing. For older kids, discuss how this "early warning system" might apply to "going too far" on a date.

Principle #3: Equip Them for Battle

Our children need to understand the devil's game plan. While we don't know exactly what he has in mind, his *modus operandi* isn't entirely unpredictable. Our kids also need to visit the spiritual armory, as Christian did, to be outfitted with protective gear and offensive weaponry.

Parental Action: Study Enemy Strategy

Discover Screwtape. The best source of information about the enemy's typical behavior is, of course, the Bible—especially passages like the one describing Jesus' temptation in the wilderness. But another resource to share with your child (ages 12 and up) is *The Screwtape Letters* by C. S. Lewis (Harper San Francisco, 2001). In this book, Lewis gives us an entertaining, often humorous look at what the battle over human souls might look like from the perspective of two low-ranking demons. The book is also available in a four-hour, abridged audio version (Audio Literature, 1999). After reading or listening together, talk about the devil's strategies. Ask questions like, "How did the devil's workers try to defeat the Christian? Do you think any of their methods might work on you? Now that you know the story, what should you watch out for?"

Watch the instant replay. Football teams often videotape games, then watch the tapes later to learn from their mistakes and to better understand their opponents' strategies. We can use the "replay" idea to help our children improve their devil-resisting skills. When you know your child has been struggling with a particular sin—say, flying off the handle every time she's disappointed—talk about it. Choose a relaxed moment, perhaps at bedtime. Ask your child to imagine an "instant replay" of the last time she gave in to this temptation. What happened? How did the skirmish begin? What was so appealing about the wrong behavior? When would it have been easiest to resist? Next time the temptation occurs, what will it probably look like? How and when can your child fight back—and how would she like you to support her efforts?

Parental Action: Give Them the Weapons

Put on the armor. To introduce young children to the idea of spiritual armor, try making the Ephesians 6 battle gear out of cardboard and tin foil. Have your child put the armor on; talk about each piece and how it stands for something we can use in our fight against evil.

Act it out. Older kids may enjoy acting out a spiritual warfare skit for the rest of the family. One such script is "The Whole Armor" by John Duckworth, found in his book *High-Impact Worship Dramas* (Group Publishing, 1999). In this humorous sketch, a sleazy salesperson tries to sell a new believer stylish but ineffective substitutes for the Ephesians 6 weaponry—including the Sash of Sincerity, the Hair Spray of Holiness, and the Tie Tack of Tolerance. After applauding your actors, discuss the fact that real spiritual armor may not be the most fashionable outfit available—but it's the only one that works.

ONWARD, CHRISTIAN SOLDIERS

Even young children can learn that God wants us to stand up against the devil—and that He gives us the strength to do that.

One of our greatest challenges as parents is to model what it means to be soldiers in a war that our culture believes is nonexistent. With Christian's example in mind, however, we can face the enemy and win—never forgetting that the battle ultimately belongs to the Lord.

"I will give thanks to the One who has rescued me from the mouth of the lion and who helped me against Apollyon," Christian vowed, still panting. And he did so, saying:

"Old Beelzebub, the captain of this fiend,
Designed my ruin; therefore to this end
He sent him well equipped; and he, with rage
That hellish was, did fiercely me engage:
But guardian angels helped me, and I,
Through shield and sword, did finally make him fly.
Therefore to Him let me give lasting praise,
And thank and bless His holy name always."

Chapter 7

THE FLESH TOO WILLING

Helping Your Child Avoid
Sexual Immorality

～ତ

When he had caught up to his good friend Faithful, Christian said, "Tell me now what you've encountered along the road so far. Surely you've met with some interesting things."

Faithful tilted his head to one side, thinking. "I escaped that swamp—the same one you fell into. I got to the gate…" He cleared his throat, looking embarrassed. "There was that person whose name was Wanton…"

"A man or a woman?"

"A woman. One who would have liked to cause me trouble."

Christian raised his eyebrows. "It's good you slipped out of her net. In the Old Testament, Joseph found himself in the clutches of such a woman. He escaped her as you did, but it nearly cost him his life." He cast Faithful a sideward glance. "What did she do to you?"

Faithful's expression was pained. "You would not believe what a flatterer she was. She kept pressing me to…take a detour with her. She promised me all kinds of…contentment."

"Hmm," mused Christian. "I assume she did not promise you the contentment of a good conscience."

Faithful blushed. "You know what I mean; all...uh...carnal and fleshly contentment."

"Thank God you escaped her."

"I..." Faithful hesitated. "I'm not sure whether I did escape her completely."

"What?" Christian asked, startled. "You didn't consent to her desires, did you?"

"No, no," Faithful was quick to reply. "I didn't defile myself. I remembered an old writing I had seen: 'Her steps take hold on hell.' So I shut my eyes, not wanting to be hypnotized by her looks. That made her angry, and she yelled at me; I went on my way."

~🍥

Sex and the Seventeenth Century

Christian has been joined by another pilgrim—Faithful. As they walk, Faithful describes trials and temptations he's faced along the way. He's managed to avoid some troubles Christian experienced, but has been nearly destroyed by others. Such was the case in his encounter with Ms. Wanton.

The word *wanton* comes from a combination of Old English terms that roughly meant "deficient of discipline." *Webster's New Collegiate Dictionary* lists such synonyms for *wanton* as *lewd, bawdy, lustful,* and *sensual.*

Ms. Wanton is a clever picture of sexual temptation. Attractive and cunning, she nearly persuades Faithful to return her advances.

Is it surprising that a seventeenth-century man would encounter sexual temptation? With our culture's overemphasis on sexuality in entertainment, advertising, and elsewhere, it's easy to assume that the lust problem began at some point in the twentieth century. We might even chart the starting point at the publication of the first issue of *Playboy* magazine, or with the showing of the first X-rated movie.

But that would be naïve, as Bunyan demonstrates. Sexual temptation was alive and well in 1678, when *Pilgrim's Progress* was written. In fact, as Christian reminds Faithful, sexual sin is at least as old as the Old Testament.

Sex and the City—and Everywhere Else

Lust is nothing new. But we parents face a huge challenge as we try to help our children avoid sexual snares in today's world. There continue to be ominous, seismic shifts in the way people view the relationship between sex, marriage, and having children.

According to the National Opinion Research Center, there has been a slight increase in the percentage of people who believe teenage premarital sex is "always wrong." That's good news. The bad news is the still-increasing number of people who believe premarital sex between *adults* is all right.[1]

One U.S. study published in 2000 indicated that 54 percent of all first marriages began as cohabitations.[2] Another showed an increase in the number of people who think there's no need to get married if you want to have children.[3]

We can't pretend, meanwhile, that premarital sex hasn't invaded the church. Christian teens encounter the same kinds of temptations that others do. Surveys confirm, as do talks we've had with numerous parents and church youth counselors, that Christian kids are having sex at a rate that approaches that of their non-Christian peers.

Our daughter Sarah has observed this sad phenomenon while working in a youth ministry. She recalls one girl in particular—let's call her Eve—who seemed to be struggling with sexual temptation. Sarah invited her out to dinner, where the two of them chatted. To Sarah's surprise, Eve was completely open about her situation. After giving it some thought, Eve said, she'd decided she was going to have sex with her boyfriend on prom night. Eve had heard sex was great—and "with life being so hard right now, I just want to do something that is fun." The girl had decided to break God's law as if she were choosing to go to a theme park—despite identifying herself as a born-again Christian and being regularly involved in church activities.

To make matters worse, we're seeing more and more Christian young people whose lives are devastated by the consequences of sexual sin. Sexually transmitted diseases (STDs) are on the rise. And too many Christian teens are embracing the deadly idea that abortion is the way out of a crisis caused by sexual immorality.

When it comes to sex, young people are only imitating the attitudes and actions of their elders. How can we expect teens to reject premarital sex when they see large numbers of unmarried adults practicing promiscuity?

We can't wait for our schools or even our churches to give our children the right attitude toward chastity. It's up to us as parents to make sure our children have a solid foundation for sexual purity.

Unfortunately, too few parents seem to take their responsibilities in this area seriously. We saw that when our two daughters, then in their early teens, were invited to a slumber party. We thought we knew the family well enough; the home was within 50 yards of ours. But later that night we heard a knock at our door. Our girls were standing on the porch.

"Why are you home so soon?" we asked.

The girls explained that the "all girl" slumber party had quickly evolved into a "make out" session when several boys dropped by. The parents who were chaperoning the sleepover actually welcomed the boys and allowed them to stay for the night—saying that teenagers were going to have sex anyway, so they might as well do it in the safety of a parent's home!

We're glad our daughters, unlike those parents, knew there are absolutes when it comes to sexual purity. Let's fortify all our kids to resist temptation—instead of seeing how close they can fly to the flame without getting burned.

Advancing Abstinence: Practical Progress for Parents and Kids

Of all the areas in which we need to prepare our children, this one probably intimidates parents most. Embarrassment about the subject, guilt over past lapses, or not wanting to acknowledge a youngster's sexuality can keep even the best-intentioned parent silent. You don't have to shed every inhibition or become an expert on the topic, however, before you can help your child develop a healthy, biblical perspective on sex. Here are some practical principles and actions to employ.

Principle #1: Motivate Them

It took effort for Faithful to resist Ms. Wanton's charms, but he was motivated to exert that effort. Why? He didn't want to "defile" himself. And why did that matter? Because it would offend and disappoint the God he loved.

All the lectures, rules, and scary statistics in the world won't keep a young person on the path of purity when the opportunity to stray arises. Real motivation is internal, and it comes from loving God and respecting those He created in His image.

Parental Action: Feed Their Relationship with God
Encouraging abstinence is more than making sure that our teens keep their pants zipped and their hands and time otherwise occupied. A love for God will guide them even when no one else is around and they're tempted by sexual pleasure.

Start early. Don't wait until adolescence arrives to begin cultivating your child's relationship with God. The goal is to make it personal—between your child and God—rather than an extension of your own spiritual commitment. To help you meet that goal, you may want to share with your child some of the many books designed to deepen his or her relationship with God. Here are just a few.

Birth to age three: *Playtime Devotions* by Christine Harder Tangvald (Standard Publishing, 2002) provides simple songs, games, rhymes, and prayers that introduce the youngest children to the God who loves them.

Preschool: *God Says I Am* by Laura Derico, *Jesus Loves You* by Diane Stortz, and *Jesus Must Be Really Special* by Jennie Bishop (all from Standard Publishing, 2002) use words and pictures to explain the Lord's attributes and His desire to have a relationship with each of us.

Elementary: *My Time with God* by Jeanette Dall, Carla Williams, and B. J. Bassett and *My Time with God, Volume 2* by Jeanette Dall and Jean Gowen Dennis (both from Tyndale, 2000) feature lively, Bible-based devotions for ages 8-12.

Middle school/high school: *LifeTraining* and *LifeTraining 2* by Joe White (Tyndale, 1998 and 2000) are packed with hundreds of thought-provoking devotions. Teens can ponder the readings on their own, or parents can use them as family devotions that include their adolescents.

Find a small group. Worship services, Sunday school, and other large-group events are important. But many parents discover that their kids' spiritual growth soars in a small Bible study—sometimes known as an "accountability group" or "discipleship group." Most commonly offered for preteens and adolescents, these programs usually include mutual support as well as Bible reading and prayer. Ask whether your church offers such a program, or would be willing to start one.

Give a promise ring. When your child makes the connection between loving God and abstaining from premarital sex, it's an occasion worth celebrating. After you've discussed the subject, or after your teen has attended a youth group meeting or other event promoting sexual purity, ask whether he's willing to commit to abstinence until marriage. If so, give him a tangible reminder of that promise—a ring, for example. Girls may prefer a necklace they can save and give to their husbands on their wedding night, symbolizing the gift of chastity they've preserved for their spouses.

Parental Action: Teach Respect for Others

When kids respect others, they don't use or betray them. Joseph's respect for his boss, among other reasons, kept him from having sex with the boss's wife; it would have been a shocking betrayal of his employer's trust. Boys in particular need to work at cherishing the girls they find attractive, valuing them and not using them as sexual objects. We need to teach kids that sex outside of marriage betrays both the other person and God Himself.

Go on a date. Younger children will enjoy the chance to "go on a date" with a parent. A son can "take Mom out" to a restaurant; Dad could do the same for a daughter. During this date, help your child practice showing respect for the opposite sex. Boys can hold the door open for Mom and let her order first, for example; girls can ask Dad about his interests, listen carefully to his answers, and thank him for buying dinner.

Face the music. Ask your teen or preteen to share with you a few favorite songs that describe male-female relationships. Then ask, "Do you think these songs show enough respect for the opposite sex? Why or why not?" Some rap lyrics, for example, depict women as little more than prostitutes; some country songs revel in revenge against unfaithful men. Next, compare these songs with ones that clearly convey a biblical view of premarital sex. One good example is "Wait for Me," recorded by Rebecca St. James—a poignant but upbeat request directed to a hoped-for spouse. Ask, "How does the singer show respect for the opposite sex—and for herself?"

Parental Action: Tell the Rest of the Story

Though the best motivation for abstinence is simply wanting to please God, facts about the risks of "safe sex" may also make teens think twice about giving in to sexual temptation. They're unlikely to hear these facts from most media outlets, so they need to hear them from you—or from resources you provide.

Show the video, read the book. With your teen, watch *No Apologies*, a powerful 30-minute video revealing the importance of purity and the risks of promiscuity. A book with the same title also gives teens strong reasons for choosing abstinence as the only true "safe sex." The video and book are available from Focus on the Family.

Talk back to TV. When you and your teen watch a documentary, panel discussion, or news report advocating "safe sex," make a list of assertions you'd like to question. For example, is the failure rate of condoms in preventing pregnancy mentioned? Does the show give the mistaken impression that condoms reliably prevent the spread of AIDS? Are other incurable STDs, some of which can't be prevented by condoms, described? Is there any mention of the emotional fallout of premarital sex? After the show, work together to compose an e-mail or letter to the producers of the program, challenging them to answer your questions.

Principle #2: Give Guidelines They'll Remember

Barry is a dad whose 11-year-old son Connor recently sat through a two-week public school course on human sexuality. Barry was careful to preview the videos and other materials used in the class, and was glad to see that they stuck to the "plumbing" of reproduction. *What a relief,* he thought. *I won't have to explain to Connor what all that stuff is.* But now Barry realizes his job is just beginning; when it comes to sexuality, Connor has to understand a lot more than biology. He needs moral guidance, and he needs it from Barry. Here are some things Barry—and you—can do along those lines.

Parental Action: Be Open

It's important to be a step ahead of our kids, ready and unashamed to discuss sexuality. We saw a good example of this when we were first married. An older missionary couple, our longtime friends, gave us a book as a wedding present. We figured it would be a Bible study or missions story. To our surprise, it was a book about how Christian spouses can have a successful sexual relationship! As much as possible, we need to get over the "blush factor" when talking to our children about sex. It'll be on their minds, so we'd better have it on our lips. God designed sex; we need to take it back from the devil and explain how God wants us to enjoy it—in His timing and His way, within the bounds of marriage.

Practice before preaching. Too often parents go it alone when preparing to talk with their kids about sex. Dad silently steels himself to broach the subject with his son; Mom grits her teeth and approaches her daughter with a sheaf of mental notes. But we need moral support at times like these. Instead of taking the Lone Ranger approach, why not sit down with your spouse and talk through what you plan to say? Need help choosing your words? Need practice using them? Your mate can listen and offer feedback. Pray together about what you plan to say, too. If you're a single parent, try this with a trusted friend or youth leader.

Take a weekend. Sex education should be a process that stretches throughout childhood, gradually giving your child information for which she's ready—not a one-time, sweaty-palmed "big talk." At the end of that process, however, it's good to summarize what you've said over the years and to launch your child into adolescence. Dr. James Dobson advocates a "Preparing for Adolescence Weekend" in which parent and preteen get away from home to address concerns about self-esteem and life direction as well as sexuality. To get ready for that weekend, you and your child can read Dr. Dobson's book *Preparing for Adolescence* (Regal, 1989) or listen to an audio series based on the book (available through Focus on the Family at 1-800-A-FAMILY).

Parental Action: Be a Good Example

The best sexual guideline Christian parents can give their kids is to have a good marital relationship themselves. Do your children see you and your spouse displaying appropriate affection—the kiss in the kitchen, the hug in the hallway? Do they see you taking time for each other, perhaps going away for an occasional weekend? They'll remember whether Mom and Dad were obviously in love, physically as well as emotionally; to some degree, your example will become their model.

Send year-round valentines. Why limit hearts and flowers to February 14 and anniversaries? Let your spouse know you love him or her the rest of the year, too. Do so in a way your kids can see—by posting homemade valentines on the refrigerator once a week, for instance. Your youngsters may pretend to ignore them, or may wrinkle their noses and say, "Ewwww!" at these "mushy" expressions of affection. But they'll know

Mom and Dad are still in love—a great source of security and healthy sexual attitudes for any child.

Get out the album. Your kids might be shocked to see how young you and your spouse once looked—and how often you posed for pictures with your arms around each other. If you have photos or video from your courtship days, wedding, and honeymoon trip, drag them out and gather the family to look at them. Serve refreshments to entice kids who are reluctant to skip down memory lane. You might even take the opportunity to ask, "If you get married, what would you like *your* pictures to look like 20 years from now?"

Parental Action: Store Up Scripture

When Ms. Wanton tried to entice Faithful, his memory bank accessed a warning. "I remembered an old writing I had seen: 'Her steps take hold on hell.'" When your son or daughter faces sexual temptation, will that memory bank be empty, cluttered with bad advice from movie stars and magazines, or filled with prudent pointers from Scripture?

Create acronyms. Make it easier to retrieve those gems of biblical wisdom by turning them into compact acronyms. Start by challenging your child to condense a verse into a principle of no more than four words. Then ask him to memorize the first letters of those words. When the moment of temptation arrives, recalling the acronym may help him remember the principle. A few examples:

- NLL—No Lustful Looks. This comes from Job 31:1: "I made a covenant with my eyes not to look lustfully at a girl."
- HCSF—Hot Coals Scorch Feet. This is based on Proverbs 6:28: "Can a man walk on hot coals without his feet being scorched?"
- WBAS—We're Brothers and Sisters. This is drawn from 1 Timothy 5:1-2: "Treat younger men as brothers…and younger women as sisters, with absolute purity."

Study David's story. David's sexual misadventure with Bathsheba (2 Samuel 11-12) stands as a flashing warning sign to young people as well as adults. See whether you and your adolescent can trace three steps in David's moral fall. Here are three we've identified:

1. He was in *the wrong place.* What was David doing hanging around the palace, when his armies needed him at the battlefront?

2. He had *wandering eyes*. He spied a gorgeous woman bathing on the rooftop of a nearby building—not an unusual practice in those days. David's eyes went where they didn't belong, and led him to lust after a woman who didn't belong to him.

3. He issued an *improper invitation*. He suggested that he and Bathsheba meet. He knew this was way out of bounds; she was the wife of Uriah, one of his faithful soldiers. Without excuse, David was putting a flame to dry gunpowder.

After studying the story, ask your son or daughter how a young person today might avoid repeating these three mistakes.

Principle #3: Help Them Avoid Temptation

Our kids need to know that when Ms. Wanton comes sashaying down the road, they should cross to the other side. Perhaps Faithful couldn't have known from Ms. Wanton's appearance what she was after, but her flattery should have made him suspicious. In a world where sexual temptation seems to lurk in every chat room and car backseat, young people must be helped to steer clear of danger zones.

Parental Action: Teach Them to Guard Their Eyes

David's eyes got him into trouble; they were looking where they shouldn't have. Faithful, meanwhile, knew what to do when he teetered on the edge of Ms. Wanton's trap: "So I shut my eyes, not wanting to be hypnotized by her looks." Let's help our children—especially our boys, whose sexual engines run on visual input—to make wise choices about what they watch.

Sing a song. Preschoolers can start early by learning the action song "Be Careful, Little Eyes, What You See." To keep the discussion age-appropriate, focus on nonsexual visual temptations like a forbidden cookie jar or an overly violent cartoon.

Get tough with the Internet. Web sites featuring pornography are easily—even accidentally—accessed by children as well as adults. Self-control may be the best Internet filter, but parents can make eye-guarding easier by taking steps like these:

- Use an Internet Service Provider (ISP) that screens out "family-unfriendly" material, or one that offers you the option of blocking inappropriate sites. You can also buy software that denies access to certain sites or allows access only to approved sites.

- Put the computer in a room with plenty of foot traffic, rather than one where a child can "hide out" and visit questionable sites without interruption.
- Avoid revealing your e-mail address online. Pornographers and other "spammers" troll for addresses, then use them to send unsolicited messages with links to their sites—links on which any child could innocently click.
- To reduce the chances that your child will open a pornographic e-mail message, use an ISP that offers a "spam-blocking" service. Since none of these services is 100 percent effective, however, use a password to access e-mail—and don't share it with your kids.
- If you suspect that your child is viewing off-limits sites despite precautions you've taken, prohibit Web-surfing unless you're present (and enforce it with password-only access). You can also track your child's Internet travels with monitoring software that keeps a record of every site visited. If your child regularly goes to a friend's house where Internet access is available, get assurance from the friend's parents that they're filtering or monitoring—or have the friend come to *your* house instead.
- Tell your preteens and teens *why* you're so careful about Internet access. As a reminder, you may want to place a sign on top of or next to your computer monitor, quoting Psalm 101:3: "I will set before my eyes no vile thing."

Skip the sleaze. Many parents do what they can to tune out offensive TV shows—blocking cable channels, checking the ratings, and declaring certain programs out of bounds. Sometimes, however, when they sit down to watch a "clean" show with their kids, they're stunned by commercials and promos for other programs filled with sexual images and innuendo. If this is a problem in your home, consider taping the shows you want to watch and fast-forwarding through commercials—or getting a VCR with a "commercial skip" feature. With older children, you may want to make this a learning experience by handing them the remote and letting them decide which commercials to "zap."

Parental Action: Help Them to Flee

When Faithful shut his eyes to Ms. Wanton's allure, she was enraged. "That made her angry, and she yelled at me; I went on my way." He could have stuck around to assure Ms. Wanton that he wasn't rejecting her personally, or to discuss the prospect of being "just friends." Wisely, he chose to flee instead. Our kids often need to do the same, and could use our help in deciding exactly how and where to run.

Share Joseph's story. Explain to your teen or preteen that Joe was a young man—and a "hunk." As Genesis 39:6 puts it, "Joseph was well-built and handsome." Imagine him miles from home, in Egypt, where nobody from his hometown could spy on him. He could have told himself, "No one will ever know." He had reason to rebel, having been sold into slavery by his own brothers. He could have said, "I deserve a little pleasure; I've had a raw deal." But when his boss's wife tried to seduce him, he resisted. And he ran. He ran so suddenly and so fast that he left his jacket behind, in the woman's hands.

Ask, "Why is running sometimes the best thing to do? How would a guy 'run' if a pornographic Web site popped up on his computer? How would he run if he found himself at a party where an 'adult' video was about to be shown? How would a girl run if she arrived at her boyfriend's house to study, only to discover that his parents were gone and he had other things on his mind?"

Plan escape routes. Just as it's best to map out specific exits and meeting places in case of a house fire, it's most effective to plan how and where your child will flee when sexual temptation strikes. If your daughter finds herself stranded with a date who's pressing her to get physical, will she have a cell phone and an invitation to call you? If your son gets caught up in sexual fantasy, will he have a list of better things to do? Ask your young person to decide which escape routes would work best for him or her; the key is to plan ahead, rather than trying to improvise solutions in the heat of the moment.

All You Need Is Love

Sexual temptation may be as old as the Bible, but the way to avoid it is just as ancient.

Our challenge as parents is to replace the attraction of sexual sin with the attraction of obeying God. With honesty, tenderness, and consistency, we can teach our young ones that sexual immorality isn't just about breaking a bunch of rules. It's about breaking God's heart.

And that matters—because He is the true lover of our children's souls.

Chapter 8

THE SHAME GAME

*Raising Your Child in a Culture
of Conformity*

~❧

"So," Christian asked Faithful, "did you meet anyone else in that valley?"

"Yes, I met with Shame. But of all the men I met with on my pilgrimage, he, I think, bears the wrong name. This Shame was too bold-faced."

"Why? What did he say to you?"

Faithful threw up his hands as he walked. "He objected to religion itself. He said it was a pitiful, low, sneaking business for a man to mind religion. He said a tender conscience was an unmanly thing; and that for a man to watch over his words and ways, keeping himself from the liberty that brave spirits enjoy, would make him the ridicule of the times."

Faithful frowned. "Shame also pointed out that few of the mighty, rich, or wise, are pilgrims. Nor are they willing to lose everything in order to gain 'nobody knows what.' He also turned up his nose at the lowliness of those who believe, as well as their ignorance and unscientific views."

"Hmm," Christian grunted.

"That wasn't all," Faithful continued. "He said it was a shame to waste time listening to sermons, to ask a neighbor's forgiveness, or to make restitution. He said great men think religious people are strange."

"And what did you say to him?" Christian asked.

Faithful paused, picked up a stone, and heaved it in frustration at the *trunk of a nearby tree.* "Say? At first I didn't know what to say. All I could do was get red in the face." *He sighed, then started down the road again.* "But at last I began to consider that what men highly esteem can be an abomination to God. And I thought, 'This Shame tells me what men are, but he tells me nothing about what God, or the Word of God, is.' I also thought that on Judgment Day we will not be doomed to death or life according to the hecklers of the world, but according to God's wisdom and law."

"A point well taken," *Christian said.*

Faithful bowed slightly in humility, but kept walking. "So, I thought, 'What God says is best, is indeed best—even if all the men in the world are against it.' I could see that God prefers a tender conscience, and that those who make themselves fools for the kingdom of heaven are wisest. I could see that the poor man who loves Christ is richer than the greatest man in the world who hates Him."

"And did you share this with Mr. Shame?"

"I said, 'Leave me, Shame. You are an enemy to my salvation. Should I choose you over my sovereign Lord? If I do, how will I be able to look Him in the face when He returns? If I'm ashamed of His ways and His people, how can I expect Him to bless me?'"

Faithful shook his head. "I thought that was the end of it, but this Shame was a bold villain. I could scarcely get rid of him. He kept haunting me, whispering in my ear about the weaknesses of religion. Finally I told him he was wasting his time, because I saw the most value in the things that disgusted him. At last he gave up. When I'd shaken him off, I began to sing:

> "The trials of those who hear God's call,
> Are many, and expected all;
> We must be careful, or we may
> Be overcome by them and cast away.
> And so let all the pilgrims then
> Be vigilant, and conduct themselves like men."

Smiling, Christian reached over and slapped Faithful on the back. "I am glad, my brother, that you withstood this villain so bravely. As you say, I think he has the wrong name. He is so bold as to follow us in the streets, trying to *put us to shame—to make us ashamed of that which is good. Let us still resist him! For all his bravado, he promotes foolishness. As Solomon said, "The wise inherit honor, but fools he holds up to shame" (Proverbs 3:35).*

Faithful returned the smile. "I think we must cry to the One who wants us to stand for truth, asking for help against Shame."

IT'S A SHAME

Mr. Shame's name was indeed something of a misnomer. He wasn't shamed by anything. But he loved making others feel that way.

In particular, he seemed preoccupied with shaming pilgrims. He struck a blow at Faithful's masculine pride; having a tender conscience that warned when sin was committed was, he said, "an unmanly weakness."

According to Mr. Shame, the whole business of worshiping God, asking for forgiveness, being repentant, and restoring broken fellowship with others was ridiculous and very much beneath him. Mr. Shame would never grovel before God or anyone else. And those who did so earned his utter contempt.

Why would a pilgrim as strong as Faithful almost buckle when he heard the arguments of Mr. Shame? Because for a moment he forgot one of the most basic truths of the pilgrim's way: "What is highly valued among men is detestable in God's sight" (Luke 16:15).

This has everything to do with the idea of shame. And it has everything to do with the way our children need to handle the Shame Game.

WHERE SHAME COMES FROM

The Greek philosopher Zeno defined shame as the fear of being disgraced. Mark Twain put it another way—that man is the only animal that blushes, or needs to.

One thing we do know: Shame was not in the Garden of Eden before the first sin. There was perfect intimacy between husband and wife, and perfect openness to God. Genesis 2:25 says, "The man and his wife were both naked, and they felt no shame."

But then sin entered the world when Adam and Eve chose to disobey

God. What had been a seamless connection of love and fellowship and openness was broken. Now there was shame.

Genesis 3:8-10 tells us,

> Then the man and his wife heard the sound of the LORD God as he was walking in the garden in the cool of the day, and they hid from the LORD God among the trees of the garden. But the LORD God called to the man, "Where are you?"
>
> He answered, "I heard you in the garden, and I was afraid because I was naked; so I hid."

There it is—shame as the ultimate cover-up. It's about hiding from each other, and hiding from God.

Shame is what we feel when we think we're about to be found out. It happens when we think people will find us to be fools, frauds, failures, or worse. It's what takes place when we think our connectedness to others, or to God, is about to be broken.

YOUR CHILD: SHAME'S TARGET

Shame is a powerful tool. Children of all ages, but especially teens and pre-teens, can be devastated by it. Peers use shame to enforce conformity—but only certain kinds of conformity.

Think about it. In most public schools, students tolerate a wide range of bizarre adornment—tattoos, blue and green dyed hair, piercing of noses and lips and eyebrows and navels, baggy pants that threaten to go south at any moment, ripped T-shirts, and strange makeup (even among the boys). These are often seen as marks of individuality. There is no shame in these differences.

But watch what happens to the kids who are "on-fire" Christian believers, who pray together and carry their Bibles. It isn't long before other students start the process of shaming them.

Teachers sometimes get in on the act too. Our son Samuel took a filmmaking class from an instructor he respected. One day, though, the teacher sent out a volley of anti-Christian rhetoric, comparing Bible believers to the Taliban. After all, he said, what's the difference between

Al-Qaeda blowing up the World Trade Center and "Christians who blow up abortion clinics"?

After the shock wore off, Samuel was faced with a dilemma. Should he respond to the attack on his faith, or just sit quietly? Finally he raised his hand and pointed out that the teacher had just expressed the kind of intolerance with which he'd charged the entire Christian church.

The instructor paused. Then a tiny smile curled his lips. Instead of attacking our son, he said that he appreciated Samuel's honest reply.

Samuel had learned the importance of Paul's words in Romans 1:16: "I am not ashamed of the gospel.…"

In the seventeenth century and in our own, Bible believers have always been fair game for ridicule. Notice how Mr. Shame indicts pilgrims as a group, calling them unfortunate, ignorant, low-income people. Just a few years ago, in an amazing parallel, a writer for the *Washington Post* categorized conservative Christians as "poor, uneducated, and easy to command." CNN mogul Ted Turner sniped that Christians were "Bozos." Some things never change.

They're not likely to improve anytime soon, either. Even if our children are homeschooled, or educated exclusively in Christian schools, and we thrust them into every church-related activity we can find, they won't escape today's shaming, clique-forming youth culture.

On one Internet bulletin board, for example, high school students identified no fewer than 24 distinct peer groups. Some were classics, like "jocks" and "druggies." Others had a "digital age" ring—"pager people," "technogoths," and "computer dweebs."[1]

There was another group, too: "Jesus freaks."

Three hundred years ago, John Bunyan called them pilgrims. Two thousand years ago they were called followers of the Way. Regardless of the label, those who belong to Christ will always be the targets of those who would shame them.

We need to show our kids that the pilgrim's way requires tough choices. At the beginning of that journey, and a thousand times along the way, we must choose to stay close to God even though it may mean ridicule from those who laugh at the Bible and think that carrying a cross is stupid.

~⊙ ⊙~

NEVER ASHAMED:
PRACTICAL PROGRESS FOR PARENTS AND KIDS

How can we prepare our children to face the Shame Game? The answer doesn't lie in trying to make Christianity less "shameful." As the apostle Paul writes in 1 Corinthians 1:18, "For the message of the cross is foolishness to those who are perishing, but to us who are being saved it is the power of God."

Or to put it another way, as Mike Yaconelli does in *Going Against the Flow*,

> The subtitle of this book is "When Being a Christian Feels Weird." Weird is a weird word. It sounds like what it means—strange, unusual, different, odd. The Christian faith feels weird because it is weird. Someone has said, "You shall know the Truth and the Truth shall make you odd." There is a built-in oddness to faith.[2]

Our children are meant to be different—in a good way. Here are some principles and actions for helping them to do that in a world that would much prefer they conform.

Principle #1: Seek God's Approval

Faithful explained, "I also thought that on Judgment Day we will not be doomed to death or life according to the hecklers of the world, but according to God's wisdom and law.... So, I thought, 'What God says is best, is indeed best—even if all the men in the world are against it.'"

In the end, God will outvote everyone else. We can help our kids take the long-range view that it's best to be on His side.

Parental Action: Picture Pleasing God

Faithful could imagine vividly the results of pleasing—and disappointing—his heavenly Father. Dismissing Mr. Shame, he said, "Should I choose you over my sovereign Lord? If I do, how will I be able to look Him in the face when He returns? If I'm ashamed of His ways and His people, how can I expect Him to bless me?" Our children, on the other hand, may need help to make the abstract concept of "pleasing God" more concrete.

Look at God's "Good List." If your kids see the phrase "God's approval" as an oxymoron, they'll think seeking His favor is pointless. Maybe it's time to balance talk of His judgment with a discussion of people who have actually pleased Him. Here are just a few examples to share with your children:

- Abel, whose offering was commended by God—even though his brother Cain was extremely displeased (Genesis 4:1-8).
- David, who—despite his flaws—earned the title of "a man after [God's] own heart" (1 Samuel 13:14).
- The woman who poured perfume on the head of Jesus, ignoring the grumbling of the disciples who thought it wasteful (Matthew 26:6-13).
- Enoch, who made God so happy that He allowed the man to leave this life without having to exit through death's door (Hebrews 11:5).

Point out that none of these people was perfect. Yet all of them pleased God. We can be "popular" with God too, by obeying Him instead of trying to fit in with those who oppose Him.

Do imitations. Have a family contest to see who can do the best celebrity vocal impressions. Let each person write down the names of three famous people (or cartoon characters) with distinctive voices. Put the names in a bowl, and let people take their best shot at mimicking the voices of the people whose names they chose. If you like, award a prize for the best impression. Then ask, "Who can do the best imitation of Jesus?" Confused silence may reign for a moment as children realize they don't know what He sounded like. Point out that we can imitate other things about Jesus—His servant attitude, His willingness to sacrifice, His compassion for people who hurt. Let each person do a silent imitation of Jesus, pantomiming something He might do. Then ask, "Why is it better to imitate Jesus than to imitate other kids? How might imitating other kids get us into trouble?"

Parental Action: Put Popularity in Perspective

It's not easy for adults, let alone kids, to ignore our culture's call to conform. Who longs to be unpopular? Children especially need guidance to see that the rewards of "going along" don't last—unlike the benefits of being a leader instead of a follower.

Show what's not hot. Many youngsters don't realize how fleeting popularity can be. To open their eyes, try creating a "Museum of Once-Popular Culture" together. Have family members scour your home for items—or pictures of items—that used to be "in" but are now "out." How about that avocado green leisure suit in the back of your closet? Or those "valuable" trading cards the kids whined for a few years ago, now collecting dust under their beds? Gather old magazine photos and album covers featuring "hot" entertainers who've entered the "Where are they now?" category. Once you've assembled your museum, use it to illustrate the fact that popularity is temporary—which means it isn't worth ignoring eternal truths to get.

Reverse peer pressure. Many kids aren't ashamed enough to abandon their faith—but shame keeps them silent, always on the defensive. They don't seem to realize that peer pressure works both ways, and that it's possible to positively influence those who'd like to drag them down. Introduce that concept to older kids by telling them the following story based loosely on Daniel 1, from *Going Against the Flow*:

> When they were in high school, four brothers named Steve, Chad, Tom, and Mike had to move from Bozeman, Montana to a Chicago suburb because their father was changing jobs. When they got to Chicago, it was as if they'd entered another world.
>
> Kids at their affluent new school gave the four "farm boys" insulting nicknames—Bozo, Clodhopper, Geek, and Dorkman. But the four made the football team, an honored place to be since the school had won every state championship for the last eight years.
>
> Soon the brothers discovered the secret of the school's success. The coach, an aggressive and demanding man, routinely encouraged players to increase their muscle mass by taking steroids. The four boys knew that taking the drugs was dangerous as well as illegal. As Christians, they decided they had to refuse.
>
> When they told the assistant coach of their decision, he shook his head. "Look, guys," he said. "I like you. But if you don't take steroids, you won't look as strong as the other players. If the coach finds out that I said you didn't have to take the stuff, he'll fire me."
>
> Steve, the oldest brother, had an idea. "Give us a test," he said.

"Let us work out and eat right, with no steroids, for the first month of the season. Then compare us with the players who are taking the drugs. Treat us according to what you see." The assistant coach agreed.

At the end of the test period, the four brothers looked and played better than any of the guys who were taking steroids. So the assistant coach let them continue playing without drugs.

The brothers were such outstanding players, in fact, that each received a college football scholarship at graduation.[3]

After reading the story, compare it with the first chapter of the Book of Daniel. Ask, "If the guys in these two stories had been ashamed of what they believed, what might have happened? How did they turn the tables and influence others? How could a Christian kid with your set of friends do something like that?"

Principle #2: Expect Criticism

"The trials of those who hear God's call,

Are many, and expected all..."

Faithful sang those words after his confrontation with Mr. Shame, recognizing that efforts to embarrass believers should come as no surprise. Children who have the same expectation won't be shocked when peers taunt or teachers condescend. Is your child ready to take such "shaming" in stride?

Parental Action: Don't Take It Personally

Share war stories. Twelve-year-old Andrea was stunned last week when one of her best friends said only "babies" don't play kissing games at parties. Andrea doesn't realize that such jibes have been making the rounds for thousands of years, and that shaming is one of the oldest games of all. She wonders whether her friend might be right; after all, if "everybody" is doing it, there must be something wrong with the "weirdo" who isn't. Andrea needs to know that most Christians have been "needled" about their convictions; she's not the only one. If you've had similar experiences—perhaps being laughed at for saying grace at a cafeteria table or for questioning evolutionary theory in biology class—share some of them with your child. If you don't have such "war stories," encourage your child's Sunday school teacher or youth leader to give group members an opportunity to share theirs.

Concentrate on issues, not individuals. It's only natural that a biblical worldview would clash with a nonbiblical one. A shamer's real quarrel is with God and His Word, not with your child. Not realizing this, many kids—and adults—desperately try to win arguments as a matter of personal pride. Instead, help your child focus on ideas instead of personalities. Ask questions like, "How does your friend's view differ from what the Bible says? Where do you think she got her idea?" Debating issues is less threatening than deflecting personal attacks, making it easier to absorb as part of a pilgrim's everyday life.

Parental Action: Be Ready to Reply

When Mr. Shame launched his verbal assault, Faithful was tongue-tied at first—overcome by anger and embarrassment. Eventually our pilgrim recovered and let fly some thought-provoking answers—which didn't convince Mr. Shame, much to Faithful's frustration. With a little work, we can help our children skip the tongue-tied and frustrated phases of these inevitable conversations.

Rehearse a response. What will your child say when a sneering peer calls him a "chicken" for not trying drugs? What will she say when a teacher smugly calls Bible believers "right-wing fundamentalists"? You can't prepare for every possible challenge, but you can talk through replies that would apply to a variety of situations. For example, here are responses a young person could make when belittled for taking the Bible seriously:

- "Could you make a list of ten mistakes you've found in the Bible? I could study them and try to come up with some answers."
- "It's okay with me if you don't want to believe the Bible. Is it okay with you if I do?"
- "Have you found an instruction book for life that's more trustworthy than the Bible? I'd like to hear about it."

Don't try to script your child's responses; simply help him come up with his own. The goal is to build his confidence and willingness to stand up to shaming.

Let God handle it. When Mr. Shame wouldn't stop pestering Faithful, the latter summarized his position and left the results to the Lord: "Finally I told him he was wasting his time, because I saw the most value in the things that disgusted him. At last he gave up." Kids who expect to "convert" shamers with a clever zinger (or even a thoughtful reply) usually will be disappointed. Encourage your child to give gentle but firm answers, to try to maintain the friendship if there is one, to leave the door open to more discussion later—and to trust God to change the person's heart.

Principle #3: Find Strength in Fellowship

One of the most powerful defenses against shaming is staying connected to other pilgrims. The isolated believer is especially vulnerable to peer pressure, often feeling outnumbered, lonely, and confused. That's what Christian discovered when he first met Faithful:

In the Valley of the Shadow of Death, poor Christian was so confounded that he did not know his own voice. When he had traveled in this disconsolate condition for a considerable time, he suddenly thought he heard a man somewhere ahead of him, saying, "Even though I walk through the valley of the shadow of death, I will fear no evil, for You are with me; Your rod and Your staff, they comfort me" (Psalm 23:4).

Then Christian was glad, for three reasons:

First, because someone else who feared God was in this valley, too.

Secondly, because God was with him.

Thirdly, because he hoped to catch up to the man ahead and thereby have some company.

Before long Christian came to a little rise in the road, built so that pilgrims might see ahead of them. Looking forward, he saw Faithful.

"Hello!" shouted Christian. "Stay, and I will be your companion!"

Faithful turned, but only for a moment. Christian could see terror on his ashen face.

"Stay till I come up to you!" Christian called again.

"N-no!" Faithful cried. "I'm running for my life! The avenger of blood is behind me!"

More than ever, Christian was determined to join his fellow pilgrim. With all his strength he sprinted up the hill. Finally he caught up to Faithful, then passed him. Smiling smugly, Christian turned to say something about his prowess as a runner—and promptly stumbled and fell.

The wind knocked out of him, Christian could only wheeze until Faithful arrived. Sheepishly Christian accepted Faithful's offer to help him up.

Getting to his feet, Christian began to chuckle at himself. A few moments later Faithful grinned, and then the two of them broke into hearty laughter. From that point they walked together.

"My honored and well-beloved brother Faithful," Christian said, "I am glad that I have overtaken you, and that God has so tempered our spirits that we can walk as companions in so pleasant a path."

Like Christian and Faithful, our children need the support of other believers if they're to withstand pressures to conform. Here are ways to help them know they're not alone.

Parental Action: Join the Club

Kids need to see how they're attached to a church—the whole body of believers throughout history, all over the world—that shares their struggles and cheers them on. There's strength in numbers, especially when those numbers follow a Savior who prayed that His disciples would "be one" (John 17:21).

Be a part of it. Are you truly part of a Christian community? If "fellowship" is just a word for you, and you have no real support group of believers, don't be surprised if your child doesn't see the value of the church connection. If possible, find a small group where you can "plug in" to your congregation. Let your child know how the accountability and closeness help you on your spiritual journey. When you urge him or her to find the same kind of support in a youth group, he or she will be more likely to listen.

Examine extreme examples. Church history is packed with role models who went "overboard" in serving God—without a shred of shame. Kids who feel a kinship with these practitioners of "extreme" faith may be bolder next time peers start sniping. Encourage them to read about Saul of Tarsus, that fanatical persecutor of Christians who became the ultimate Jesus freak of his day—a sold-out, ocean-crossing, empire-defying apostle named Paul. And don't forget more recent examples like missionaries Amy Carmichael and Jim Eliot.

WE NEED NOT BE ASHAMED

The things that the world loves most, Jesus warned us, God hates.

That's strong language. But God wants us to choose between loving Him and merely craving the things He created. In choosing Him, we find blessings beyond our wildest dreams.

The shamers want our kids to choose second best. When we help our children discover the truth—that the real shame is in missing a close relationship with God—the blessings for us as parents are pretty indescribable too.

Chapter 9

VANITY FAIR

Steering Your Child Away
from the Worthless

⤚ﻌ

*When they got out of the wilderness, Christian and Faithful peered down the
road. There they saw a town called Vanity—the home of a year-round festival
named Vanity Fair.*

*Why is it called Vanity Fair? Because the town is lighter than vanity—
and because everything sold there, or that comes there, is meaningless. As goes
the saying of the wise, "Everything to come is meaningless" (Ecclesiastes 11:8).*

*This fair is no new-erected business, but a thing of ancient standing. Here
is a bit of its history:*

*Almost five thousand years ago there had been pilgrims walking to the
Celestial City, as Christian and Faithful were now doing. When Beelzebub,
Apollyon, Legion, and their companions saw the path the pilgrims took
through this town of Vanity, they contrived to set up a fair that would sell all
sorts of pointless goods.*

*Now this fair offers such merchandise as houses, land, trades, places, hon-
ors, preferments, titles, countries, kingdoms, lusts, pleasures, and delights of all
sorts—harlots, wives, husbands, children, masters, servants, lives, blood, bodies, souls, silver, gold, pearls, precious stones, and whatnot. There are also jug-
gling, cheating, games, plays, fools, apes, knaves, and rogues—as well as thefts,
murders, adulteries, and lying.*

As in other fairs of less importance, there are rows and streets in which wares are vended—for example, Britain Row, French Row, Italian Row, Spanish Row, and German Row.

Since the way to the Celestial City lies just through this town, pilgrims cannot avoid it. The Prince of princes Himself, when here, went through this town to His own country. Beelzebub, chief lord of this fair, invited the Prince to buy some vanities, even offering to make the Prince lord of the fair if the Prince would worship him. Beelzebub took the Prince from street to street, quickly showing Him all the kingdoms of the world, trying to lure that blessed One to buy; but the Prince cared nothing for the merchandise, and therefore left the town without spending a penny.

Now it was the turn of Christian and Faithful to go through Vanity Fair. As soon as they entered the town, the place was in an uproar. The townspeople, shocked at how different the pilgrims' clothes were from their own, stared at them and called them fools, lunatics, and outlandish men. It didn't help that the pilgrims' language was foreign, either. Worst of all, Christian and Faithful refused to look at the wares in the marketplace; in fact, when the merchants tried to get their attention, the two men would put their fingers in their ears, and cry, "Turn my eyes away from worthless things" (Psalm 119:37). Then they would look upward, signifying that their trade and traffic was in heaven.

～❧

TOO LONG AT THE FAIR

Vanity Fair, it seems, can't be avoided. Pilgrims like Christian and Faithful can't reach their destination, the Celestial City, without passing through this place. When Satan and his demonic cronies realized that, they decided to set up their carnival of temptations, libations, and misrepresentations in order to trap unsuspecting travelers.

Notice the activities and merchandise being sold at Vanity Fair. Bunyan gives us a list that might describe Jimmy Stewart's hometown in *It's a Wonderful Life*—after it had became "Pottersville" and had gone bad.

But Vanity Fair hits much closer to home. It is us; it is where we are today as a culture. Bunyan gives us a snapshot of the worthless goods the world offers in the twenty-first century, and it isn't pretty.

The apostle John knew about Vanity Fair too. He identified three kinds of vanity that threaten to take pilgrims off the path:

> For all that is in the world, the lust of the flesh, and the lust of the eyes, and the pride of life, is not of the Father, but is of the world. (1 John 2:16, KJV)

Satan may be clever, but God tells us he is predictable. These three areas of enticement—the lust of the flesh, the lust of the eyes, and the pride of life—have been around since the fall of man in the Garden of Eden.

THE LUST OF THE FLESH

This phrase doesn't refer only to sexual sin; it includes any allurement that appeals to the physical body, and which threatens to capture our love.[1] For instance, Satan tried unsuccessfully to use this approach after Christ had fasted for 40 days in the wilderness; the devil tempted the hungry Jesus with bread (Matthew 4:2-3).

In the decade ahead, our children also will be assaulted with appeals to the pleasures and senses of the body. Recent movies like *American Pie* and *Road Trip*, targeting teen audiences with the message that sex is nothing more than a recreational activity, indicate that things will get worse before they get better.

Meanwhile, children will *not* see some important truths in Hollywood's output. They won't be told, for example, that sexual promiscuity destroys lives and results in a rate of syphilis and gonorrhea in the U.S. that is 50 times greater than in Sweden.[2]

Another sensory indulgence—getting "high" on illegal drugs—will continue to escalate as society lacks a consensus on how to stop it. According to the Trends Research Institute, one of the top 10 upcoming issues in America will be the controversy over whether drugs should be decriminalized.[3] If you think drugs can't be a problem for your children, think again. Illegal drug use has spread to Christian families, too.

Will we and our children hold fast to the Bible's instructions to avoid intoxication, excess, and lack of self-control? Will we be filled instead with the Holy Spirit, living under God's influence (Ephesians 5:18)? Will our children respond to Vanity Fair as Christian and Faithful did, showing no interest in its worthless offerings?

The Lust of the Eyes

This second temptation entices our children with the visual appeal of fashion and possessions. Ten-year-old Mitchell, for example, seems to go into a trance whenever he sees a remote-controlled toy on TV. The shiny chrome, the sleek lines mesmerize him as the glint and curves of a sports car might hypnotize his father. The result can be viewed in Mitchell's room—which is cluttered with a robot dog, robot spider, radio-controlled cars, and an army of battling robots, all rarely used.

Visual temptation is no recent invention, of course. Satan offered Jesus all the kingdoms of the world, displaying them in "their splendor" (Matthew 4:8). Imagine the special effects the devil must have used in his failed effort to impress the King of Kings. But Jesus turned down the trinkets of the world, as did Christian and Faithful.

Enslavement to fashion is another result of our society's overemphasis on visual appeal. One popular Internet site regularly reveals how to "steal the look" of celebrities. Preteen girls wear the garb and makeup of streetwalkers, imitating female pop stars who are barely older than they are.

Yet as Christian and Faithful walked through Vanity Fair, their dress was so different—probably more modest and less luxurious—from others' clothing that everyone stared in disbelief.

That doesn't mean our children have to dress like "geeks" or deliberately be out of fashion. But it does mean we must help them get used to looking different—and to looking differently at the visual lures of the twenty-first century.

The Pride of Life

Lastly, our children will encounter "the pride of life" in Vanity Fair. The New International Version translates this phrase as "the boasting of what [man] has and does."

The consequences of this temptation can be devastating, but its beginnings are subtle. Look at how Satan tried to get Jesus to prove His power and heavenly authority. The devil suggested that Jesus simply demonstrate His divine nature by throwing Himself off the top of the great Herodian temple in Jerusalem, permitting angels to save Him at the last moment (Matthew 4:5-6).

Such a stunt would have been impressive. The temple was always busy with priests, scribes, and other workers, providing plenty of witnesses. Furthermore, the structure was incredibly high. When the two of us first visited Jerusalem, we were impressed with the mammoth, golden Dome of the Rock that now sits where the temple used to be—and the temple was several times taller than the Dome.

But Jesus resisted the temptation to "blow His own horn"—to arrogantly display His divine power. Later He would show His divinity through many miracles of healing—but to exhibit God's compassion, not for personal glory. Jesus was a servant, not a self-promoter.

That approach contrasts sharply with Vanity Fair. Merchants were selling "honors, preferments, titles, countries, kingdoms"—in other words, everything that appeals to pride.

The Bible doesn't teach self-hate; it tells us to love others in the same way that we love ourselves (Matthew 19:19). But Satan and our culture beckon our children to be little gods—free of moral or social restraints. During the 1960s and 1970s in America, radical thinker Saul Alinsky epitomized the student movement when he stated that Satan was a hero because he was the first rebel against the moral establishment.[4]

Now, decades later, we are reaping the harvest of a belief that equates limits with oppression. Civility seems to have collapsed; 89 percent of schoolteachers have reported regularly facing abusive language from *grade school* children.[5] "Comics" like Tom Green have built careers on vulgarity and crudeness, ridiculing social norms by violating them in front of millions of viewers.

The pride of life has an even darker side, as seen in the defiant last words of Oklahoma City bomber Timothy McVeigh, who before his execution quoted these lines from William Ernest Henley's poem "Invictus":

I am the master of my fate,
The captain of my soul.

When you believe you are the "captain" of your own soul, it seems you need not worry about the innocent children who are slaughtered in the wake of your vengeance.

Society urges our young people to seek self-exaltation and to cast off moral restraint. As Christian parents, we can't let this appeal go unchallenged.

VALUE AND VANITY:
PRACTICAL PROGRESS FOR PARENTS AND KIDS

How can anyone escape the lure of Vanity Fair? John Bunyan provides hints later in the story, when Christian talks with Hopeful, a former Vanity resident:

As they traveled, Christian began to ask questions of Hopeful, a former resident of the town of Vanity. "How did you come to do what you do now?" Christian began.

For a moment Hopeful looked puzzled. "Do you mean, how did I come to look after the good of my soul?"

"Yes, that's what I mean."

A rueful expression crossed Hopeful's face. "For a long time I delighted in the things that were seen and sold at Vanity Fair. Had I continued in them, they would have drowned me in perdition and destruction."

"What things were they?"

"All the treasures and riches of the world," Hopeful replied. "Not to mention rioting, reveling, drinking, swearing, lying, uncleanness, Sabbath-breaking, and other things that tend to destroy the soul. But at last I heard from you and Faithful about the things of God, and that my disobedience was marking me for death."

"And were you convinced of this right away?"

Hopeful gave a humorless chuckle. "No. I didn't want to know about the evil of sin, nor the condemnation that follows it. I tried to shut my eyes to the light."

"Why?"

Hopeful squinted at the sky. "I suppose there were four reasons. First, I didn't realize it was God who was working on me. Second, I liked sinning and didn't want to leave it. Third, I didn't know how to leave my old friends behind. And fourth, thinking about the subject made me miserable."

"Were you able to forget about it?"

"Sometimes," Hopeful said. "But then it would come into my mind again. And I'd be as bad as—no, worse than—before."

"What brought your sins to mind again?"

"Oh, many things." He held up a hand and began to count them off on his fingers. "If I ran into a good man on the street…if I heard anyone reading the Bible…if my head began to ache…if I were told that some of my neighbors were sick…if I heard the bell toll for the dead… if I thought of dying myself…if I heard that someone else had died suddenly…"

Hopeful turned to face Christian. When he spoke, his voice was soft but emphatic. "And especially when I thought of myself, that I must quickly come to judgment."

The mindset that helped Christian, Faithful, and Hopeful resist the pull of Vanity Fair is one we need to cultivate in our kids. Here are some ways to do that.

Principle #1: Control the Cravings

The New International Version of the Bible translates "the lust of the flesh" as "the cravings of sinful man" (1 John 2:16). How do we help our kids control their cravings when the culture urges them to indulge? The following actions can help.

Parental Action: Adjust Appetites

Most of us don't need to eat, drink, or buy nearly as much as we think we do. Many parents inadvertently encourage their kids to develop voracious appetites for pleasure and material things by giving them too much, too soon. Reversing the process isn't easy, but the following ideas are worth a try.

Shrink that stomach. When we go on diets, we may feel famished in the beginning—until our stomachs contract and it's easier to feel full. In the same way your kids can learn to be satisfied with less, though the process may be uncomfortable. If you want your child to stop expecting that you'll rent a video every Saturday night, for instance, cut back a step at a time. Rent a video every *other* week, substituting a no-cost family activity on the "off" weeks. Then cut back to once a month if you like, perhaps borrowing library books for your child to read instead. Chances are that, in time, what once seemed like a necessity will be all but forgotten.

Satisfy real needs. Why do people buy the baubles of Vanity Fair? Because they're trying to meet deep-down needs for intangibles like security and love. Meet the real needs, and the hunger for cheap substitutes will vanish. If you want to keep your daughter from seeking acceptance in the arms of a boy, make sure she knows you love her unconditionally; if you want your son to reject marijuana, keep the communication lines open so that he doesn't try to mask unspoken pain with a hand-rolled cigarette.

Parental Action: Strengthen Self-Control

When our children were young, we took them to see their grandparents—affectionately known as Grannie and Papa. During one particular visit, the kids saw a TV ad for a "celebrity hotline" that promised to share a secret about some teen idol. They called the 900 number on the screen; the "secret" turned out to be useless information. When the recording at the end revealed that their grandparents would be charged $10 for the call, the kids broke into a cold sweat.

Then they confessed. Grannie, ever the picture of grace and wisdom, kissed them all and thanked them for their honesty. She didn't stop there, however. Firmly but gently she said, "The four of you will pay our house the total sum of $10 that you had charged to our telephone." Then she added, "You will learn, I hope, that foolishness and sin come with a price tag."

It took weeks for the kids to gather the money, but they did it. They still remember the cost of pursuing worthless trinkets.

Grannie knew how to help children learn self-control. As parents, we won't always be there to make our kids' buying decisions at Vanity Fair. But if we've helped them develop self-control, our influence will linger. Here are some ways to help your child tame his own cravings.

Take a brake. Get in your parked car with your child. Demonstrate how the brake pedal and emergency brake work; let him or her try these if it's safe to do so. Then talk about how people have brakes too—a way to stop themselves from doing things that might hurt them. The brakes are called self-control. Ask, "How could you 'put the brakes on' if a friend asked you to shoplift a CD? If you were saving up for a bike, but were tempted to blow it all on an afternoon at the arcade? When do we need to use the regular pedal of self-control, and when do we need to use the emergency brake?"

Window shop. Take your child to the mall. Explain in advance that you're going to *look* in a couple of stores—no buying. Window shop in a store your child isn't interested in, like a jeweler's or office supply mart. Then do the same in a toy store or candy shop. Afterward, ask which window-shopping experience was harder, and why. What did your child have to tell herself in order to keep from buying or asking to buy? Did it help to know in advance that no purchases would be made? Did it help to think, "I can't buy anything today, but maybe another time"? Explain that reminding ourselves of limits like these is a way of exercising self-control.

Principle #2: Look Past the Glitter

The seventeenth-century marketing wizards of Vanity Fair were cunning, but Christian and Faithful didn't bite. Why? Because they knew the difference between gold and fool's gold, and knew that only a fool would sit through a sales pitch for the latter. Our children need the same discernment in a world where fool's gold is more cleverly disguised and hyped than ever.

Parental Action: Shut Out the Come-ons
"Christian and Faithful refused to look at the wares in the marketplace; in fact, when the merchants tried to get their attention, the two men would put their fingers in their ears, and cry, 'Turn my eyes away from worthless things' (Psalm 119:37). Then they would look upward, signifying that their trade and traffic was in heaven."

Today's pilgrims may need more than blindfolds and earplugs to ward off insistent merchants. Still, our kids can learn to filter out at least some of the temptations that will bombard them in the years to come.

Auction action. If you have access to an Internet auction site such as e-bay, go online with your child and search for items he or she isn't interested in—like oriental rugs, fishing lures, or Frank Sinatra records. Examine the gushing descriptions sellers have written to entice customers. Ask, "Why would anyone want this item? What words do sellers use to get attention?

Is everything really 'a must-have' or 'rare' or 'a steal'? Why not? What should we watch out for in advertisements for things we *do* want?"

Muted merchandise. To help your child separate salesmanship from substance, watch some TV commercials together with the sound off. Then take an old magazine and cut the text from the advertisements, leaving only the pictures. Talk about how it's usually less exciting to look at a hamburger, lipstick, or handheld video game than it is to see or hear an ad claiming that the object will change your life for the better. In the end, you're left only with the object—not the empty promises.

Parental Action: Determine True Value

No doubt everything displayed in Vanity Fair was shiny, sweet-smelling, breathtaking, racy, tasty, or clever. But Christian and Faithful based their buying decisions on other criteria. The following activities can help set your child's sights on things above, too.

What would Jesus buy? Walk with your child through a favorite store, making a list of things he or she thinks Jesus might buy there. Gently challenge your child's choices with questions like, "What would Jesus do with that? Would He keep it or give it to someone else? How would having this fit in with what He was trying to do on earth?" Afterward, talk about whether our buying decisions are—or should be—different from those we think Jesus would make.

Christian consumer reports. Cut pictures of "hot" products (toys, snacks, electronics, running shoes, etc.) from magazines and glue each on its own sheet of paper. Have your child rate each item (zero to five stars) according to the following criteria:
  • Ability of product to last forever
  • Ability of product to help people have eternal life
  • Usefulness of product in glorifying God
  • Usefulness of product in feeding starving people
Talk about the ratings your child chose. Ask, "Do people usually use ratings like these to help them decide what to buy? Should they?"

Principle #3: Go Back to the Future

All his life Hopeful had delighted in the trinkets of Vanity Fair. But when he contemplated his future—his own eventual death—he realized that the fair and all it offered were trivial. Even hearing that someone was sick was enough to remind him that this world's pleasures would be of no help in the next.

While we don't want our kids to concentrate morbidly on death, they do need to understand that this life and its flimsy attractions will end someday. Preschoolers, not truly grasping the concept of death, are not ready for this concept—but elementary students and teens certainly are.

Parental Action: Acknowledge Our Destiny

How can you help your child understand that earthly life won't last forever—without frightening or depressing him? Try the following suggestions.

Make a timeline. Tape several sheets of paper to the wall, end to end. Using a crayon, draw a horizontal line on the paper to represent all of history—from creation into eternity. Working with your child, make marks on this timeline that stand for major events—the Flood, Jesus' ministry, World Wars I and II, the first moon landing, etc. Then mark the births and projected life spans of family members, including your child. Next, step back and see how short our earthly lives are in the grand sweep of history. Ask, "How do you feel when you see that we don't have much time on earth? How might that affect the way you live?" Finally, extend your child's "lifeline" into eternity, using another color to draw to the edge of the paper. Ask, "How does it feel to know your life will last forever if you belong to Jesus? How might that affect the way you live?"

Visit a cemetery. Walk with your child through a cemetery, being careful not to disturb others who might be meditating or grieving. Read inscriptions on tombstones; if any relatives are buried there, be sure to view their markers and tell their stories. Afterward, encourage your child to share her feelings about the experience. You may hear words like "creepy" or "scary" or even "boring." Ask, "How would you like people to remember you when you've gone to heaven? What are some things you'd like to get done before then?" End the discussion on a positive note, reminding your child that for those who put their faith in Jesus, death is a door to a new and better life with God.

Parental Action: Get Ready to Run

In light of our limited time on earth, we can't afford to let Vanity Fair distract us from what's important. Do your kids understand the need to "travel light" on the road to the Celestial City, leaving behind the junk that would only weigh them down? Here are activities to help you make that point.

Run the race. Stage a race—perhaps a 50-yard dash—at a nearby field or playground. The catch: Each family member must wear a backpack filled with "stuff" from his or her room. After resting briefly, run the race again without the burdens—and talk about how much easier it was to sprint the second time. Read Hebrews 12:1: "Therefore, since we are surrounded by such a great cloud of witnesses, let us throw off everything that hinders and the sin that so easily entangles, and let us run with perseverance the race marked out for us." Ask, "How could having lots of stuff make it harder to follow Jesus? Do you own things, or do things own you? How can you tell?"

Sell what you have. Next time you have a garage sale, use it as an opportunity to talk about getting rid of things that complicate our lives. As you choose items to sell, discuss how some of them seemed so valuable when you bought them—and now seem almost worthless. Ask, "If you knew that everything you bought would end up in a garage sale someday, how would it change your buying habits?"

MAKING IT THROUGH

Our children must pass through Vanity Fair. But so did the Prince of Peace—and He left town without spending a penny on Beelzebub's goods.

In the end, Jesus is our ultimate tour guide through this bizarre bazaar. Hebrews 2:18 says, "Because he himself suffered when he was tempted, he is able to help those who are being tempted."

By following His example, and by calling on Him to help them to say no to the worthless wares being hawked from the carnival booths on every side, our children can make it—even through Vanity Fair.

Chapter 10

THE HEAVENLY GOODS

Teaching Your Child About Absolute Truth

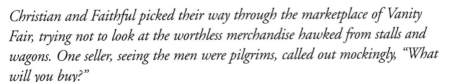

Christian and Faithful picked their way through the marketplace of Vanity Fair, trying not to look at the worthless merchandise hawked from stalls and wagons. One seller, seeing the men were pilgrims, called out mockingly, "What will you buy?"

Looking gravely at him, they said, "We buy the truth."

The merchant scowled. Another, having overheard, shook his fist at the pilgrims. Word passed down the street that Christian and Faithful were confounding the order of Vanity Fair, showing disrespect and threatening business. More and more sellers took up the drumbeat, showing how much they despised the pilgrims by mocking, taunting, and reproaching them.

"Too holy for us, are you?" shouted one businessman.

"Your money's no good here!" yelled another.

"A rap on the head should set them straight!" bellowed still another.

Soon the whole town was in a hubbub. Word was brought to the ruler of the fair, who quickly dispatched some of his most trusted friends to take the two strangers into custody.

Christian and Faithful were hauled in for questioning. "Where did you come from?" asked one of the town fathers, sneering.

"What is your destination?" demanded another.

"Why do you wear such unusual outfits?" asked a third.

The two men explained that they were pilgrims and strangers in the world, and that they were going to their own country, which was the heavenly Jerusalem. Speaking quietly but firmly, Christian added, "We have given no occasion to the men of the town, nor to the merchandisers, to abuse us."

"All we did," Faithful continued, "was to answer, when asked what we would buy, that we would buy the truth."

The town fathers scoffed. "They are mad," one declared.

"Worse," said another. "They are here to sow confusion, to destroy our way of life."

～◎

THE MARKETPLACE OF IDEAS

Our two pilgrims are knee-deep in the confusion of Vanity Fair. From every side, hawkers are urging them to buy.

We can imagine the noise and chaos, having wandered through a crowded Mexican marketplace some years ago. Straw baskets hung from booths; strings of lights glowed overhead; brightly colored rugs were everywhere. Tiny, jammed-together shops displayed leather boots and shoes, painted pottery, and beautiful silver jewelry. We waded through the maze, surrounded by running children who dodged in and out of shops, and shouting merchants who urged us to "come look—there is no harm in looking!" Others beckoned us to negotiate, crying, "Give a price, any price!"

In an atmosphere like that, it would have been easy for the pilgrims to say, "What harm is there in picking up a small bit of merchandise from this place, just to make the shop owners happy? If I feel guilty about what I buy, I can get rid of it later."

But Christian and Faithful didn't give in. Why not?

Because they knew in advance what they were looking for. Before encountering the persistent and crafty salesmanship of Vanity Fair, they had decided that the only commodity worth investing in was "the truth."

TRUTH DECAY

Unfortunately, that attitude is all too rare today. Christians, especially Christian children, are suffering a "truth crisis." The crisis is that they neither understand nor believe in the idea of absolute truth.

In 1994, a survey of thousands of Christian teens in the U.S. verified that only about 9 percent consistently believed in absolute truth.[1] Six years later, another study found that the percentage of born-again teenagers who believed in absolute moral truth was still at 9 percent.[2]

What's the cause of this dismaying statistic? Much of the responsibility must lie with parents; that same study revealed that 56 percent of all born-again *adults* aren't certain that moral absolutes exist.

When it comes to truth, the world seems to be having a greater effect on the church than the church is having on the world. That ought to be sobering news for every Christian parent.

HOW WE LOST THE TRUTH

Why do we find ourselves in this situation?

An important contributor to today's moral confusion (though certainly not the only one) was Joseph Fletcher, a clergyman who published his book *Situation Ethics* in 1966. His concept of moral relativism is now so ingrained in our culture that it's hard to believe it wasn't always popular.

A few years after the publication of *Situation Ethics,* Joseph Fletcher spoke at the liberal arts college we attended. He was a small man, soft-spoken, with wire-rim glasses and a courtly, courteous demeanor. But the concept he advocated sent shock waves into churches across America. According to Fletcher's philosophy, we should not be guided by moral rules—including those found in the Bible. Rather, we should be directed by the concept of "love," which will lead us to different choices depending on the situation with which we are faced. Love may lead us to lie, cheat, or steal in one situation but not another. "Love" may even lead us to extinguish another person's life if he or she appears to be suffering.

In other words, Fletcher divorced *love* from *truth*. With no sense of the absolute, no authoritative communication from God in the form of the Bible, we are left only with "love" as the ultimate guide.

The trouble is that God links love and truth throughout Scripture. Jesus is described as the embodiment of love—*and* as "the truth" (John 14:6). Christians are urged to speak the *truth* in *love* (Ephesians 4:15).

When truth is stripped from love, you get bizarre results. We saw this happen years ago in a public park on a Sunday afternoon. A large group of self-styled "hippies" had gathered, and soon much of the park was filled with a noisy, free-wheeling, tie-dyed crowd. A lone police squad car eventually showed up; the officer explained that the group did not have a permit for exclusive use of the park, and would have to disperse. Soon dozens of these "counterculture" representatives surrounded the police vehicle and angrily pounded their fists on the windows and doors—all the while yelling, "Love, love, love, love, love!"

When you dislodge *love* from the anchor of *truth*, you can use "love" as an excuse for anything. For many people, that's a highly attractive prospect.

THE LURE OF RELATIVISM

Truth often makes us uncomfortable. Dodging the idea of absolute truth, on the other hand, can provide comfort—at least temporarily. As author and youth speaker Josh McDowell has observed, relativism promises instant gratification; you can do what you like, when you like. The trouble happens when the consequences of immorality come home to roost, as they always do.[3]

As if relativism's natural appeal weren't enough, it's been pervasively marketed. That wasn't the case 50 years ago, when neighborhood parents would let you know if your children were out of line. There were shared values, despite differing spiritual or social backgrounds. Church leaders were respected as moral guardians of the community; public schools generally reinforced parents' views of right and wrong.

That's no longer the case. When our daughter Sarah attended her first day of eighth grade in a public school, she encountered a math class that turned out to be a battleground over absolute truth.

"Close your books," the teacher announced. "We are not going to be talking about mathematics right now. Not exactly. We are going to be talking about non-number values."

Sarah was perplexed. The teacher went on to explain that they were going to play a game; the purpose was to show how moral values, unlike number values, were not absolute.

The students were to imagine themselves on a lifeboat, survivors of a ship that had just sunk. The lifeboat was in the middle of the ocean. There was room for only two more passengers, but in the water were several others looking for safety—a pregnant teenager, an unemployed African-American man, a Christian fundamentalist, a famous scientist, and a criminal.

Students were to decide which two of this group deserved a place on the lifeboat—and which would drown. They were to write their answers on paper and send them to the front of the room.

We had discussed this kind of "values clarification" exercise before with Sarah, telling her that it promoted values that conflicted with the Bible. But we'd never heard of it being used in a math class!

As the other students toiled over their answers, Sarah jotted this down:

> Morals are absolute, not situational. Therefore I do not feel comfort-
> able doing this exercise. I pass. If you have any questions on this,
> please call my father at his law office at...

Sarah passed her paper to the boy in front of her to give to the teacher. The boy read her note, then turned quickly to Sarah.

"Hey," he said, "you can't do that. Can you?"

"Sure I can, and so can you," she said cheerfully.

The boy, who said he was also disturbed by the exercise, wrote down a response similar to Sarah's and passed both to the teacher.

The teacher read the two papers, wide-eyed.

It was the last time a values clarification exercise was attempted in that class.

Schools are not the only arena in which relativism has gained a foothold. In the battle over truth, the entertainment media are no longer the help they once were, either. Remember when television viewing was limited, and content was strictly guarded? Mouseketeer Jimmy Dodd ended each episode by singing a tune with a strong moral lesson, and the policemen of *Dragnet* were portrayed as heroes. Movies' use of sexual situations and vulgar language was tightly restricted. Obscenity on the printed page was banned, and no one would have been able to find a radio station that aired indecent lyrics.

Today, TV programming routinely includes explicit sexuality, blasphemy, violence, and regular attacks on Christian views. There are almost no limits to the sexual content and sadism found in movie theaters and on music CDs. The message is that anything goes; the only absolute is profit.

"BUT I HAVE FAITH!"

Relativism can have a devastating effect on our children's moral choices. But it can also twist their understanding of what it means to be a Christian. John Bunyan makes this clear in a dialogue between Christian and Ignorance, a fellow who thought it unnecessary to base his faith on absolute truth:

Ignorance, a young man who seemed impressed by the quality of his own mind, had been hanging back on the road. But Christian finally drew him into conversation. They had been talking a while when Ignorance said, "Tell me—what do you think are good thoughts, and what kind of life is according to God's commandments?"

Christian clasped his hands behind him as he walked. "There are many kinds of good thoughts. Some are about ourselves, some about God, some about Christ, and some about other things."

"What are good thoughts respecting ourselves?"

"Those that agree with the Word of God," said Christian.

Ignorance stroked the little mustache under his nose. "And when do our thoughts about ourselves agree with the Word of God?"

"When we pass the same judgment on ourselves that the Word passes," Christian replied. "For instance, the Word of God says of persons in a natural condition, 'There is no one righteous, not even one' (Romans 3:10). It also says that 'every inclination of the thoughts of [man's] heart was only evil all the time' (Genesis 6:5). And again, 'Every inclination of [man's] heart is evil from childhood' (Genesis 8:21). When we think that way of ourselves, then our thoughts are good ones—because they are according to the Word of God."

Ignorance made a face as if he smelled something unpleasant. "I will never believe that my heart is that bad," he said.

"Then you've never had one good thought concerning yourself in your

life," Christian said wryly. "But let me go on. As the Word passes judgment on our hearts, so it passes judgment on our actions. When our thoughts and actions agree with the judgment the Word gives both, then both are good."

Ignorance looked impatient. "Explain your meaning," he said.

"Why, the Word of God says that man's ways are crooked—not good, but perverse. It says people are naturally off the good path, that they have not known it. Now, when a man realizes this about himself, with sensible heart-humiliation, he's having good thoughts—because they agree with the judgment of the Word of God."

Ignorance sighed. "What are good thoughts concerning God?" he asked doubtfully.

"Those that agree with what the Word says of Him—that is, when we think of His being and attributes as the Word has taught. We have right thoughts about God when we think that He knows us better than we know ourselves, and can see sin in us when and where we can see none in ourselves. Our musings are good when we realize He knows our inmost thoughts, and that our heart, with all its depths, is always open to His eyes—and when we agree that our righteousness stinks in His nostrils, and that He can't abide to see us stand before Him in any confidence on our own, even in all our best performances."

Christian's commitment to absolute truth offended Ignorance, who wanted a relationship with God on his own terms. But as Francis Schaeffer wrote, a person must have an understanding of truth before he can knowingly, intentionally accept Jesus as Savior and Lord.[4] Receiving Christ is not just a matter of having a nice feeling inside, and one can't begin a relationship with Him without believing the truth that He really lived, died on a cross, and was raised from the dead.

This is another reason why we must teach our children that God's Word gives us reliable, objective truth—not just options.

WHAT TO DO?

How do we counter our culture's message that everything is a "gray area"? How can we help our children believe in absolute truth?

One way to begin is to monitor the entertainment our kids see and hear. Another is to maintain a constant, loving, hands-on relationship so that we can respond immediately when we see the influence of relativism seeping in. We can also demonstrate by our actions that *we* believe in absolute truth, doing the right thing even when it costs us.

Our children are watching to see what kind of shopping we do in Vanity Fair. Will we say, with Christian and Faithful, "Thanks, but no thanks; I'm in the market for truth"?

~◉ ◉~

NOTHING BUT THE TRUTH: PRACTICAL PROGRESS FOR PARENTS AND KIDS

The phrase "absolute truth" may sound lofty and complicated, but you don't need a doctorate in philosophy to address the subject with your children. You can help them see that, no matter what others say, God has set some unchanging standards—and that He's done it for our own good.

Principle #1: Encourage a Reasoning Faith

As he travels the road to the Celestial City, Christian engages in countless—and lengthy—conversations with friends and foes alike. These exchanges aren't small talk; they're deep dissections of discipleship, doctrine, and doubt. Christian is a thinker, and his commitment to truth grows from his well-examined faith. To the degree that he or she is capable, your child also needs to think through the reasons for believing in truths that never change.

Parental Action: Know What and Why You Believe

Objective truth flows from a God who is supreme, is perfect, and communicates with His creations. But why believe in this God, much less in absolutes? Give your young person good reasons to believe in a world that thinks faith is always blind.

Read (and watch) all about it. For teens, the video *My Truth, Your Truth, Whose Truth?* is an excellent way to introduce the subject of absolutes; the Randy Petersen book with the same title (Tyndale, 2000) uses an entertaining "chat room" format to construct a solid case for Christianity. Both video and book are available from Focus on the Family (1-800-A-FAMILY). Check the nearest Christian bookstore for other resources like the following:

- *Don't Check Your Brains at the Door* by Josh McDowell and Bob Hostetler (Word, 1992)
- *Evidence That Demands a Verdict: Historical Evidences for the Christian Faith* by Josh McDowell (Volume 1) (Thomas Nelson, 1999)
- *Know What You Believe* by Paul E. Little (ChariotVictor, 1999)
- *Know Why You Believe* by Paul E. Little (InterVarsity Press, 2000)
- *Right from Wrong* by Josh McDowell and Bob Hostetler (Word, 1994)
- *Who Should I Listen To?* by Kevin Johnson (Bethany House, 1993)

Parental Action: Let Them Question

Angelina loves teaching her daughter to cook. When her daughter asks how long to knead pie crust or how much pepper to put in mashed potatoes, Angelina doesn't panic. She smiles and says, "If you don't ask questions, how will you learn?" This rule doesn't seem to apply, however, when her daughter asks why Christians should follow the Ten Commandments instead of "something newer." Angelina's eyes widen, her throat goes dry, and she stutters about getting answers someday when we're in heaven. This may silence her daughter temporarily—but will it prepare the girl to face a relativist culture?

Have "I'd like to know" nights. Instead of avoiding questions, try seeking them out. Every month or so, hold a family meeting; ask each person to come up with a question about God, the Bible, or following Jesus. One child might wonder why God didn't let more people into Noah's ark; another might ask why your family doesn't watch certain TV shows that the neighbors think are okay. Let these questions set the agenda for your family devotions or other times of seeking answers together. For help, see the books listed earlier, along with Bible commentaries and volumes like *The Quest Study Bible* (Zondervan, 1994), which is packed with both questions and answers.

Principle #2: Make the Case for Absolute Truth

In John Bunyan's society, appealing to biblical truth carried weight. In ours, relativism is the default mode. Very young children may accept a parent's assertion that something is true "because God says so," but the longer a child spends in our culture, the more reasons she will need to reject the prevailing philosophy. A two-pronged approach—revealing relativism's weaknesses and Scripture's strengths—can help.

Parental Action: Show Where Relativism Leads

Joseph Fletcher seemed to believe that absolutes weren't necessary for a "loving" society. But without objective standards from an all-powerful God, who's to say love is important? Who's to say Hitler was wrong? Help your child understand what's at stake by tracking relativism to its logical conclusion.

Imagine there's no heaven. John Lennon's song "Imagine" claimed that the world would be better off without religion and its rules. Ask your child to imagine what might really happen if everyone did what he or she pleased—and if everyone believed there was no God to reward or punish people. For older kids, play a recording of the song if possible—and discuss it.

Take a vote. At the dinner table, ask family members to vote on questions like these:

- "Should _____ [name of family member] be grounded for a year?"
- "Should we put maple syrup in our car's gas tank?"
- "Should we start robbing banks to pay our bills?"

After getting the results, ask, "When more than half the people in a town or country think something is a good idea, does that mean it really is? Why or why not?"

Use this activity to challenge the assumption that truth can be determined by majority vote. You may also want to share these thoughts from the book *My Truth, Your Truth, Whose Truth?*:

> The question is, does a group's majority opinion determine what's true?
>
> Some say yes. There's no such thing as bottom-line truth, they declare. Every society gets to come up with its own. What matters is the "solidarity" of the group, the way it hangs together.
>
> But what if the group hangs together by torturing everyone whose last name begins with "K"? What if the group votes...to buy and sell slaves?

What if the group decides next year to reverse its decision? Which decision was right? And on what factors does the group base its decisions in the first place?

If you're looking for truth you can count on, truth that doesn't change, you won't find it by polling a group. Groups are fickle. They pick leaders and crucify them within a week.[5]

Explain who gets hurt. Our culture tells your child, "Do what feels good, as long as nobody gets hurt." But as Randy Petersen goes on to say, "We don't always know what hurts. And we aren't always honest about what we mean by hurting." Share that concept with your younger child; with an older child, go into more detail along the following lines, as adapted from *My Truth, Your Truth, Whose Truth?*:

When people live by the Rule of Not Hurting, what are they really saying? Usually they're saying it's okay to cheat on a test because no one gets hurt. They're saying it's okay to smoke dope, because who are you hurting?

What they *really* mean is something like this:

"*It's okay as long as it doesn't hurt anybody...very much.*" When you cheat on a test, you're hurting others at least a little. It's like cutting in line.

"*It's okay as long as it doesn't hurt anybody...right away.*" Having sex might seem harmless. But what happens six months from now when you "fall out of love" with that person, and the breakup hurts even more because you've given yourselves to each other, body and soul?

"*It's okay as long as it doesn't hurt anybody...except yourself.*" If you get drunk or high on drugs, who are you hurting except yourself? Maybe no one. But isn't your body worth taking care of? Aren't your thoughts worth thinking clearly?

"*It's okay as long as it doesn't hurt anybody...this time.*" You tell your parents you're going to the mall, but you and your friends sneak into a concert with fake IDs. You hear a great band and get home late. "After the mall I went to Ty's house to watch TV," you lie. No harm, no foul, right? But next time your driver might have a few drinks and get you all wrapped around a tree on the way home.

"It's okay as long as it doesn't hurt anybody...individually." You get an extra five bucks back in change at the music store. Why not keep it? Who gets hurt? Just some corporate conglomerate. But everybody has to pay a little more to make up for it. And what does your little brother or sister learn from your example?[6]

Parental Action: Show Why Scripture's Reliable

In addition to reading books on the Bible's trustworthiness, some of which have already been listed, try the following ways to equip your child to stand firmly for scriptural truth.

Give 'em five. It can be hard to remember all those great arguments for the Bible's veracity that you read six months ago, especially when you're being heckled by peers at Vanity Fair Middle School. Try reducing the information you gather to no more than five easily recalled points. Here's a sample list:

> TOP FIVE REASONS FOR BELIEVING THE BIBLE
> 1. Archaeologists keep digging up evidence that Bible events really happened.
> 2. The Bible predicted lots of things that came true later—even hundreds of years later.
> 3. We have ancient manuscripts for the Bible, showing the Book hasn't been tampered with over the years.
> 4. Jesus' disciples were so convinced that they were willing to die rather than retract their stories.
> 5. More people and cultures have been changed by the Bible than by any other book.

Dig up evidence. On slips of paper, write examples of how archaeologists keep finding evidence confirming biblical stories (you'll find some in the books previously listed). Here are a few to get you started, from *My Truth, Your Truth, Whose Truth?*:

- Scholars used to doubt that Old Testament character David really existed, but recent digs have found his name inscribed on ancient stones.

- Experts used to scoff at the idea that Moses wrote the "books of Moses"—the first five books of the Bible—because supposedly no one knew how to write back then. Wrong again. Examples of early writing have been found in Egypt and elsewhere, and if Moses was educated in Pharaoh's court, he surely would have had that skill.
- In his gospel, Luke says Jesus was born "while Quirinius was governor of Syria" (Luke 2:2). But archaeological records showed that Quirinius left office five years earlier, before Herod was king—long before Jesus could have been born. "Aha!" crowed the skeptics. "Luke goofed." But then they found another inscription. It seems Quirinius had two terms of office, and the second one corresponded with the time of Jesus' birth.[7]

After preparing a dozen or so of these slips, roll them up and secure them with rubber bands. Do the same with an equal number of blank slips.

Now hide the slips—either burying them in a sandbox or concealing them in the yard. Challenge family members to find the slips; whoever gets the most wins a prize (blank slips don't count). Then read and talk about the evidence people found.

Principle #3: Live Out the Truth

Early in Bunyan's story, the pilgrims encounter a hypocrite named Talkative. Faithful asks him, "Do your life and conversation match? Or is your religion all word and tongue, not deed and truth?...To say 'I am thus and thus' when all my neighbors tell me I lie, is great wickedness."

Faithful knew that a commitment to truth means more than a commitment to talk about it. Does your child understand what absolute truth looks like in the real world? Does he realize that living it can be hard—and opposed even by those who profess to believe in it?

Parental Action: Demonstrate Truth at Work

Like it or not, you're a role model. Years from now, your kids won't remember your speeches about absolute truth; they'll recall the times you did the right thing because it was right, not convenient. You can help them do the same by clarifying through word and deed what it means to live a life based on objective truth.

Share tough decisions. Do your kids know when you've followed a biblical absolute even though you didn't feel like it? When obeying a tax law costs you money, or obeying a speed limit makes you late, don't keep it a secret. When refusing to lie to a client costs you a promotion, or helping a stranded motorist makes you miss a meal, let your kids know. To avoid the appearance of bragging, share your stories as part of a conversation in which all family members are encouraged to talk about tough decisions they've had to make.

Link big truths with little ones. Truth is a big concept! Kids often need help figuring out what absolute but abstract truths have to do with everyday choices. To help, share this question and answer from *My Truth, Your Truth, Whose Truth?*:

Q. I believe in the Bible, but it doesn't tell me what's true in every situation—like what TV shows to watch, or how much to spend on clothes. How am I supposed to know the truth about these things?

A. The Bible gives us general guidelines about our priorities, attitudes, and actions. The Holy Spirit offers moment-to-moment help in applying those guidelines to our lives.

The Bible might not tell you exactly how much to spend on clothes, but it has plenty to say about the fact that God isn't as concerned with our outward appearance as He is with our hearts. It also tells us to be careful about the power of money and possessions, and the importance of using some of our money to care for the poor and to support God's work....

The same pattern applies to TV shows and other entertainment. The Bible doesn't mention broadcast or cable; it talks about purity of heart, making good use of our time, and not totally removing ourselves from the world. In Philippians 4:8, we're told to focus our minds on whatever we find that's good or noble or true or excellent. That gives us some leeway, but also challenges us to pay attention to what goes into our brains.

God's truth is absolute in the biblical principles He gives us. But He allows us some flexibility in how we work those out.[8]

Parental Action: Prepare for Opposition

Was Christian caught flat-footed when Mr. Ignorance and the merchants of Vanity Fair bridled at his loyalty to truth? Hardly. He stayed calm, his replies firm but not harsh. Our children will be able to do the same if we prepare them for the challenges of swimming against today's relativist current.

Store up replies. How will your child answer the classmate who whispers, "Why not cheat if you won't get caught?" What will your child say to the teacher who dismisses abstinence as "just one of many valid perspectives"? To ready your older child for such encounters, get a book like one of the following and read it together, writing down replies you want to remember:
- *Answers to Tough Questions Skeptics Ask About the Christian Faith* by Josh McDowell and Don Stewart (Tyndale, 1986)
- *Keeping Your Cool While Sharing Your Faith* by Greg Johnson and Susie Shellenberger (Tyndale, 1993)
- *True for You, but Not for Me: Deflating the Slogans That Leave Christians Speechless* by Paul Copan (Bethany House, 1998)

Check that attitude. Some kids would rather lose their allowance for a year than defend aloud the idea of absolute truth. Others are only too eager to wage "holy war" on peers who don't accept the Bible's authority. To help your older child understand how to treat those who don't believe in absolutes, share the following thoughts from *My Truth, Your Truth, Whose Truth?*:

> If you believe in ultimate truth, how can you communicate it in a world that doesn't want to hear it?
>
> Very carefully....
>
> *Relationship first.* It's possible to lose a friend by winning an argument. It's not your job alone to convince people of God's truth; His Holy Spirit can do that. This doesn't mean that you should approve of or participate in stuff that God considers sinful, but you don't need to be scolding people all the time. Love people even when you disagree with them. Take time to listen to them, help them, pray for them. If they ask your opinion, give it—gently. Remember, it's easier to *love* someone toward God's truth than to *argue* them there.
>
> *Humility always.* Jesus saved some of His harshest words for

religious people who believed in absolute truth and were trying to get everyone else to live by it. What was their problem? They were proud of themselves. The Pharisees' whole deal was showing that they were better than others. Maybe they were trying to be good examples, but it was all about *them*. Be willing to admit that you're not perfect, and that you have questions and doubts about truth. God's strength can shine through your weakness.

Live a life worth wanting. If you're a Christian, how does knowing the Truth Himself make your life better? What happiness does knowing Jesus bring you? Sometimes Christians seem like they're not having fun because…they aren't! This doesn't mean you should pretend that being a Christian is more fun than it is. It means asking God to help you develop the qualities He already wants to grow in you—like love, joy, and peace. It might help to hang out with a fun group of Christians, too.

Stay connected. Keep going back to God's Word and talking to Him in prayer. It's easy to twist the truth, even if we don't mean to. Staying connected to God and His Book helps keep us honest.

If you take a stand for God's truth, you *will* be misunderstood. Some people won't like what you have to say.

It takes courage, but it takes love, too.

After all, if we stop loving, we've missed the whole point of God's truth.[9]

AND THAT'S THE TRUTH

In the final analysis, there's only one reason to build our lives on the belief that God's Word is absolutely true. Christian shared it with a traveling companion in this exchange:

"Come, neighbor Christian," said Pliable. *"Since it's just the two of us, tell me more about the place to which we are going."*

Christian tapped his own forehead with his index finger. "I can better imagine it than describe it," he said. "But, since you asked, I'll read about it from my book."

Pliable watched as Christian drew the book from his coat. "And do you think that the words of your book are certainly true?" Pliable asked.

"Definitely," Christian replied. "For it was made by the One who cannot lie."

When we help our children trust that One more fully each day, they'll understand why He alone deserves to be called the Truth—absolutely.

Chapter 11

ON TRIAL

Preparing Your Child to Face Persecution

ʚ

The men of Vanity Fair took Christian and Faithful and beat them, smeared them with dirt, and put them in a cage—so they might be made a public spectacle. There the two pilgrims lay for some time as the objects of any man's sport, malice, or revenge. And the ruler of the fair laughed at all that befell them.

But Christian and Faithful were patient, giving good words for bad and kindness for injuries. Some men in the fair—those more observing and less prejudiced than the rest—tried to stop their fellow townspeople from abusing the pilgrims.

This only made the abusers angrier than ever. "You're as bad as the men in the cage!" they shouted. "You must be confederates, and should share their misfortunes!"

The less hot-headed merchants, meanwhile, said, "These men are quiet and sober, and intended nobody any harm. Many who have traded at our fair were more worthy to be put in the cage—and pilloried, too—than these men!"

Before long, fighting broke out among the townspeople. Christian and Faithful behaved themselves the whole time, but again they were blamed for the hubbub and brought in for questioning. The interrogators beat the pilgrims pitifully and led them in chains up and down the streets—making them an example to anyone who might want to speak on their behalf.

Christian and Faithful received the shame with so much meekness and patience that several men were won to their side. This put the majority into a greater rage, and they demanded that the two pilgrims be put to death. "Neither cage nor irons are enough!" said the men's tormentors. "They should die for the abuse they have done, and for deluding the men of the fair!"

So the pilgrims were thrown in the cage again, and their feet locked in the stocks. While they were in this position, they called to mind what they had heard from their friend Evangelist—that they would suffer. The pilgrims comforted each other, each secretly hoping that he would have the honor of suffering for his Redeemer. Yet they committed themselves to the will of the One who rules all things, content in their condition.

When the time was come for their trial, they were brought before their enemies and arraigned. The judge's name was Lord Hate-good; their indictment read, "They are enemies to, and disturbers of, the trade; they made commotions and divisions in the town, and won a party to their own most dangerous opinions, in contempt of the law of our prince."

Faithful responded: "I have only set myself against that which has set itself against Him that is higher than the highest. As for disturbance, I make none, being a man of peace. The parties that were won to us, were won by seeing our truth and innocence, and have turned from the worse to the better. And as to the king you talk of, since he is Beelzebub, the enemy of our Lord, I defy him and all his angels."

Then the judge proclaimed, "Anyone who has something to say against the prisoner at the bar should now give his evidence."

So there came in three witnesses: Envy, Superstition, and Pickthank. "Do you know the prisoner?" the judge asked. "What do you have to say for our lord and king against him?"

Envy stood first. With great drama he declared, "My lord, I have known this man Faithful a long time, and will attest upon my oath before this honorable bench, that he is—"

"Just a moment," said the judge, and turned to the bailiff. "Swear him in."

When Envy was sworn in, he continued. "My lord, this man—notwithstanding his plausible name—is one of the vilest men in our country. He neither respects prince nor people, law nor custom, but does all he can to possess men with certain of his disloyal notions, which he calls principles of faith and holiness. I heard him once claim that Christianity and the customs of our town of Vanity were diametrically opposite, and could not be reconciled! By saying that, my lord, he not only condemns all our laudable doings, but us in the doing of them!"

The judge nodded. "Have you any more to say?"

Envy folded his hands and gazed at the ceiling with a look of great innocence. "My lord, I could say much more, but do not wish to bore the court. If the words of the other gentlemen do not provide enough evidence to condemn this man, I will enlarge my testimony against him."

"Then stand by," said the judge.

After similar testimony from Superstition and Pickthank, the judge announced, "Gentlemen of the jury, you see this man about whom so great an uproar has been made in this town. You have heard what these worthy gentlemen have witnessed against him. You also have heard his reply and confession. It's up to you to hang him or save his life.

"First, though, I will instruct you in our law. There was an act made in the days of Pharaoh the Great—servant to our prince—that, lest those of a contrary religion should multiply and grow too strong for him, their males should be thrown into the river. There was also an act made in the days of Nebuchadnezzar, another of our prince's servants, that whoever would not fall down and worship his golden image should be thrown into a fiery furnace. There was also an act made in the days of Darius, that anyone who called upon any god but he should be cast into the lion's den.

"Now, this rebel has broken these laws, not only in thought but in word and deed. He deserves to die!"

Then the jury went out. Mr. Blindman, the foreman, said, "I see clearly that this man is a heretic."

"Away with such a fellow from the earth," cried Mr. No-good.

"Yes," agreed Mr. Malice, "for I hate the very looks of him."

"I could never endure him," said Mr. Love-lust.

"Nor I," said Mr. Live-loose, "for he would always be condemning my way."

"Hang him! Hang him!" said Mr. Heady.

"A sorry scrub," muttered Mr. High-mind.

"My heart rises against him," said Mr. Enmity.

"He is a rogue," said Mr. Liar.

"Hanging is too good for him!" yelled Mr. Cruelty.

"Let's get rid of him," said Mr. Hate-light.

Mr. Implacable was the last to speak: "Even if all the world were given to me, I could not be reconciled to him. Therefore let us speedily bring him in guilty of death."

And so they did. Faithful was condemned to the most cruel death that could be invented.

First they scourged him. Then they beat him. Then they lanced his flesh with knives. After that, they stoned him, then pricked him with their swords. Last of all, they burned him to ashes at the stake.

Thus came Faithful to his end.

~◉

A PRICE IS PAID AT VANITY FAIR

While passing through the streets of Vanity Fair, Faithful boldly proclaimed his beliefs in response to questions from suspicious merchants. That started an uproar. But upon learning that Beelzebub was king of that region, Faithful went further—fearlessly proclaiming that he would obey only God, not the laws of the devil.

Faithful and Christian were arrested, shackled, and thrown in a dungeon to await trial.

Their court proceeding could hardly be called a trial, however. The judge was biased; his instructions to the jury all but sealed the pilgrims' fate. There was no hope of justice from the jury, either—all of whose members obviously resented the pilgrims' fidelity to a higher law.

And so Faithful paid the ultimate price for his faith.

THE PERSECUTED PREACHER

John Bunyan was no stranger to persecution. In his stirring account of Vanity Fair's kangaroo court, he was writing from experience.

After Bunyan became a born-again Christian, he aligned himself with the Noncomformists, a group that preached directly from the Bible and did not adhere to the Church of England's traditions. He began to preach in his hometown of Bedford, England.

Though not formally schooled, Bunyan was a powerful preacher. The vice-chancellor of Oxford University, John Owen, was so impressed that he would often go to hear this humble "tinker from Bedford" preach the gospel there.

After the ousting of Oliver Cromwell, King Charles II was restored to the throne—reestablishing the Church of England as the only official church. A few months later, in November 1660, Bunyan was arrested by a local magistrate for preaching in the fields without a license.

Asked by the magistrate to promise that he wouldn't preach again, Bunyan refused. This led to his imprisonment, off and on, for the next 12 years.

Inside his Bedford jail cell, Bunyan began to write *The Pilgrim's Progress*. Perhaps as he created the character of Judge Hate-good, Bunyan was thinking about the Bedfordshire magistrate, Sir John Kelynge, who had persecuted him so harshly.

PERSECUTION AND OUR CHILDREN

As we've noted in previous chapters, our kids are likely to face opposition from a hostile culture in the decade ahead. They can count on the occasional jeer about "religious fanatics" and "right-wing fundamentalists." They may find themselves running afoul of school districts that want to limit prayer or Bible study on school grounds. As they get older, they may lose friends, prestige, or jobs because of their faith.

Our family has encountered this kind of opposition. When the two of us were asked to assume a leadership role in a statewide controversy over homosexuality, we did so—appearing on television, on radio, and at rallies in support of a pro-family position. Often our four children would accompany us.

Our position earned us some hate mail, and a death threat was left on our answering machine. One night, when we returned from a rally, we discovered that our newly remodeled home had been severely vandalized. The form of vandalism was the trademark of a radical homosexual group.

This kind of opposition doesn't compare, of course, with the torture and death faced by too many believers around the world. Some of this persecution involves young people. In 1999, the two elementary-age sons of missionary Graham Staines—along with their father—were burned to death by a mob of Hindu radicals in India. The attackers were retaliating for the conversions of Hindus to Christianity there.[1] In the same year, in the U.S., teenager Cassie Bernall was among those killed in the Columbine High School massacre at Littleton, Colorado. Some witnesses reported that Cassie was shot after affirming her belief in God, leading many to call her a modern-day martyr.

God willing, the chances are slim that children in our society will have to die for their faith. Is it necessary, then, to tell them about the persecution of Christians?

The answer is an emphatic yes. For one thing, it's impossible for our children to understand the Bible or the history of Christianity without understanding persecution. The Book of Acts and the Book of Revelation are among those in which martyrdom plays a central role. In the Roman Empire, Christians were regularly executed for their faith—and during the Reformation, Protestants died by the sword and at the stake.

Second, understanding persecution reminds our kids that their destination is somewhere else—somewhere eternal. It encourages them to keep the kingdom of God foremost, and to put up with inconveniences that pale in comparison to the suffering many believers have endured.

Third, and by no means least important, understanding persecution leads our children to identify with, pray for, and aid Christians who are suffering today.

PERSECUTION: THE BIG PICTURE

At any given moment, somewhere in the world, a follower of Jesus is being arrested, beaten, mistreated, or killed for the sake of the gospel.

Yanus Murang, a former Muslim converted to Christianity, was arrested in December 2000 for bringing Bibles into the country of Brunei. He went on to serve a prison sentence.[2]

In China, on October 16, 2000, 21-year-old Liu Haitao died for his faith. He had been arrested by authorities during a Christian training session and jailed for several weeks. During that time he was regularly tortured and beaten.[3] As he lay in his mother's arms, dying as a result of his injuries, his last word was "amen."

We've seen firsthand the reality of persecution—when we visited a certain Middle Eastern country in 2001. A Muslim nation, it has incorporated

Islamic law into its legal system. It is illegal there to preach the gospel to a Muslim; a Muslim who decides to follow Jesus can be executed, as can the Christian who shared the gospel with him.

During our visit we met a Christian couple who ran a mountaintop retreat for young people. The husband explained to us that one of their buildings had been set on fire by angry Muslims. The couple had also received regular death threats.

Was he afraid of further retaliation? He responded to our question with a broad smile. As we stood with him in the warm breeze, overlooking the valley below, he answered with calm assurance: "If my blood is shed, may it water the seed of the gospel in this land."

Our children need to hear the stories of people like these. Our kids need to know that their focus should not be on the names they're called by peers, or the bruises they might receive, or even—if God permits—the blood they might shed.

With God's help, their focus can be that of Peter and the other disciples after they were arrested, beaten, and warned never to preach about Jesus again. After being released from jail, "Day after day, in the temple courts and from house to house, they never stopped teaching and proclaiming the good news that Jesus is the Christ" (Acts 5:42).

THE BLOOD AND THE SEED:
PRACTICAL PROGRESS FOR PARENTS AND KIDS

How can you prepare your child for the possibility that she will be persecuted for her faith? How can you alert him to the reality of persecution in other parts of the world? Here are some precepts and strategies.

Principle #1: Tell the Whole Story
"So the pilgrims were thrown in the cage again, and their feet locked in the stocks. While they were in this position, they called to mind what they had heard from their friend Evangelist—that they would suffer."

In leading the pilgrims to Christ, Evangelist hadn't soft-pedaled the certainty that they would run into trouble. Has your child been given the same forecast, or has she been led to believe that following Jesus guarantees fair weather? Our children need to know that the narrow road isn't the path of least resistance.

Parental Action: Remember the Cross

"If anyone would come after me, he must deny himself and take up his cross daily and follow me. For whoever wants to save his life will lose it, but whoever loses his life for me will save it" (Luke 9:23-24). When Jesus spoke these words, He wasn't referring to cross-shaped jewelry. He was talking about the real thing—heavy, awkward, dangerous. Christians used to mention the "old, rugged cross" more than they do today; as parents, we need to acquaint kids with the painful sacrifice Jesus made and the sacrifices we may be called upon to make for Him.

Wander in the woods. Take your child on a field trip to a lumber yard. Look at the boards, trying to find some that your child thinks might be like those used to make the cross on which Jesus died. Does she think they were rough? Smooth? Then go to the nail department. What are the biggest spikes you can find? Does your child think the nails used at the Crucifixion were like these? Afterward, talk about the fact that the cross was real, as real as the boards and nails you just saw. Ask, "When you think about Jesus being nailed to a cross, how do you feel? What's something you would be willing to do for Him?"

Look at lyrics. Get a hymnal and search out songs that refer to the cross. Read the lyrics with your child, explaining words as needed. Look especially for descriptions of Jesus' sacrifice, and our response to it. For example, the fourth verse and refrain of George Bennard's "The Old Rugged Cross" includes a pledge Faithful would have appreciated:

> To the old rugged cross I will ever be true,
> Its shame and reproach gladly bear;
> Then He'll call me some day to my home far away,
> Where His glory forever I'll share.
>
> So I'll cherish the old rugged cross,
> Till my trophies at last I lay down;
> I will cling to the old rugged cross,
> And exchange it some day for a crown.

Other hymns referring to the cross include "The Story of the Cross," "Beneath the Cross of Jesus," "Lead Me to Calvary," "Near the Cross," "O Sacred Head, Now Wounded," "When I Survey the Wondrous Cross," and "In the Cross of Christ I Glory." For more contemporary songs about the Crucifixion, try "Lamb of God," "Known by the Scars," "Via Dolorosa," and "Rise Again."

Parental Action: Remember the Martyrs

Stories of those who've given their lives for Jesus may be too disturbing for younger children, but those ages eight and older can benefit from hearing about these heroes of the faith.

Go on report. Make it a family project to find out about one or more Christian martyrs from history—like Polycarp, William Tyndale, and Jim Eliot. Each family member who's old enough to read could be assigned a different person. Help kids to research their subjects on the Internet, in an encyclopedia, and in biographies from the church library. Try to find answers to questions like these:

- Did the person have a family?
- How and why did this person die?
- What kind of personality did he or she have?
- How did this person get the strength to give up his or her life?
- What was the result of this person's martyrdom?

Let researchers present their reports at a family meeting. For "extra credit," they may even want to dress up as those on whom they're reporting.

Hear a hero. Teens and preteens can listen to the Radio Theatre production of *Bonhoeffer: The Cost of Freedom.* This Peabody Award-winning dramatization tells how theologian Dietrich Bonhoeffer resisted the Nazis because of his faith, and lost his life as a result. The presentation is available on CD or cassette from Focus on the Family.

Parental Action: Become World Christians

Persecution isn't just history; it's current reality for Christians in many parts of the world. Your family can get the facts—and get involved in helping those who suffer—through the following resources.

Listen to the voices. Several organizations specialize in telling the stories of those who suffer for Christ. Here a just a few you can contact for information, products, and suggestions on how to help:

- The Voice of the Martyrs
P.O. Box 443
Bartlesville, OK 74005
(918) 337-8015
(800) 747-0085 (for ordering)
Web site: *www.persecution.com*

In addition to publishing a magazine, this organization offers a program called LINK International, a way for parents and children to learn together about God's work in restricted nations. The children's Web site, *www.linkingup.com,* provides information on the LINK newsletter and other materials. The organization's main Web site features news, prayer requests, and ways to get involved with persecuted believers—including a "Blankets of Love" program aiding needy Christian families in the Sudan.

- Open Doors with Brother Andrew
P.O. Box 27001
Santa Ana, CA 92799
(949) 752-6600
(888) 5-BIBLE-5 (for ordering)
Web site: *www.opendoorsusa.org*

Open Doors strengthens, equips, and encourages the persecuted church —especially in the Muslim world, and throughout Asia, Africa, and Latin America.

- International Day of Prayer for the Persecuted Church
Web site: *www.persecutedchurch.org*

Besides encouraging Christians to observe a special day of prayer for suffering believers, this organization offers on its Web site a daily "prayer point" and suggests ways to help those who are oppressed due to their faith.

Pray around the world. Can your child find the country of Yemen on a map? Does he know that in that nation of more than 18 million people, only about a hundred are thought to be Christians? Does he know it's illegal—and dangerous—for a Muslim to become a Christian there? Your family can learn about and pray for believers and nonbelievers across the globe through Operation World (*www.gmi.org/ow/*). Visit the Web site for information on the organization's prayer handbook, CD-ROM, world map, desk calendar highlighting key points and concerns for 122 countries, and other resources.

Principle #2: Prepare for the Possibility

As Christian and Faithful awaited trial, they mentally prepared themselves for what might happen: "The pilgrims comforted each other, each secretly hoping that he would have the honor of suffering for his Redeemer. Yet they committed themselves to the will of the One who rules all things, content in their condition." Even if your child never faces physical harm for following Jesus, he or she will benefit from thinking through the cost of being a "living sacrifice" each day (Romans 12:1).

Parental Action: Examine Your Commitment

Judge for yourself. If you have older children, try staging a mock trial in which family members take turns as defendants. The charge: being a Christian in a country that outlaws the faith. Rotate the roles of judge, prosecutor, and defendant; the size of your jury, if any, will depend on the size of your family. The prosecutor's job is to prove that the defendant is a Christian; the defendant may choose whether to challenge the prosecutor in order to evade punishment. Prosecutor and defendant may call any family member as a witness; the defendant can testify on his own behalf. After the judge or jury has rendered a verdict, talk about what family members might do in such a situation. Would they deny being Christians? Would there be enough evidence to convict them?

Take the challenge. Two book-and-music combinations can help your teen identify with persecuted believers and assess his or her own spiritual commitment:

- *The Narrow Road* (Revell, 2001) is a youth edition of the classic *God's Smuggler* by Brother Andrew with John and Elizabeth Sherrill. The book features a CD-ROM with recording artists Jars of Clay, testimonies from persecuted Christians, information about nations in which oppression is a problem, and "imagine this" scenarios. Check the nearest Christian bookstore or call Open Doors at (888) 5-BIBLE-5.
- *Jesus Freaks* (Albury, 1999) tells stories of those who have stood for Jesus despite opposition—and encourages kids to do likewise. An

album of the same name, recorded by the group dc Talk, is also available. Consult your local Christian bookstore or contact The Voice of the Martyrs (VOM) at (800) 747-0085. *Extreme Devotion*, a youth devotional presenting 365 stories of Christians who risked everything for their faith, is also available from VOM.

Parental Action: Live Sacrificially

The idea of "losing everything" for one's faith is hard to grasp if you've never had to give up anything. If self-denial is a concept foreign to your kids, try the following.

Lose something. Choose a frequently used household item that you'll "lose" for a week. It might be the TV, can opener, microwave oven, or every spoon in the house (you may want to present options to your family and take a vote). Put the item(s) into storage. Explain that when family members think about the "loss" during the week, they can use it as a reminder to think about what they're willing to lose for Jesus—and what people in some countries are already losing for Him.

Transfer funds. After your family has learned about the needs of persecuted Christians, try raising money to help (consider the aforementioned organizations and others as potential recipients). But find the money by giving up something for a month—dessert, restaurant meals, soft drinks, video rentals, visits to a public pool, etc. At the end of the month, talk about how minor your sacrifice was in comparison to the suffering some Christians undergo. Are family members willing to extend the experiment for another month? Six months? Are they willing to try giving up something else instead?

REMAINING FAITHFUL

Faithful's death was not in vain, as Bunyan reminds us:

But there stood behind the multitude a chariot and a couple of horses waiting for Faithful, who was carried up through the clouds with the sound of a trumpet. It was the most direct way to the celestial gate.

As for Christian, he was taken back to prison. But He who rules all things saw to it that Christian was released and went his way.

And as he went, he sang, saying,

> *"Well, Faithful, you have faithfully professed*
> *Unto your Lord, with whom you will be blest,*
> *When faithless ones, with all their vain delights,*
> *Are crying out under their hellish plights:*
> *Sing, Faithful, sing, and let your name survive;*
> *For though they killed you, you are yet alive."*

Christian's walk along the pilgrim's path was mightily affected by the courageous faith of his fellow traveler to the Celestial City. As we and our children learn the stories of yesterday's and today's martyrs, we can learn to be more faithful too.

Chapter 12

FAIR-SPEECH

*Helping Your Child Speak Up in an Age
of Political Correctness*

❧

*Soon after Christian and his new companion Hopeful escaped from Vanity
Fair, they overtook one who was ahead of them. His name was By-ends, and
his red velvet coat, dignified manner, and expansive waistline indicated that
he was no beggar.*

*"What country are you from, sir?" they asked him. "And how far are you
going this way?"*

*"I am from the town of Fair-speech, and I am going to the Celestial
City." But he did not tell them his name.*

"From Fair-speech?" said Christian. "Does any good live there?"

*By-ends looked down his nose at the pilgrims. "Yes," he said dryly. "I
hope so."*

"Sir, what may I call you?" said Christian.

*"I am a stranger to you, and you to me," the man said, vaguely waving a
hand in the air. "If you are going this way, I will be glad for your company. If
not, I will live with it."*

*"This town of Fair-speech," said Christian, "I have heard of. They say it's
a wealthy place."*

*"Yes," By-ends said smugly. "I can assure you it is. I…have many rich
relatives there."*

Christian looked at him intently. "Who are your relatives there, if a man may be so bold?"

By-ends smiled. "Almost the whole town. In particular, my Lord Turn-about, my Lord Time-server, my Lord Fair-speech (from whose ancestors the town first took its name); also, Mr. Smooth-man, Mr. Facing-both-ways, and Mr. Anything. The parson of our parish, Mr. Two-tongues, was my mother's brother on my father's side."

"Are you a married man?" Christian asked.

"Yes, and my wife is a very virtuous woman, the daughter of Lady Feigning. True, my wife and I somewhat differ in religion from those of the stricter sort, but only in two small ways. First, we never strive against the popular tide. Second, we are always most zealous when religion goes in his silver slippers; we love to walk with him in the street, if the sun shines and the people applaud him."

Christian stepped aside and whispered to his friend Hopeful. "It just occurred to me," he said, "that this may be By-ends of Fair-speech. If so, we have as big a scoundrel in our company as lives in these parts."

"Ask him," Hopeful whispered back. "I doubt he's ashamed of his name."

Christian caught up with the man again, and said, "Sir, you talk as if you knew something the rest of the world doesn't. If I'm not mistaken, you're Mr. By-ends of Fair-speech."

By-ends frowned. "This is not my name, but a nickname given by some who can't stand me. I must be content to bear it as a reproach, as other good men have borne theirs before me."

"Did you ever give people a reason to call you by this name?" Christian asked.

"Never, never! The worst I ever did was to keep up with the times, and to gain thereby. If I've received a few things in that way, let me count them a blessing. But malicious people shouldn't load me with reproach because of that."

"I thought you were the man I'd heard of," Christian said. "Frankly, I fear this name belongs to you more properly than you're willing to admit."

By-ends pouted. "Well, if you wish to think that, I can't help it. But you'll find me fair company, if you'll let me travel with you."

Christian's voice turned steely. "If you go with us, you must go against wind and tide. You must also own religion in his rags, as well as when in his silver slippers—and stand by him, too, when bound in irons, as well as when he walks the streets with applause."

"You must not impose," By-ends sniffed, "nor lord it over my faith. Leave me to my liberty, and let me go with you."

Christian shook his head. "Not a step further, unless you will do as we do."

By-ends put his nose in the air. "I shall never desert my old principles, since they are harmless and profitable. If I may not go with you, I will go by myself—until I find someone who appreciates my company!"

At that, Christian and Hopeful left the man behind. But soon one of them, looking back, saw three men following Mr. By-ends. The men's names were Mr. Hold-the-world, Mr. Money-love, and Mr. Save-all. By-ends bowed to the trio; they gave him a compliment in return.

When they had thus saluted each other, Mr. Money-love asked Mr. By-ends, "Who are the two on the road ahead of us?"

"They are a couple of far countrymen," By-ends said disdainfully. "They are, in their fashion, going on pilgrimage."

"Why didn't they stay?" Money-love asked. "I should hope, after all, that we are all on pilgrimage."

"Indeed," replied By-ends. "But the men before us are rigid, and love their own notions, and think little of others' opinions. A man may be ever so godly, but if he doesn't agree with them in all things, they thrust him out of their company."

"Hmph," said Save-all. "I've read of some who are overly righteous. Their rigidity makes them judge and condemn all but themselves. On what exactly did you differ?"

By-ends threw a look of contempt in the direction of Christian and Faithful. "Why, they feel it is their duty to rush on their journey in all kinds of weather; I wait for wind and tide. They want to hazard all for God at a clap; I take all advantages to secure my life and estate. They are for holding their opinions even if all other men are against them; I am for religion insofar as the times and my safety will bear it. They are for religion when he is in rags and contempt; I am for him when he walks in his silver slippers, in the sun-shine, and with applause."

"Don't Rock the Boat!"

After witnessing Faithful's cruel execution in Vanity Fair, Christian is released by the authorities. Soon he meets Hopeful, newly converted to the faith through the examples of Faithful and Christian. Hopeful and Christian pledge to make the journey to the Celestial City together.

The two pilgrims soon meet By-ends, who might also be called "Mr. Crafty." He describes his hometown of Fair-speech in great and boastful detail. It becomes clear that Fair-speech is a place where religion fits comfortably into the culture, and where the greatest commandment is "Thou shalt not rock the boat, nor say anything controversial." In Fair-speech, religion conforms to cultural and social norms instead of transforming them.

When Christian reminds Mr. By-ends that the pilgrim's way sometimes requires swimming against the cultural tide, it's too much for By-ends. He separates himself from Christian and Hopeful, preferring more "moderate" companions.

The Power of Words

Today, too, there are many places along our journey where people expect Christian truth to be the slave of cultural norms. Our children already face this problem, and will do so increasingly in the near future.

Imagine the following scenario. One day your children come home from school. You hug them as they toss down their backpacks and book bags and head to the kitchen for a snack. You sit down at the kitchen table with them.

"Did you learn anything new today?" you ask.

They brighten up. "Oh, yes!" cries Johnny.

"A whole *bunch* of new things!" says Suzie.

"We learned that it's not nice to call people bad names," Johnny declares.

You smile. *It's nice to know the schools are teaching good manners*, you think.

"Yeah," Johnny continues, "bad names like 'homosexual.' The right word to use when two men love each other is 'gay.'"

Your smile is fading fast.

"And it's not nice to say that people who have sex but aren't married are doing something *sinful*," Johnny adds. "That makes people uncomfortable."

Before you can think of a response, Suzie chimes in. "My class talked about religions around the world. And guess what?"

Your mouth is open, but no words come out.

"We learned," Suzie says, "that God is not just a *He*. To say that is *gender bias*! We should be able to call God a *She*. Isn't that cool?"

Far-fetched? Not at all. In California, a preschool teacher was recently ordered to instruct her small subjects in the normalcy of having "two daddies" and "two mommies." In the same state, a fifth-grade male teacher proudly explained to his students that his "boyfriend" had given him the flowers on his desk.[1] And a recently published hymnal supplement "updates" the idea of a heavenly Father with references to our "Mother God" and the "mothering Christ."[2]

In the cultural battles of our day, language is the weapon of choice. The current trend is to use language to stifle those who hold traditional values. This form of oppression is more subtle than the outright persecution of Vanity Fair. It doesn't set the Christian faith on fire or hang it from a noose. Instead, it tries to slowly suffocate it.

TRUTH IN A STRAITJACKET

It's been called "political correctness," or "PC." It's the insistence that what we think, and how we express it, must conform to the popular idea of "truth." When we break this unwritten code, we're punished.

Here are a few examples from our own contacts:

- A college professor was investigated by his university for suggesting that homosexuals can change their behavior. Another underwent scrutiny after he said that public school textbooks might be biased against traditional religion.
- An elementary student was banned from putting Jesus' name on a valentine at school; a high school student was barred from bringing a Bible to class because it might make others uncomfortable.
- Christian groups on college campuses were threatened with expulsion unless they agreed to adopt a "nondiscrimination" policy regarding homosexuals and those of other faiths.

- Christians placing ads to rent rooms to "Christians" have been sued for housing and rental discrimination—thereby facing huge fines and attorneys' fees, as well as mandatory diversity training to make them more sensitive to other beliefs and lifestyles.

Much of the "PC" trend originated in the halls of academia. Now it infects the media, industry, commerce, and community life.

The most popular target of the PC scourge, it seems, is conservative Christianity and those who promote traditional family values. When John Ashcroft, a conservative Christian, was nominated by President Bush to serve as U.S. Attorney General, one national magazine emblazoned the words "Holy War" next to the nominee's photo on the cover. When the Promise Keepers movement called men back to their biblical roles as spiritual leaders in their families and communities, a nationally syndicated newspaper cartoonist lampooned a "promise keeper" as a club-wielding caveman, dragging his wife by her hair.

THE BITTER ROOTS OF PC

There are several reasons why our children must be prepared to face increasing pressure from the inhabitants of "Fair-speech."

First, our culture has become convinced that "sensitivity" is more important than morality. Our children are told that their most important duty is to avoid offending, rather than trying to do what's right in the biblical sense.

Make no mistake: We *should* teach our children to respect other people. Every person is created in God's image, and has worth. But that's not the same as muzzling the truth because it may make someone uncomfortable.

Some might ask, "But wasn't Christ the epitome of compassion toward other people?" The answer is clearly yes. But political correctness disguises political sympathies to look like true moral compassion.

The second reason our children must deal with the PC plague is the new ethic of "tolerance." Janet encountered this when she was on the television program *Hardball with Chris Matthews*, debating pro-promiscuity comments made by a nominee for the post of U.S. Surgeon General. A *Time* magazine reporter on the show claimed that condemning sex before marriage was judgmental; after all, didn't Jesus talk a lot about "tolerance"? The fact is that Jesus never preached "tolerance" of the twenty-first-century kind anywhere in the Gospels. As Janet pointed out on the program, while Jesus forgave the adulteress (John 8:1-11), He also told her to stop sinning.

Josh McDowell and Bob Hostetler have noted that once upon a time, tolerance meant respecting the other person even though you didn't share his or her beliefs. Now tolerance has been redefined to mean considering all beliefs equal; it is "intolerant" to tell someone else that his or her actions or beliefs are wrong.[3] Our children will be called "intolerant" if they cite what the Bible says about sin.

The third reason why our culture has embraced PC is a fear of religious "extremism." Being "outside the mainstream" brands you with a scarlet letter of shame. The citizens of Fair-speech are highly suspicious of those who take absolute stands. If our children say that Jesus is the only way to God, or that the Bible is God's infallible Word, they'll be increasingly branded as "fundamentalists"—another way of saying "bigoted right-wingers."

OUR MANNERS, HIS MESSAGE

If a tidal wave of political correctness is heading toward our children, how do we prepare them?

The apostle Paul offers two complementary guidelines. First, he urges Christians to be gracious in the *manner* in which they communicate:

> Let your conversation be always full of grace, seasoned with salt, so that you may know how to answer everyone. (Colossians 4:6)

Our children need to know that their speech and conduct should always reflect the truth that the other person has value because God loves him or her. We tried to teach our four children how to handle, in grace, those who maligned them because of their stand on spiritual or moral issues. We reminded them not to view their persecutors as "the enemy," but as those who may have been captured by the enemy. And we told them the wise words of D. L. Moody, who advised remembering that we could be spending eternity with that "unsavory" other person.

Our children appear to have taken this teaching to heart. All of them have had homosexual friends or coworkers whom they've treated with compassion and respect. Yet these same people can explain exactly what our kids believe about the sinfulness of homosexual activity—and why they believe it. That's because our children have spoken the truth—in love.

Second, and just as important, Paul points out the necessity of never watering down the *message* of the gospel with human "wisdom":

> My message and my preaching were not with wise and persuasive
> words, but with a demonstration of the Spirit's power, so that
> your faith might not rest on men's wisdom, but on God's power.
> (1 Corinthians 2:4-5)

What might this graceful but uncompromising approach look like? Consider the accusations of "political incorrectness" against Faithful during the Vanity Fair trial, and his responses to them:

Then they called Superstition as a witness, and bid him look upon Faithful. The judge asked, "What can you say for your lord the king against the prisoner?"

After Superstition was sworn in, he began. "My lord, I have no great acquaintance with this man, nor do I desire to have further knowledge of him. But I know he is a pest, from a conversation I had with him the other day. He said our religion was for nothing, and no man could please God by it! And you know, your lordship, what that means: That we worship in vain, are yet in our sins, and finally shall be condemned!"

Then Pickthank was sworn in. "This fellow I have known a long time," he declared. "I have heard him speak things that ought not to be spoken. He has railed against our noble prince Beelzebub and spoken contemptibly of his honorable friends—the Lord Old Man, the Lord Carnal Delight, the Lord Luxurious, the Lord Desire of Vain Glory, my old Lord Lechery, Sir Having Greedy, and the rest of our nobility. He has even said that none of these noblemen should have a place in this town!"

Pickthank turned from the assembled crowd to address the judge. "The accused has not been afraid to criticize you, my lord, calling you an ungodly villain and other vilifying terms with which he has bespattered most of our town's gentry."

When Pickthank had told his tale, the judge directed his speech to the prisoner at the bar. "You heretic and traitor! Have you heard what these honest gentlemen have said against you?"

Faithful, in chains, lifted his head. "May I speak a few words in my own defense?"

The judge curled his lip. "Sir, you deserve to live no longer, but to be executed immediately! But so that everyone may see our gentleness toward you, let us hear what you—vile as you are—have to say."

Faithful cleared his throat. "I say, then, in answer to Mr. Envy's earlier statement, that I never said anything but this: Any rule, law, custom, or people who oppose the Word of God are diametrically opposite to Christianity. If I am wrong in this, convince me of my error and I'll recant.

"As to Mr. Superstition's charge against me, I said only this: In the worship of God a divine faith is required. But there can be no divine faith without a divine revelation of God's will. Whatever is thrust into the worship of God that does not agree with divine revelation can only be done by a human faith which will not lead to eternal life.

"As to what Mr. Pickthank said: The prince of this town and all his attendants are more fit for living in hell than in this town and country. And so the Lord have mercy on me."

WAR OF THE WORDS:
PRACTICAL PROGRESS FOR PARENTS AND KIDS

Teaching our kids to be graceful yet uncompromising in their speech is no small task, especially in a world that prods them to do the opposite. Here are some ideas to prepare them for living in a PC society.

Principle #1: Have a Winsome Manner

Despite his suspicions about Mr. By-ends, Christian addresses him as "Sir." Even when Christian's suspicions are confirmed, his tone is still respectful: "Frankly, I fear this name belongs to you more properly than you're willing to admit." Our kids need to watch their tone too.

Parental Action: Teach True Tolerance

Tolerance used to mean "agreeing to disagree." It meant showing respect for those who hold other views—not necessarily respecting the views themselves. You can help your child practice this kind of tolerance—instead of the kind that shuts off debate.

Model respect. Take your child to hear a speaker with whom you disagree—or watch such a person on TV, or listen to one on the radio. Take notes, especially on points with which you differ. Afterward, go over your notes with your child, being careful not to say anything negative about the speaker—only about his or her views. Ask, "What kinds of experiences might have led the speaker to feel so strongly about this point? What could we learn from this person? If you met this person face-to-face, what's something positive you could say to him or her?"

Practice listening. As a family, sit in a circle. Give each person one of the following assignments:

- Tell us why you think our family should get a cat.
- Review the last movie you saw.
- Explain why you shouldn't have to do any chores for a week.
- Try to convince us to eat asparagus.

After each person speaks, ask the rest these questions:

- Did you agree with the speaker?
- What were the person's main points?
- Is it easier to listen carefully to someone with whom you agree than someone with whom you don't?

After family members answer these questions, ask the speaker, "Did the rest of us hear what you really meant? What does this tell us about listening to people with whom we disagree?"

Live with differences. Your child may wonder what to do when a winsome attitude doesn't change a friend's mind. Does the friendship have to end? Should your child avoid talking about God in order to keep the peace? Share this advice from Randy Petersen, as found in *My Truth, Your Truth, Whose Truth?*:

Q. I have a good friend who belongs to a different religion. I want to keep him as a friend, not get in a big argument. Sure, I'd like it if he agreed with me about what's true, but what if he doesn't? Can't I just let it drop?

A. Yes. Don't stop caring about him, but drop the arguing. It's more likely that your relationship—not your arguments—will win him over. The Bible tells you to "Always be prepared to give an answer to everyone who asks you to give the reason for the hope that you have" (1 Peter 3:15). Be ready. Maybe your steel-trap mind can help sweep away one of your friend's questions at some point, but it's your love that will help attract him toward Jesus. That same verse urges Christians to speak to others "with gentleness and respect." Be sensitive to how God's Spirit is guiding you about when and how to talk about your faith.

Take some time to learn about your friend's religion. What elements of God's truth do you find there? Can you build a bridge from his beliefs to your belief in Jesus?

Check out what the apostle Paul did while visiting Athens (Acts 17). Before speaking to the Athenians, he walked their streets to get a feel for what they believed. Then, instead of criticizing their multi-god religion, he used it to help them understand Christ. Paul had found a shrine "To an Unknown God"—the One they didn't know yet, the One Paul had come to tell them about.

Like the Athenians, people of many religions are reaching out to know what they can about the Creator. With love and sensitivity, you can help introduce them to Jesus.[4]

Parental Action: See Yourself as Others Do

Who decides whether our manner is winsome? Those we're trying to "win." Unfortunately, people have noticed a few flaws in the approach of some Christians. Here's a way to help your child avoid some of those mistakes.

Look in the mirror. According to Randy Petersen, many people think Christians...

1. are ignorant;
2. are stuck in the past;
3. are afraid to really live;
4. feel guilty about everything;
5. hate people who aren't like them;
6. don't want anyone to have fun;
7. want to control what everyone does and thinks;
8. think they know it all.

As a result of these stereotypes, many people don't take our "odd" views seriously. Petersen writes, "Sometimes Christians *earn* [these stereotypes].... Try asking yourself: *Do any of these descriptions sound like me?*"[5]

Next time you need a topic of conversation at the dinner table, ask how your family could show your neighbors that not all Christians fit the preceding list. For example, inviting a family of a different faith over for dinner might help with #5; coordinating a block party might help with #6.

Principle #2: Have an Uncompromising Message

Christian wasn't rude to By-ends, but made it clear where he stood: "If you go with us, you must go against wind and tide. You must also own religion in his rags, as well as when in his silver slippers—and stand by him, too, when bound in irons, as well as when he walks the streets with applause." Your child can gain a similar understanding of what's negotiable, and what isn't.

Parental Action: Identify the Essentials

"Choose your battles wisely," Dr. James Dobson has said concerning the parenting of teens. The same holds true when confronting a politically correct culture. Help your child decide which biblical truths to defend on the narrow road.

Boil down the gospel. Kids can be overwhelmed by the idea of taking unpopular stands—especially if they think they must speak up on every issue from Bible interpretation to body piercing. Start them with the basics—the Good News about Jesus. See whether they can express the gospel in five words or less. A few examples:

- "Believe in Jesus, live forever."
- "Jesus, the Door to heaven."
- "Ask Jesus, He'll forgive you."

Draw the line. Try this activity with teens and preteens. Draw a horizontal line in the middle of a piece of paper. As you read the following "politically incorrect" principles, your young person should write each one above or below the line. Those above the line are those your youngster thinks shouldn't be compromised; those below the line are less absolute. Here are the principles:

- Jesus is the only way to heaven.
- Abortion is wrong.
- Girls shouldn't ask boys out on dates.
- God created the world.
- Research on embryonic human stem cells shouldn't be allowed.
- Women shouldn't serve in military combat roles.
- God hates divorce.
- Homosexuals aren't "born that way."
- Students should be allowed to pray before school football games.

When you're done, talk about the results. Rather than correcting your child's choices, ask him to explain them—and whether they're supported by the Bible. Then ask, "Do you agree with all of these principles? Which ones would you defend to your friends or in a class? How far would you go in doing that?"

Parental Action: Practice the Preaching

Speaking up is easier if you've done it before—even if it was only a "dry run." Help your child prepare by trying these activities.

Have a chat. In the book *My Truth, Your Truth, Whose Truth?*, a Christian teenager with the screen name "Tim4U" finds himself attacked in an Internet chat room for his politically incorrect views:

Hulkster:	You don't think about sex?
Tim4U:	I just choose not to focus on it, OK?
wonderboy:	It's a religious thing, right? Maybe you Christians want to pretend that sex doesn't exist, but I've got news for you.
Tim4U:	I'm just saying sex isn't a joke. And it's just for people who are married.
r2d2:	Married?
Hulkster:	Are you for real?
Tim4U:	God says sex should be reserved for marriage.
r2d2:	Maybe YOUR God says that.
Tim4U:	I didn't make this up. The Bible says it.
Hulkster:	So?

r2d2:	I know what it is. You're gay, aren't you?
Tim4U:	No!
r2d2:	Not that there's anything wrong with that.
Tim4U:	Well, now that you mention it…
wonderboy:	Oh, so you hate gay people too.
Tim4U:	I don't hate gay people.…
r2d2:	Explain yourself, Tim.
Tim4U:	You're just going to crucify me on this point, too.
butterfly:	No, Tim. Tell us what you think.
Tim4U:	It's not what I think. It's what God thinks.
r2d2:	What YOUR God thinks. Or what you THINK he thinks.
Tim4U:	What He says in the Bible.
butterfly:	But isn't that a matter of interpretation?
Tim4U:	No, it's pretty clear. God loves everybody, but He puts certain kinds of sexual activity out of bounds.
wonderboy:	No offense, but you're hopeless. Only bigots are against being gay now.
butterfly:	I have a friend who's gay, and he's the most caring person I've ever known.
wonderboy:	So what do you say to that, Timmy?
r2d2:	Timmy the Intolerant.
Tim4U:	I knew I should have stayed in bed this morning.[6]

After letting your teen read the preceding exchange, ask, "If you were in Tim4U's place, what would you have said in the chat room? Was Tim4U bound to have trouble no matter what he said? Why or why not?"

Say it your way. Has your child thought through how he or she would stand up for an unpopular truth? A little rehearsal can go a long way toward building confidence. Rather than handing him or her a speech to memorize, though, help your child come up with a few points that reflect his or her own ideas and way of talking. Role-play a conversation in which you play the part of a skeptical (but not hostile) friend. One good topic for both younger and older children is "Why I Believe Jesus Is the Only Way to Heaven." Teens may be encouraged to decide and articulate what they believe about issues like abortion, divorce, and euthanasia.

A Different Drummer

When our oldest was a teen, she came back from a Christian conference with a great T-shirt. On the front was a cartoon depicting a school of fish, all swimming in one direction. Swimming in the opposite direction was a lone fish in the shape of the Christian "IXTHUS." The shirt bore this message: SWIMMING AGAINST THE CURRENT.

The tide of political correctness is rising. But our children can rise above its influence by getting used to their "differentness" as they carry a distinctly different message.

Paul's two guideposts—a winsome, gracious manner and an uncompromising message—will help our children withstand the pressures of Fair-speech. When the townsfolk of that crafty place turn up the heat, our children can respond by shedding the light.

Chapter 13

THE MONEY TRAP

Guiding Your Child to Reject Materialism

~๑

A little bit wiser and warier, Christian and Hopeful put the town of Fair-speech behind them and set out again along the Pilgrim's road. In time, the path led them across a broad plain. On the far side of this plain, sharply out-lined against a pale, yellowish sky, rose a solitary green hill.

"What is this place?" asked Hopeful, leaning on his staff and wiping his brow.

Christian shaded his eyes against the sun and studied the landscape with a frown. In the side of the hill he saw a gaping black hole. Out of this hole rose a faint cloud of dust and smoke and the sounds of iron scraping against the deep rock.

"It looks like a place I've heard described," he said. "And if I'm right, Hopeful, I don't think we want to get detained here. Keep moving and stay sharp."

They pushed on then. And as the road drew near the hill, they became aware of a man who stood there, between the path and the pit, waving vigor-ously and calling out to them in a loud voice.

"Hello!" he shouted, smiling broadly. "Over here! This way, my friends! I have something to show you!"

Hopeful paused and shot Christian a questioning look. But Christian quickly stepped in front of his companion and barred his advance with his staff.

"Who are you?" he shouted back. "And what could you possibly have to show us? We're just a couple of poor pilgrims!"

The man laughed. "My name is Demas," he answered. "And unless you're anxious to remain poor, I think you'll find my information extremely interesting. Do you see that?" he said, pointing to the hole. "It's a silver mine! Just think of it! Full of wealth, and all to be had for the taking! Even now it's crowded with industrious souls who know what to do when opportunity comes knocking. Why don't you join them? You'll never have another chance like this to line your purses so richly and with so little effort!" At this, he plunged both hands into his own pockets and brought them forth again simply dripping with brightly shining coins.

Hopeful cocked an eyebrow at Christian.

"Let's go see," he said.

THE DEFECTOR

Demas. Does the name sound familiar?

In the New Testament, Demas had been a companion of the apostle Paul. That in itself tells us a great deal about the level of his dedication to the Lord. You don't travel in Paul's company without having made a fair amount of progress down the road to the Celestial City.

But something happened to Demas. Somewhere along the way something changed, for in his second letter to Timothy, the apostle tells the young pastor, "Demas, because he loved this world, has deserted me" (2 Timothy 4:10).

Paul doesn't expand, so we're left to guess at the exact nature of Demas's "love for this present world." But Bunyan, with a touch of creative license, takes the liberty of assuming that his defection had something to do with the lure of money.

His point in doing so is clear: Temporal wealth, and the particular brand of ease and security it offers, are liabilities for the serious disciple. Jesus, in His famous Parable of the Sower, spoke of the "deceitfulness of wealth" (Matthew 13:22; Mark 4:19). He underscored this theme when He said, "It is easier for a camel to go through the eye of a needle than for a rich man to enter the kingdom of God" (Mark 10:25).

Jesus knew that money has tremendous power to deceive and deflect—not because material wealth is wicked in itself, but because of the deceitfulness of the human heart, which tends to attach itself to almost anything *but* God. This is why Paul warned Timothy, "The *love* of money is a root of all kinds of evil," adding that "some people, eager for money, have wandered from the faith and pierced themselves with many griefs" (1 Timothy 6:10, emphasis added).

The Demas of the Bible "wandered from the faith" when he cast his lot with the solidity of temporal things. Bunyan's Demas follows in this tradition when he invites Christian and Hopeful to take a detour off the King's Highway on the chance of picking up some easy cash.

LUCRE'S LURE

Our children come up against this temptation every day. Take Taylor, age 11, who comes home from school with a breathless announcement: "Mom! I can get this really cool radio-controlled car—for nothing!"

Mom cocks an eyebrow. "Oh, really? How?"

Taylor takes off his backpack and pulls out a stapled sheaf of papers. "See?" he says. "I can earn the car by selling 75 magazine subscriptions to raise money for the school. And everybody who sells at least 12 subscriptions gets out of class for a pizza party!"

If the school district needs money, why don't they just ask for it? Mom thinks, gritting her teeth. She's tired of pressuring neighbors, relatives, and coworkers to buy overpriced cans of popcorn, candy bars, and gift wrap—just so Taylor doesn't miss the prizes the school uses to lure young "salespeople."

It's hard enough to convince him he doesn't need more toys, Mom tells herself. *Why does the school have to make it harder?*

Or take sisters Erin and Linda, ages 12 and 13, who spend hours in front of the computer—playing the CD-ROM versions of *Who Wants to Be a Millionaire*. Half the time their competitions end in fights, even though the money is imaginary. Judging from their TV viewing habits—mostly programs like *Survivor*, *Weakest Link*, and *Wheel of Fortune*—their aim in life is to get "something for nothing" by becoming professional game show contestants.

And then there's little Andre, age four, who toddles into the mall arcade with his dad. Andre sees something that looks like a treasure chest under glass, a machine holding heaps of shiny tokens. "I wanna play that one!" he says. Dad dutifully buys a handful of tokens and gives them to his son, who plops them one at a time into a slot. Each token rolls down a track and onto a numbered circle.

Looks like a roulette wheel, Dad thinks absently. He's right. There's no skill involved in this game—only chance. Andre frowns as the first three tokens yield no tickets. Then he smiles as the fourth hits a "jackpot," and a dozen tickets reel into his little hand. Dad may not realize it, but his son is being conditioned to play "real" gambling games when he's old enough—when the urge to get something for nothing may cost him his livelihood, home, and family.

In short, the pull of easy money—and materialism in general—may be stronger on our children than it's ever been. And it's getting worse.

THREE ALARMING TRENDS

The lure of "lucre" and materialism will be an increasing problem for families in the coming decade. Here are three economic trends pointing in that direction.

Trend #1: More kid-oriented marketing. Children, more than ever before, are driving their families' consuming habits. That's why marketers created commercials like those for "Parkay Fun Squeeze" margarine, a spread that comes in attractive kid colors like blue and pink, to be shown amid Saturday morning cartoons. It's why bright green ketchup is being sold in containers specially designed to fit small hands—a strategy yielding tidy profits for the Heinz company.[1] It's why Journeys, a shoe retailer, installed pay phones and TV sets in the middle of its stores to attract teen customers.

Perhaps most disturbing of all, credit companies are creating new kinds of "plastic money" aimed specifically at young people—in some cases, kids as young as 13. In the U.S., at least 7 percent of high school students and 55 percent of college students are now using major credit cards of their own.[2]

Trend #2: Fewer role models of financial responsibility. To put it bluntly, many of us have been poor models: Kids are being taught by their parents' example to overextend themselves financially. In Bunyan's terms, many of us have already slipped into Demas's pit, and we're dragging our children down with us.

Debt has become a way of life, especially in America. Between 1952 and 2001, household debt in the U.S. mushroomed by a staggering 800 percent—from about $1 trillion to $8 trillion! The average American household now has four times the credit card debt it had in 1990, and *twice* as much of that money is being spent on luxury items today than 20 years ago. Most Americans spend only about half as much of their income on daily necessities as they did in 1980.[3]

No wonder contemporary kids see little reason to resist the temptation to spend money they don't have on things they don't need. They've watched Mom and Dad do it a hundred times! Whatever parents (even Christian parents) may be *saying* during their lectures on the evils of materialism, their *actions* are communicating a clear message: Personal value is to be measured by the value of the things we possess.

Trend #3: Greater financial angst. It's that nagging anxiety, the feeling that, however much stuff and money we manage to beg, borrow, steal, invest, or warehouse, it can never *really* be enough. Ironically, this fear is the natural fruit of money's unsubstantiated promises: security and stability.

Children may not understand money markets or the ups and downs of Wall Street. But when Mom starts chucking items out of the grocery cart after adding them up on her calculator, those wide little eyes don't miss a trick. When Dad cancels that planned vacation and decides that the family is going to stay home instead, kids immediately prick up their ears. They sense the money mood in the house pretty quickly; they're practically gurus when it comes to emotional economics.

There's good reason to believe that financial angst will worsen over the next two or three decades. The economy, increasingly global in scope, may "boom" on an international scale, but will become more volatile and subject to sudden downswings. This principle was dramatically illustrated on September 11, 2001, when hijacked airliners crashed into the World Trade Center in New York City and into the Pentagon. When the twin towers crumbled into dust and tangled steel, the stock market plummeted with them—further underscoring the linkage between world events and home-town financial solvency.

Our children are likely to live in an increasingly uncertain world. As the anxiety index rises, the urge to acquire, grasp, gamble, and hoard—the temptation to "get while the getting's good"—may prove overwhelming for those who are not prepared.

WHAT TO DO?

Christian parents face an urgent challenge. Our mission? To instill in our children a healthy wariness of roadside Demases...*and* a strategy for rebuffing enticements to "get rich quick."

How can we help our children hold their ground when Demas approaches with his silver-tongued lies? How do we keep them from falling into the "money trap" set by financial angst? For a hint, let's go back to Bunyan's allegory and see how Christian handles this challenge.

Again Christian put out a hand and restrained his friend. "Now I'm certain that I've heard of this place before!" he said in a low voice. "It's the Hill of Lucre—Money. It looks inviting...but it has a fearsome reputation."

"Why so?" asked Hopeful.

"Because its treasure is a snare—a trap! If the reports are true, many pilgrims have lost their lives seeking it. As for those who succeed in their quest, the prize merely tarnishes and rots their minds and bodies in the end."

Demas interrupted him with another loud cry. "Look closer, friends!" he shouted. "I'm only asking for a small investment of your time. You'll soon be on your way again, loaded down with easy money!"

Christian turned and faced the man. "But the place is dangerous—isn't it? Haven't many people wrecked or lost their lives here?"

"Dangerous?" sniffed Demas, dropping the coins back into his pockets, and swinging his arms nonchalantly at his sides. "Oh, not very. Not except to those who are careless."

Christian turned to Hopeful with a grim smile. "Exactly," he shouted back at Demas. "And careless is something we don't intend to be! Our goal is the Celestial City, and we have no wish to forfeit our chances of reaching it by falling into that pit of yours. A good day to you, sir!"

He gripped his walking stick with one hand and with the other seized his companion by the sleeve.

"Come on, Hopeful," he said, turning his face away from the hill and peering determinedly down the road. "We're moving on."

ESCAPING THE MONEY TRAP: PRACTICAL PROGRESS FOR PARENTS AND KIDS

Bunyan's hero handles himself admirably in this sticky situation. Despite his failings at other points along the road, in this case he manages to thrust temptation aside, lead his friend away from the brink of disaster, and get back to the business of being a pilgrim without the loss of another precious moment. And he does it by applying three principles.

Principle #1: Question That Sales Pitch

First, Christian refuses to take the claims of Demas at face value, asking, "But the place is dangerous—isn't it? Haven't many people wrecked or lost their lives here?" He remembers the warnings he's heard about the Hill of Lucre. Though the story doesn't give us specifics, it's obvious that *someone* has taken the trouble to prepare Christian for this moment. The warnings he's received are anything but vague: "Its treasure is a snare—a trap! If the reports are true, many pilgrims have lost their lives seeking it. As for those who succeed in their quest, the prize merely tarnishes and rots their minds and bodies in the end."

Parental Action: Encourage Skepticism

We can do the same for our children, teaching them to question the materialistic messages our culture sends. Here are some activities to try:

Mall crawl. Take your kids to a nearby shopping center for a scavenger hunt. Ask them to find and write down the names of items like these: an arcade game that encourages kids to waste money; an article of clothing that's a bargain; a toy nobody would buy if it weren't tied into a TV show or movie; the best deal on a soft drink; a package that makes a product look bigger or more exciting than it really is. Then end your outing with a snack in the food court, where you can discuss your findings.

Ad analysis. Watch a kid-targeted TV show together. During commercials, have children pay close attention to the sales pitch presented. Ask questions like these: What was this ad trying to sell you? What reasons did it give for buying the product? Do you think the product would make you as happy, cool, or flabbergasted as the people in the commercial? Why or why not?

No free lunch. Challenge kids to come up with a way to get something for nothing. Then point out the hidden costs in their schemes. For instance, sending away for a "free" toy might require buying several boxes of cereal and collecting the tops; entering a contest might mean writing an essay and buying a postage stamp and envelope; a "two for one" dinner deal would require driving to the restaurant and purchasing the first meal.

Parental Action: Ring Out a Warning

Just as Christian has been warned about the Hill of Lucre, you can alert your children to the dangers of materialism. Here are two ideas to get you started:

Point out parables. Sit down with your kids and read them Jesus' parable of the Rich Fool (Luke 12:13-21). Then tell them the story of the Rich Man and Lazarus (Luke 16:19-31), where the Lord makes it clear that the things we acquire in "this present world" have nothing to do with our security and comfort in the world to come. Follow up with questions like these: Is getting rich a good goal? Why or why not? What would you be willing to do for a million dollars? What would you refuse to do? Has wanting money or things ever made you do something you were sorry for later?

Share cautionary tales. Characters from literature—Charles Dickens's Ebenezer Scrooge, for instance, or George Eliot's Silas Marner—can help you make the point that chasing riches causes grief. High-quality Radio Theatre dramatizations of *A Christmas Carol* and *Silas Marner* are available on CD or cassette from Focus on the Family. After listening together, talk about how loving money led to trouble for Ebenezer and Silas.

Principle #2: Heed the Warning

Christian doesn't allow the warnings he's heard to remain a matter of mere theoretical or theological speculation. He takes them to heart and *does* something about them. It would be easy to take a few steps off the road to get a closer look at the silver mine—just for curiosity's sake, of course. In the same way, it's easy for us to treat Jesus' hard-hitting assertions about the dangers of wealth as mere conversation pieces. Bunyan's hero doesn't waste time playing such games. Instead, he takes his friend by the arm, turns on his heel, and walks away from the temptation.

Parental Action: Rehearse Those U-Turns

When you discuss the lure of "lucre" with your child, he or she may give all the right answers. But when confronted by temptation itself, what will your child do? One good way to prepare for those crucial times of decision is to rehearse "walk away" strategies. For example:

Impulse purchases. Say to your child, "Pretend you're at the store. You're almost out the door when you see a sign that says, '50% Off.' You look on the shelf and see a _____ (toy, pair of jeans, video game). It's not something you've planned to buy. You don't want it enough to pay full price. But half off seems like such a good deal! Something tells you there are better things to do with your money, but you're afraid if you don't act now you'll miss your chance. What do you do?" As needed, suggest such plans as praying about the choice, calling a parent or trusted friend for advice, going home and making a list of pros and cons about the purchase, or taking a day or two to think about it. Let your child pick the strategy he or she likes best.

Media messages. Discuss actions your child can take when he or she is bombarded with sales pitches in TV commercials. Some possibilities: changing the channel; laughing at an ad's claims; turning off the set; talking back to the announcer. Practice your child's favorite strategy next time you watch TV together.

Parental Action: Teach Stewardship

Besides encouraging kids to reject the rush for riches, we need to teach them how to handle the money and possessions they *do* have. Then these things can be what God intends them to be: tools to be used for good purposes and applied to the practical challenge of living a wise and peaceful life. Here are a few ways to help your children develop a sensible, intentional approach to handling their own money matters:

Five-step program. When it comes to spending, help your kids memorize this sequence: working; earning; saving; intelligent shopping; and, finally, buying. Stress the idea that it *doesn't* work the other way around!

Make the connection. Try giving your children "commissions" rather than "allowances." This helps to establish a direct connection between the money they receive and the work they do to earn it. Encourage them to see themselves as essential participants in the family enterprise—not just "hangers-on" who are living "on the dole." This fosters self-control and self-reliance.

Use the resources. Check your local Christian bookstore for guides to helping kids learn stewardship. One is *Financial Parenting* by Larry Burkett and Rick Osborne (Moody Press). Or try playing the board game called *Money Matters for Kids* (Rainfall Toys).

Principle #3: Keep Your Eyes on the Prize

What enables Christian to walk away when offered the chance to dip his hand into a silver mine? It's knowing he's destined for bigger and better things—things that surpass the glitter of gold as the sun outshines a tarnished copper penny. Like the Lord Jesus Himself, Christian knows where he's come from, to whom he belongs, what his purpose is, and where he's going (see John 13:1). With his heart set on gaining the Celestial City, he doesn't have time for the petty distraction of trying to "win" by "dying with the most toys."

Parental Action: Model Trust

How can we help our children see things from Christian's eternal perspective? The first step is to have that perspective ourselves.

It comes down to *trust.* Do you really believe God loves you, cares for your family in practical ways, and has your best interests at heart? Do you pay attention when Jesus says, "Do not worry, saying, 'What shall we eat?' or 'What shall we drink?' or 'What shall we wear?'" Do you think He's credible when He promises, "Seek first his kingdom and his righteousness, and all these things shall be given to you as well" (Matthew 6:31, 33)?

If you *do* believe these things, you can make a point of acting and talking like it. When the first of the month arrives and there isn't quite enough money to go around, don't fret and fume and take out your frustrations on the rest of the household. Instead, practice saying things like, "I don't know how we're going to cover everything this month, but God does. He's aware of our needs and He'll provide for us. Meanwhile, we'll cut back a bit and do the best we can."

Imagine having this conversation with one of your children:

YOU: It looks like we won't be taking that trip to Sea World after all, Tommy.

TOMMY: Why not?

YOU: Well, it's been a rough year. I was out of work for a while last fall. Some of our investments fell through. The transmission went out in the van and cost us $1,900. The money just isn't there.

TOMMY: Oh, no! Can't you do something? Isn't there some way to get more money? What about the lottery? Or a bank loan? Maybe we could borrow from Grandma and Grandpa. Or sell the dog. Anything! We've just *got* to make that trip!

YOU: I suppose we *could* try some of those things. But I don't think we will.

TOMMY: Why not?

YOU: Because I don't believe we need to worry about it right now. Money isn't everything. Neither are trips to Sea World. Things may change in time. But for right now, I have a feeling that God has something else in mind for us. Let's just wait and see what it is.

What would happen to financial angst if our kids saw that kind of faith reflected in our words, actions, and attitudes? It might mean a revolution in the next generation's orientation toward the value of material things.

Parental Action: Store Up Treasure in Heaven

Our children need to understand the "heavenly bank account" to which Jesus points in Matthew 6:19-21: "Do not store up for yourselves treasures on earth, where moth and rust destroy, and where thieves break in and steal. But store up for yourselves treasures in heaven, where moth and rust do not destroy, and where thieves do not break in and steal. For where your treasure is, there your heart will be also."

How? Here are two suggestions:

Tithe early. The sooner you help your child develop the habit of giving 10 percent (or more) of his or her money to God's work, the better. If your church doesn't provide offering envelopes, construct some of your own as a family project—making them as creative and colorful as possible to reflect the joy of being a "cheerful giver" (2 Corinthians 9:7).

Pick a person. Adopt a missionary or a needy child, possibly through an agency like Compassion International. Write letters. Exchange photographs. Get your children involved in the stories and lives of the people their gifts are supporting. In so doing, you'll show what it means to make a solid investment in the "unseen world."

"Give, and it will be given to you. A good measure, pressed down, shaken together and running over, will be put into your lap. For with the measure you use, it will be measured to you" (Luke 6:38).

That, in the final analysis, is the very best way to escape "the money trap."

"WE'RE MOVING ON"

In the years ahead, your child may be targeted by the slickest pitchmen in history. But with your prayerful preparation, he'll remember that there's no permanent place for a Christian along the side of the road. His purpose is to move farther on—unshackled by any chains, no matter how brightly they glitter, that might hold him down.

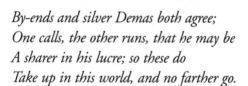

By-ends and silver Demas both agree;
One calls, the other runs, that he may be
A sharer in his lucre; so these do
Take up in this world, and no farther go.

Chapter 14

OUT TO PASTURE

Keeping Your Child from Dangerous Detours

At this point the river and the road parted ways. Christian and Hopeful were sorry to leave the river, but dared not leave the road.

Unfortunately, the path began to grow rough, and their feet were tender because of all their travels. The weary pilgrims sighed, and their sighs turned to groans. "If only there were a better way," they said.

Just then they noticed a pasture—By-path Meadow—on the left side of the road. There was a set of steps leading into it, over a fence.

"Hopeful!" Christian said excitedly. "This meadow will be easier going. Come, let's go over the fence."

Hopeful stared at the pasture, doubt wrinkling his forehead. "But what if this path should lead us out of the way?"

"That is not likely," said Christian. "Look. Doesn't the meadow run right next to this road?"

Hopeful shrugged. "Very well," he said, and followed Christian over the fence.

Sure enough, the meadow path was far easier on their feet. Soon they spied another traveler ahead of them, a man named Vain-Confidence.

"Excuse me," called Christian. "Where does this way lead?"

"To the Celestial Gate," Vain-Confidence called back.

"See?" Christian said to Hopeful. "Didn't I tell you so? This is obviously the right way." So they followed Vain-Confidence.

Eventually night came on, and it grew very dark. Christian and Hopeful peered ahead, but lost sight of their erstwhile leader.

Suddenly they heard a crash. Vain-Confidence, unable to see the way before him, had fallen into a deep pit—one built by the owner of the property to catch vain-glorious fools. Sadly, Vain-Confidence was dashed to pieces in his fall.

Christian and Hopeful heard groaning, then silence. "What happened?" Christian cried. "What's the matter?"

But there was no answer—only darkness.

Hopeful shivered. "Where are we now?" he asked.

Christian did not speak. The fear in his eyes, however, made it clear that his conviction about the rightness of this path had evaporated.

At that moment it began to rain—first a sprinkling, then a downpour. Thunder boomed, lightning flashed, and the water began to gather around their feet. Soon it had reached their ankles.

"If only I'd stayed on the right path," Hopeful said, his voice barely audible.

Christian flinched as the thunder and lightning drew closer. He lifted his soggy shoes out of the water, but there was no dry place to stand. "Who could have thought this path would lead us astray?" he asked, and then blushed at the foolishness of the question.

"I was afraid of it from the beginning," Hopeful said. "That's why I gave you that gentle caution. I would have spoken more plainly, but you are older than I."

Christian sagged as the flood rose higher, the water nearly touching their knees. "Good brother, I am sorry," he said. "I have led you off the right road, and put you in imminent danger. Please forgive me! I didn't do it with evil intent."

Hopeful put a hand on Christian's shoulder. "Be comforted, my brother. I forgive you. And I believe this will be for our good."

"I am glad I have such a merciful companion," Christian said. He looked around and swallowed hard. "But we can't stay here. We must try to find our way back."

"I'll go first," said Hopeful.

Christian put up a hand. "No, please. Let me. If there's any danger, I'll face it first. After all, this is my fault."

High Road, Low Road

Christian and Hopeful had made the right choice—or so it seemed. The narrow way had grown rocky; their legs and feet were throbbing. Then, just at the right moment, they spotted a shortcut.

It was By-path Meadow, a "low road" through a pleasant field along the river. It seemed to parallel the path they'd been traveling, and looked so much easier and more convenient than the pilgrim's road, which was getting harder by the minute.

Who can blame them for taking an alternate route? Not us! As Type A personalities, we can appreciate this pragmatic choice. Wasn't it a matter of efficiency and practicality?

Unfortunately, the shortcut turns out to be anything but a time-saver. Christian and Hopeful are left in the dark when their "guide" falls into a trap. They're caught in a torrential rainstorm, in danger of drowning in the cold, swirling waters.

John Bunyan may have lived in an era of horse-drawn carts, but his point here is particularly relevant to our digital age: What seems to be the quickest way can prove to be the most dangerous detour.

The Fast Track

The high-tech world has come on us so quickly, it's hard to believe that just a few decades ago none of us were using computers, cell phones, e-mail, or microwave ovens.

Even "fast food" used to have a different definition. Having grown up in the same town, the two of us remember when the first McDonald's arrived in our area. There was no "drive-thru"; you had to walk inside and wait about 15 minutes to get your hamburger. It seemed like a revolution in convenience at the time.

Today, though, we get impatient if we have to wait five minutes in our car to get a Big Mac. We tap our fingers with irritation if our computer is slow in connecting us to the Internet. Efficiency and immediacy are two reigning values of the twenty-first century.

Efficiency has its benefits, of course. Remember how, if you played summer sports as a child, the coach would hand out a mimeographed schedule? If a game was cancelled, the coach had to pick up the phone and call you personally. Nowadays the Little League has a sophisticated Web site listing games, teams, and statistics.

For the busy parent, that may be an improvement. But have we stopped to consider how living on the high-speed technology highway will influence our children in the next decade?

The Quick Fix

In 1998, 17 million kids were online. In 2003 an estimated 42 million were expected to be in cyberspace.[1] Currently about half of all teens are hooking up on the Internet, using e-mail as a form of instant communication.[2]

Social scientists are beginning to grapple with the effects of this technology. Some experts predict that we'll see less emotional intimacy in relationships, as the lure of immediacy causes us to put more and more technology between ourselves and those with whom we're communicating.[3]

But living in an instant world will have an even bigger price tag. As life gets faster, one important casualty will be our sense of moral responsibility.

Researcher George Barna observes that families are becoming more inclined to jettison anything that's too time-intensive—like keeping promises. As we increasingly prize efficiency, we'll be tempted to avoid commitments that are inconvenient, time-consuming, or that don't yield immediate benefits.[4] Barna's survey indicates that we're becoming more concerned with results than with biblical guidelines.[5]

According to John Naisbitt, author of *Megatrends*, our preoccupation with the immediacy that technology brings has created a kind of cultural inebriation. As we become numb to things of real, intrinsic, and permanent value, we demand a quick fix—in the spiritual realm as well as in physical health.[6]

In our conversations with teens, we've seen this played out in heartbreaking terms. We know Christian young people from Christian families who have made the tragic choice to have an abortion instead of bringing an unborn child to term. Their reasoning was simple: In the panic of the moment, they sought a "quick fix" for their "problem pregnancy." Immediacy triumphed over morality. Pragmatism won out over biblical principle.

THE VALLEY OF DECISION

How can we help our children avoid shortcuts that turn out to be dangerous detours? The first step is to understand how kids make decisions.

Child psychologists tell us that children go through stages in developing decision-making skills. At first they're "concrete operational"—making decisions based on what's physically in front of them. The beautifully decorated cake Mom has made for dinner presents a real temptation for the child who opens the refrigerator door looking for a snack. The child may look around to see if Mom is lurking nearby; satisfied that she isn't, he grabs a piece of cake. Consequences are usually not on the young child's radar screen.

As children enter their teen years, they develop "abstract" thinking. They can understand the importance of rules, and the fact that actions have consequences. But there's still a problem. Even though the teen may know why the cake ought to be left alone—that Mom has worked hard to make it and wants to save it for dinner, and that it's important to submit to parental authority—knowing and acting are not the same thing.

That's why, in a Human Growth and Development class, teens may be able to write the correct answers on an exam about the negative consequences of premarital sex—yet remain sexually active. Many such programs in public schools, warning young people about sexually transmitted diseases and pregnancy, have failed to lower sexual activity. One reason is that abstract reasoning is not enough to guide teens. Without a moral framework for their choices, mere information will only give them additional data for making bad decisions.

Josh McDowell, writing about the moral crisis among Christian youth, notes that kids *are* using their critical thinking skills. That's not the problem. The problem is that they're using them to make decisions that are based on a counterfeit view of the world. It's a worldview that prizes immediate benefits and instant gratification.[7] Cheating on a test, for example, can garner a good grade and avoid the hassle of an angry parent at report card time.

Without a powerful moral counterbalance, immediacy and convenience can be the decisive factors in our children's decisions—as they were when Christian and Hopeful saw the sign for By-path Meadow.

TIME AND ETERNITY

The second step in helping our children to avoid tragic shortcuts is to put time in perspective.

None of us feels we have enough time. Its drumbeat is constantly in the background as we rush to get ready in the morning, take the kids to school, meet our responsibilities in the home or marketplace, pick up the kids, and drive them to their game, meeting, or church activity. Dinner is a microwave affair, often resembling the fueling of a race car in an Indy 500 pit stop.

Guess where our children are picking up the idea of making a "mad dash" for the immediate and convenient?

We'll be the first to admit that the two of us have struggled with this "time management" crisis throughout our child-raising years. The clock is an unforgiving master in our world, too.

So how do we slow it down?

We can begin by taking a different view of time. We can stop seeing it as the enemy—the sweaty guy in the bottom of the slave ship who beats the drum as we, chained to our bench, row to his unceasing metronome. We can begin to see it as a commodity—precious and limited, but not something to be counteracted with slapdash decision-making and quick fixes.

We need to teach our children that time can be a tremendous source of blessing if we fill it with important relationships, rather than focusing on shortcut results.

Miles Stanford, in his classic *Principles of Spiritual Growth*, points out the importance of time in God's plan for spiritual maturity. Stanford notes that a deep relationship with God does not develop primarily from a crisis or other event, but from spending time with God over a long period. Reviewing the lives of spiritual giants like D. L. Moody, Hudson Taylor, and Amy Carmichael, he concludes that each spent an average of at least 15 years in the maturing process before feeling he or she was beginning to know God in an intimate way.[8]

God uses time to bring us to spiritual maturity. As parents, we need to show our children the role of time in making wise decisions rather than snap judgments.

ENTICING—OR ENDURING?

The third step in steering our kids away from detours is to put up strategic signposts.

When Christian and Hopeful left the narrow road, they departed from a well-worn path trodden by thousands of pilgrims before them. That in itself was a red flag indicating they were making a mistake.

Consider Jeremiah 6:16:

This is what the LORD says: "Stand at the crossroads and look; ask for the ancient paths, ask where the good way is, and walk in it, and you will find rest for your souls."

Our two pilgrims left the "ancient paths" because they'd been lured away by the seeming convenience of a shortcut. They nearly lost their lives as a result.

Our children, too, will make decisions in the next decade with potential for great personal growth—or disaster. How do we encourage them to stick to the "ancient paths" when our culture grabs their attention with the new, the faddish, the popular, and the flashy?

We can put up signposts pointing them to the old ways that generations of Christians have found valuable: reading the Bible, having devotional time with God, avoiding sexual impurity, being careful with conversation as ambassadors for Christ, cultivating positive friendships with Christians, avoiding the influence of those who would drag them down, being bold sharers of the faith, dealing forthrightly with sin in their lives...

These are some of the basics. They've been part of the pilgrim's path for thousands of years. Living by those principles brings joy and spiritual victory. And of course we want that for our children.

Unfortunately, when we put up these signposts, we sometimes make them less than enticing. We say, "You really ought to …" or "These are the rules …" or "You've got to stop …" When we're so gloomy and negative, it should be no surprise if our children find the enduring principles of the Christian life tedious.

Notice what God says in the verse from Jeremiah. In the ancient paths "you will find rest for your souls." That's the positive message we often forget to impart. God's ways are laid before us, not so He can push us around like a cosmic bully, but for our protection and our benefit. That's the kind of signpost our children need to see.

~◦◦~

SKIPPING SHORTCUTS:
PRACTICAL PROGRESS FOR PARENTS AND KIDS

Is it possible to teach our kids the patience and self-control needed to resist quick fixes? Yes—and here's an example.

Our daughter Rebekah always has been bright, athletic, and competitive. But as she grew up, she was impatient, too—and easily distracted. When this started causing problems in one of her classes, Janet came up with an idea. She dug up an old-fashioned key, tied a beautiful ribbon to it, and presented it to Rebekah.

This key, Janet told her, would be the key of "self-control and patience." Whenever Rebekah felt tempted to lose patience or talk in class, she should touch the key and remember that God would give her the self-control she needed. After all, self-control was a "fruit of the Holy Spirit," according to Scripture.

Rebekah wore that key around her neck the rest of that semester, tucking it under her blouse. By the end of the year her teacher reported that Rebekah had made tremendous progress.

More recently, Rebekah ran the Marine Marathon in Washington, D.C.—all 26 miles of it! As she ran, she thought about that special key. Through it she'd learned a lasting lesson about perseverance and patience.

Here are more principles and suggestions to use in teaching your child to avoid risky detours.

Principle #1: Teach Decision-Making Skills

Remember how Christian and Hopeful made the decision to take the shortcut?

"Hopeful!" Christian said excitedly. "This meadow will be easier going. Come, let's go over the fence."

Hopeful stared at the pasture, doubt wrinkling his forehead. "But what if this path should lead us out of the way?"

"That is not likely," said Christian. "Look. Doesn't the meadow run right next to this road?"

Hopeful shrugged. "Very well," he said, and followed Christian over the fence.

The pilgrims rushed into this choice. Christian acted impulsively; Hopeful stifled his misgivings. We can help our children do better by showing them how to think through decisions—and outcomes.

Parental Action: Link Choices with Consequences

The younger the child, the more likely she is to miss the connection between cause and effect. How can you show kids that today's choices often determine their tomorrows? Try the following.

Plant a seed. Have your preschool or early elementary child help you plant a garden, even if it's only in a window box or milk carton. Choose herbs or fast-growing flowers, using stakes or seed packages to remind you of what you planted. Let your child water the garden regularly; he should let you know as soon as any plants emerge. When this happens, talk about how you knew in advance what kind of plants would come up. Explain that making a decision is like planting a seed; it usually leads to a predictable result, one that may take a while to observe.

Ditch the dice. Pick a board game your family enjoys, one that features a path down which players "travel" after rolling dice or spinning a spinner. Some possibilities: Candyland, The Game of Life, or Monopoly. This time, though, leave out the element of chance. Let kids choose the squares they land on. After playing this way, talk about how players' choices affected the outcome. Ask, "How is this like real life? What decisions do we make that shape the way our lives turn out?"

Parental Action: Build a Moral Framework

Pondering decisions carefully is good—but doesn't guarantee good choices. Kids need moral compasses that point to values more lasting than efficiency and convenience. Here are some ways to set those compasses in place.

Appoint an ethics chair. Some universities create a "chair," or office of a designated expert, on issues like ethics. You can do the same at home, naming one of the chairs at your dinner table the "ethics chair." Let a different person sit in the chair each night for a week; he or she is to weigh in on the right and wrong of subjects discussed at the table. Other family members are free to talk about ethics too, but the "chairperson" makes sure that at least one moral issue is raised at each meal. If your "expert" takes a questionable stand, resist the urge to overrule him; simply ask him to explain how his position fits with what the Bible says.

Have family nights. Moral frameworks aren't built in a day—or a month. An ongoing effort works best, as long as it's enjoyable. Once a week or so, schedule a "family night"—an active, fun alternative to traditional devotions. Heritage Builders, a ministry of Focus on the Family, can help you use family nights to pass on biblical principles and moral values to your children. For resources, go to the Heritage Builders Web site at *www.heritagebuilders.com.* And check local Christian radio listings to see whether the one-minute feature "The Family Night Guy" is heard in your area. This program offers ideas for activities and general tips for shaping a family's spiritual life.

Principle #2: Put Time in Perspective

Christian and Hopeful apparently thought they could shave hours from their journey by taking the "low road." Not until later, when flood waters rose around their knees, did they realize how shortsighted they'd been. Time pressures can lead our kids to make poor choices too—unless we show them through word and example that we need not be tyrannized by the clock.

Parental Action: Slow Down

Today's frantic lifestyles teach children to rush. By slowing down, we can show our kids that speed isn't the most important value—and strengthen family relationships at the same time. Researchers have discovered that teenagers, for example, want more of their parents' time—and yearn for more parental involvement in their lives.[9] Time spent together in building relationships can balance the results-oriented push our kids will feel from the rest of the world.

Take them along. When our children grew old enough to endure travel and a little boredom, we constantly looked for opportunities to bring at least one with us when we had to go out of town for a speech, a legal case, or a meeting. It wasn't always possible to do that. But we tried to ask ourselves when planning a trip, "Can we include one of the children in this?" Consider whether bringing your child along might buy you some rare time together.

Make the world go away. In our family, we tried to make dinner a sacred time of fellowship. No phone calls, no interruptions were allowed. We could count on that time nearly every day—a time to gather together, break bread, share what had happened at school or work, and remind ourselves that family was of utmost importance. During your dinner hour, try turning off cell phones and pagers, and letting voice mail or an answering machine get other calls. Ignore faxes, handheld digital organizers, alarm clocks, beepers, radio, TV, and e-mail. The silence may take some getting used to, but before you know it you'll probably be filling it with relationship-building conversation.

Parental Action: Reward Patience

"Good things come to him who waits," the old saying advises. But our society hates to wait, and caters to those who crave plug-and-play computers and overnight delivery. How can you help your child see the benefits of being patient?

Serve too-fast food. To show that speedier isn't always better, take "quick cuisine" to the extreme. If kids are old enough, let them help you do the cooking. For the first course, heat canned soup in the microwave—but only for a minute. Chill soft drinks—but only for a minute. For dessert, serve half-baked cookies—a cut-up stick of refrigerated dough that you've microwaved for a minute. When family members turn up their noses at this fare, use the opportunity to talk about how we often try to rush things—

with unfortunate results. Then work together to heat up the soup, ice the drinks, and bake the cookies—no matter how long it takes.

Plan ahead. Figure kids can only think short-term? Try working together on a long-term project that shows the advantages of slow, methodical planning over quick-fix decisions. For instance, include older children in planning a family vacation one year in advance. Assign them the job of researching places to visit. Give them a budget, time guidelines, and other practical limits. What a great chance to learn that careful preparation and wise planning can be rewarding as well as fun!

Principle #3: Set Up Signposts

Here's what happened when Christian offered to lead the way back from the dangerous detour to safety:

"No," said Hopeful. "You will not go first. Your mind is troubled, and it may lead you off the path again."

Just then, even amid the crashing of the thunder, they heard a voice saying, "Set up road signs; put up guideposts. Take note of the highway, the road that you take. Return, O Virgin Israel, return to your towns" (Jeremiah 31:21).

But by this time the waters were greatly risen, making return very dangerous. It was clear that losing one's way is easier than finding it again. Still, the pilgrims were determined to go back—even though it was so dark, and the flood so high, that going back might drown them nine or ten times.

Road signs and guideposts like those in Jeremiah 31:21 might have prevented the pilgrims' watery plight. As parents, we can post pointers that lead our children away from risky routes—and toward the Celestial City.

Parental Action: Point Out the Beaten Path

There's only one problem with the old ways—they're old. Instead of seeing the well-worn path as proven, kids in our culture are likely to see it as boring. They want to blaze new trails, to go where no pilgrims have gone before.

Here are some strategies for introducing kids to tried-and-true spiritual disciplines—without turning them off.

Meet "cool" pilgrims. If you have teens, do they associate discipleship with "dorkiness"? They may not realize that some cutting-edge Christian recording artists adhere to old-fashioned practices like Bible reading and prayer. Help your young person discover the spiritual commitment of these musicians by subscribing to magazines like *Campus Life*, *Breakaway*, and *Brio*. Or check the nearest Christian bookstore for books by or about popular Christian artists. Here, for instance, are some co-authored by Michael W. Smith:

- *This Is Your Time* with Gary Thomas (Thomas Nelson, 2000)
- *Old Enough to Know* with Fritz Ridenour (Thomas Nelson, 2000)
- *Your Place in This World* with Michael Nolan (Thomas Nelson, 1998)
- *It's Time to Be Bold* with Bob Laurent (Word, 1997)

Reinvent the old ways. The beaten path may be the best route, but your child may have a unique way of walking it. Encourage him to come up with his own approaches to devotions, faith-sharing, prayer, and more. Here are some examples:

- After reading the 10th chapter of Revelation, one 12-year-old boy fired up the family computer and created a short animation featuring the apostle John, an angel, and the eating of a scroll.
- Tiring of repeating the same prayers every night, one child said, "I need to pray with more *oomph*"—and resolved to tell God what he was really thinking and feeling.
- Instead of listening to his father lead another family devotion, a seventh-grader volunteered to present one himself—and did so, complete with flip chart, clips from a VeggieTales video, and readings from the Book of Exodus.

Parental Action: Keep Guidelines Positive

Chuck Swindoll shares the unnerving estimate that in the average home there are 10 negative statements for every positive one![10] When it comes to the decisions our children will be making during the next decade, we need to be overwhelmingly positive. Specifically, we need to focus on the positive aspects of the ancient moral road that God has mapped out from eternity.

Turn around the Ten. As a family, read the Ten Commandments from Exodus 20. Since most of the commands are phrased as "thou shalt not" prohibitions, children may get the impression that God's moral instructions are negative. Help them understand that the results of obeying the commands are positive. Have a contest to see who can name at least one positive consequence of following each commandment. For example, those who don't steal (Exodus 20:15) will get to stay out of jail; they'll have the peace that comes with a clear conscience; they'll learn how to make an honest living. If you like, give a prize to the child who comes up with the longest list of positive results. You may also want to have a contest to see who can list the greatest number of negative results of ignoring the commandments.

Have a Proverbs party. The Book of Proverbs is filled with signposts pointing pilgrims to the right path. Celebrate the wisdom in this book by having a family Proverbs Party. Here are some activities you might want to include:

- Come dressed as your favorite proverb. A girl who likes Proverbs 20:15, for instance, might wear lots of costume jewelry; a boy who picks Proverbs 20:29 might put cornstarch in his hair. After giving each other a chance to guess the verses they've chosen, family members should reveal and explain their picks.
- Serve food found in Proverbs—like honey, apples, and cinnamon.
- Using charades or Pictionary-style drawing, give clues to a proverb and let others guess. Then talk about the meaning of the proverb, and how following its advice could help a person avoid dangerous detours.

DON'T WALK THIS WAY

We can show our children how decision-making, done God's way, is part of building a relationship with our heavenly Father. Through that relationship we learn to value time over convenience—and recognize the benefits that come from enduring moral standards rather than the shoddy quick fixes marketed by our culture.

If we do our job, our children will know that the sign saying "By-path Meadow" really points to a dead end.

Chapter 15

ESCAPE FROM DESPAIR

*Protecting Your Child from
Depression and Suicide*

⁓◉

*The rain poured slanting down. The thick darkness was sliced raw at sudden
intervals by the lightning's searing edge. Thunder crashed appallingly. The
river swelled, rose, overtopped its banks, and spread out across the low and
soggy ground of By-path Meadow with frightening rapidity.*

*By now Christian and Hopeful were convinced that they had made a ter-
rible mistake. They made a brave effort to get back to the stile and onto the
King's Highway again. But it was no use. So high was the water and so black
the night that they were all but drowned nine or ten times before they finally
gave up the attempt and sought shelter under a small overhang of rock on a
bit of rough, high ground. There, completely exhausted and overwhelmed, they
threw themselves down and slept.*

*They were awakened early—and rudely—by the shaking of the rocks and
the rasp of a great, huge voice, grim and surly.*

"So! Trespassers, is it?"

*Christian and Hopeful rubbed their eyes, raised themselves on their
elbows, and looked up into the face of the speaker: a huge, scowling, bulbous-
nosed face, with a chin like a moss-grown boulder and eyebrows like a pair of
unruly gorse bushes. The face of the Giant Despair.*

"Trespassers it is!" he thundered in answer to his own question. Then he

stretched out his powerful arms—arms like the knotted and burled limbs of an ancient oak—and lifted them up, each by the nape of his neck.

"Please, sir," said Christian, squirming in the giant's grasp, "we meant no harm. We're only poor travelers who have lost our way and…"

"Trampled and trespassed my land! Aye!" said he. "And now you'll come along with me to await my pleasure!"

And so they did. Indeed, they had no choice. They could see that they were no match for him in size and strength.

To his castle he drove them then—Doubting Castle, it was called—a morbid, forbidding pile of gray stone on the top of a steep, bleak hill. Once inside, he threw them down into the dungeon, where he starved them and beat them from Wednesday morning until Friday. At the end of that time Christian and Hopeful were in a sorry state indeed, almost too weak and sore to turn themselves on the dank and putrid floor. Christian's plight was espe-cially pitiful. He couldn't help blaming himself for their predicament. It had, after all, been his idea to follow the by-path.

On Friday morning they heard the great key rattling in the lock again. The heavy door squealed on its rusty hinges. At the sound they cowered against the wall, shielding their faces behind their arms, expecting the worst. But it never came. Instead, the giant withheld his cudgel and made them a proposal.

"Face it," he growled. "You're a couple of miserable wretches! Miserable! You'll never get out of here alive! So why not make a quick end of it? Why not do away with yourselves? The knife, the rope, or the poison: what'll it be?" He turned with a grunt and left them to mull it over.

"What do you think, Hopeful?" moaned Christian when the giant had gone. "I know I'd rather be strangled than live another minute in this stinking hole. Should we take his advice?"

～◉

THE BIGGEST BULLY OF THEM ALL

Overnight, our heroes have fallen prey to an almost unbelievably radical reversal of fortune. This is perhaps the darkest of all the dark moments Christian has encountered. After one false move—an ill-advised attempt to find an easier road—our two pilgrims suddenly find themselves under the domination of the biggest bully of all time.

His name is Despair. He's strong, nasty, ugly, and totally lacking in sympathy for any other living thing. Bunyan portrays him as a powerful giant who maintains a prison and torture chamber deep beneath his Doubting Castle, apparently out of pure meanness. Here he pummels his victims to the very verge of death—and then strongly "suggests" that they take the final plunge over the edge themselves.

We don't talk much about *despair* anymore. Nowadays we tend to use the word *depression*. But a bully by any other name is just as troublesome. And the threat he poses to young pilgrims is every bit as formidable as it was in Bunyan's day—if not more so.

In his book *Bringing Up Boys* (Tyndale House, 2001), Dr. James Dobson provides this real-life example:

> A mother called me a few weeks ago to say she was extremely concerned about her twelve-year-old son, Brad. She had found him crying two nights earlier and pressed him to tell her why. The boy reluctantly admitted through his tears that he didn't want to live and that he had been looking for a way to kill himself. He had read that toothpaste could be harmful if swallowed, so he was considering eating an entire tube. This family is one of the strongest and most impressive I have had the privilege of knowing, yet right under the parents' noses, their precious son was considering suicide. Brad had always been a good boy who had many friends, yet he had encountered a problem with which he couldn't cope. After working their way through the crisis, the parents learned that a boy at school had been making fun of Brad's ears because they protruded a bit. The bully had made him feel like the most stupid-looking person in school. When they passed in the hall, the harasser would put his hands behind his own ears and press them forward.
>
> ...Most of us have been taunted or ridiculed by our peers. But we must never underestimate the distress that can occur in what looks like "no big deal" to an adult, especially for kids who are already wounded from other sources. In Brad's case, it even took away his desire to live.[1]

CULTURAL SUICIDE

Depression and despair have been around for a long time. Moses, for instance, became so distraught with the obstinate children of Israel that he begged God to take his life (Numbers 11:14-15). Even Jesus, the Son of God, plumbed the depths of human emotional experience as He approached the agony of the cross. "My soul is exceedingly sorrowful, even to death," He told His disciples in the Garden of Gethsemane. "Stay here and keep watch with me" (Matthew 26:38).

But despair often presents itself under a different guise today. It's become more than a matter of one's ups and downs. It's become a matter of *fashion*.

Ever since the days of Nietzsche and Sartre and the early existentialists, *nihilism*—a philosophy assuming that human existence is meaningless—has been gaining ground in the West. The idea that nothing means anything—that there is nothing worth living for—has tightened its grip on the popular imagination.

It all started slowly, and mainly among the *avante garde* of the intelligentsia. But by the 1950s, beatniks in black turtlenecks and berets were composing bleak verses about the Bomb and chanting them in backstreet bistros. By the 1970s, the Sex Pistols, pioneers of the punk-rock movement, were singing, "There's no future for you, no future for me." By the 1980s and 1990s, rudderless urban rappers were advocating the murder of policemen.

Today this view has taken hold among many of the rank-and-file. It's mouthed regularly by the most ordinary people, especially teenagers. Despair has become as popular on high school campuses as poodle skirts were in an earlier era. "Goth" girls dress in black and carry purses made in the shape of coffins. Suicide, to an alarming degree, is not only acceptable and intellectually respectable—it's actually kind of trendy.

In the U.S., the teen suicide rate has increased dramatically over the past several decades. It jumped 300 percent between 1950 and 1990. Suicide is now the third leading cause of death for young people between the ages of 15 and 19.[2] One psychiatrist who studied adolescent depression concluded that one in four American teenagers contemplates suicide.[3]

Even under ideal circumstances, adolescence can be a rocky stretch on the road to adulthood. But it doesn't take a rocket scientist to figure out that nihilism, along with other aspects of contemporary society like terrorism and a soaring divorce rate, have combined to aggravate the situation.

No wonder so many kids feel compelled to listen when the Giant Despair says, "What's the use? You'll never get out alive anyway!" It's not unreasonable to suppose that increasing numbers of our children—and our children's children—will be persuaded to take his advice in the decades ahead.

CONFRONTING THE GIANT

So what's a Christian parent to do? How do we protect our pilgrims from despair? At this point Christian and Hopeful have something important to teach us. Let's see how they found their way out of the dungeon.

Twice more the giant pressed his counsel upon them. At last he threatened to do away with them himself if they refused to follow through. He took them into his courtyard and showed them the bones of all the other hapless pilgrims whose bodies he had torn limb from limb in that dismal place. Then he cast them back into their hole and left them alone with their thoughts. It was Saturday night.

About midnight, Christian and Hopeful began to pray. They hardly knew where they found the strength or breath, but they prayed and prayed throughout the rest of the night. They prayed until the dawn began to break.

Then, as the light began to grow—a thin gray thread trembling almost imperceptibly into view beneath the door of their cell—Christian suddenly straightened up and clapped his hand to the side of his head.

"Idiot!" he laughed. "Fool that I am!"

"What is it?" said Hopeful, sitting bolt upright. "What's the matter?"

"To think that we've been lying here for days in this rotten dungeon—beaten, starved, hopeless, crushed—when all the time the key was in my pocket!" He reached inside his shirt and pulled it out—a small, star-like golden key that gleamed darkly in the gloom.

"Key? Pocket? What key?"

"The Key of Promise! Hopeful! Don't you remember? This Key will open any door—any door in this old Doubting Castle, anyway! Come on! Let's try it!"

In the next moment he was fitting the key into the lock and tumbling back the bolt. Then the two of them were dashing down the dim, dripping corridor to the prison's outer door, past the great iron gate, and across the open fields that sparkled with dew in the early morning sun. Before they knew it, they were over the stile and back on the King's Highway.

Back on course and beyond the reach of Giant Despair.

BEATING THE BULLY:
PRACTICAL PROGRESS FOR PARENTS AND KIDS

What's the lesson of the Key of Promise? Simply this: Some Christians who suffer under the hand of the Giant Despair do so unnecessarily. There are many exceptions, of course, and we'll mention those shortly. But first, let's take a look at how we might use the principles in this story to help our children avoid needless scrapes with depression, despair, and suicidal self-doubt.

Principle #1: Stay on the Road

Giant Despair is a little like Defector Demas: He waits for his victims at the side of the road. Pilgrims who stick to the Narrow Path are far less likely to run into him than those who go astray.

Christian and Hopeful need not have fallen into the giant's hands in the first place. They landed in his dungeon as a result of their disobedience. Had they paid closer attention to instructions and kept to the right road, they probably would have bypassed Doubting Castle without even seeing it.

Sin, John Bunyan seems to be telling us, can lead to depression. King David's experience bears this out; Despair attacked him when he fell into sin and tried to cover it up:

> When I kept silent, my bones wasted away
> Through my groaning all the day long.
> For day and night your hand was heavy upon me;
> My strength was sapped as in the heat of summer.
>
> (Psalm 32:3-4)

We've spoken to many Christian parents who would agree. Their children's poor choices—drugs, alcohol, premarital sex, criminal activity, vandalism, gangs, cheating, or simply drifting away from a close personal relationship with God—brought despair to both generations.

This is not to say, of course, that all depression is caused by wrongdoing. In his book *Dark Clouds, Silver Linings*, Dr. Archibald Hart notes that some depressions are *endogenous*, coming from within the body. "They are generally understood to be caused by biochemical disturbances in the brain, the hormonal system, or the nervous system. Some are the direct consequence of disease or infection." Other depressions are *exogenous*, or "from without." "They are reactions to loss—part of a grieving process in which we come to terms with that loss," Dr. Hart writes.[4]

Some losses are unavoidable. But those caused by sin can be bypassed through skipping the sin itself. The question is, what can we do to help our kids keep their wheels on the road? How can we spare them the agony of making wrong choices?

Parental Action: Steer Them Straight

To help children see the link between sin and despair, try these ideas:

Moral of the story. Expose your kids to soundly constructed tales pointing out the connection between sin and consequences. Bible accounts in this category would include those of Ahab and Jezebel, Samson and Delilah, and King Nebuchadnezzar. If your children like fables, try "The Boy Who Cried Wolf," "King Midas and the Golden Touch," and Hans Christian Andersen's "The Red Shoes." Classic television programs like *Leave it to Beaver* and *My Three Sons* also tend to link actions and consequences—unlike a great deal of contemporary movie and television fare. With older children, discuss real-life stories in the news—for example, criminals sentenced to prison and sports stars whose careers are ruined by drugs or gambling.

How do you feel? Next time your child does something wrong, don't just administer a penalty. Ask, "How do you feel?" The child may feel angry at being caught, fearful about punishment, or guilty over disappointing you or God. Help your child to see how these feelings could have been avoided by avoiding the wrongdoing. The idea is to set this simple concept in concrete:

Sooner or later, *doing* bad makes you *feel* bad. In more ways than one, obedience is in our own best interests.

Principle #2: Stand on the Promises

Bunyan's second point is this: Once in the dungeon, Christian and Hopeful need not have remained there. Like Dorothy in *The Wizard of Oz*, Christian possessed the power to "go home"—or get back on track—at any time. He carried the Key of Promise, symbolizing God's promises given to believers in His Word.

Here is a powerful image for children *and* adults who find themselves pinned down by depression or despair. When the giant has finished beating them, when he grabs them by the shirt collar and thrusts them up against the cold stones of the prison wall, when he fills their nostrils with his stinking breath and says, "You're finished," they can choose to see their situation from another point of view:

> Who will bring any charge against those whom God has chosen? It is
> God who justifies. Who is he that condemns? Christ Jesus, who
> died—more than that, who was raised to life—is at the right hand of
> God and is also interceding for us. Who shall separate us from the
> love of Christ? Shall trouble or hardship or persecution or famine or
> nakedness or danger or sword?... I am convinced that neither death
> nor life, neither angels nor demons, neither the present nor the
> future, nor any powers, neither height nor depth, nor anything else
> in all creation, will be able to separate us from the love of God that is
> in Christ Jesus our Lord.
>
> (Romans 8:33-35, 38-39)

Does this mean our kids should be expected to "snap out of" depression by simply recalling God's promises? No. In *Dark Clouds, Silver Linings*, Dr. Hart asks,

> Is depression a failure to trust God's promises? This is another idea
> often suggested by well-meaning but uninformed Christian writers.
> Again let me say that it's not the depression itself but what leads up
> to it that can be a failure to trust God's promises. For example, we

may not be trusting God in the area of values or security. The depression that follows is a consequence or symptom of that failure. But the depression itself is a normal and natural reaction to the failure, and it must run its course.[5]

Overcoming depression is seldom a matter of pulling oneself up by one's bootstraps, even if those bootstraps are connected to Bible verses. Still, knowing and believing God's promises can be a protective "gas mask" for our children as they live in an increasingly poisonous atmosphere of hopelessness.

Parental Action: Pass on God's Promises

When the nihilism of our culture tries to discourage your children, will they know where to find that golden Key of Promise? Here are some ways to ensure that they do:

Memorize Scripture. There are plenty of promises worth hiding in a child's heart. Here are just a few to start: Jeremiah 29:11; Romans 8:31; Hebrews 13:5, 6. For young children, try sitting on the edge of your son's or daughter's bed and working through a verse or two. Older children can be encouraged to write verses on index cards and post them around the house to help them memorize.

Don't promise too much. Paradoxically, a culture that believes life is ultimately meaningless also tells our children, "Follow your dreams! You can be anything you want to be!" These overblown claims carry the seeds of disillusionment and despair. What about the hundreds of thousands of young people who *don't* get accepted to medical school, who *don't* make it to the Olympics, who *don't* find the perfect mate? Help children to understand that while *our* dreams don't necessarily come true, *God's* do. By His grace, we can and will become what He wants us to be.

Parental Action: Share Your Promises, Too

Do your children know *you* love them? Do they understand *your* unconditional, lifelong commitment to them? The security that comes from knowing how much your parents value you is a powerful anchor in an unstable world. To affirm the promise of your love, try the following suggestions.

Spend quantity time. Love your children in practical ways. That means spending time with them—and not just snippets of "quality time." Play together, work in the yard together, fold laundry together. Eat together as often as possible; statistics indicate that children from homes where the family shares evening meals at least three times a week are dramatically less likely to become involved in self-destructive behaviors like drug and alcohol abuse, premarital sex, criminal activity, and suicide.

Write a love letter. Dr. Hart writes in *Dark Clouds, Silver Linings*:

> Keep affirming the potential of your child. It can be very helpful to give a letter to your child during times of depression, expressing your affirmation and love in written form. Such a letter can become a prized possession. I know one adult who received such a letter from his parents when he was in a deep depression as an adolescent, and he keeps the letter in his Bible as a constant reminder that he is deeply loved. Whenever he feels depressed, he reminds himself of the depth of his parents' love. That's especially precious to him, because both his parents have now gone to be with the Lord.[6]

Don't wait until your child becomes depressed to write that letter. Now's the time to express your love. It literally could be a lifesaver further down the road.

A Note of Caution

We can prepare our children to reject the message that life isn't worth living. Still, when depression occurs, it's serious business. If you believe your child may be depressed, don't hesitate to get help from a qualified counselor. Here are some symptoms of childhood depression, as listed by Dr. Hart in *Dark Clouds, Silver Linings*:

- Sadness
- Withdrawal—the child will not converse or play with friends
- No interest in regular activities or games
- A profound loss of energy
- Complaints about being tired all the time
- Little capacity for pleasure

- Many physical complaints, ranging from stomachache to headache to vague pains all over the body
- Complaints about feeling unloved or rejected
- Refusal to receive comfort or love, even though protesting not being loved
- Many thoughts about death and dying
- An increase in aggressive behavior, bickering, and negativity
- Many sleep disturbances, including insomnia
- A change in appetite, either overeating or refusing to eat favorite foods[7]

Dr. Hart also warns parents to watch for *anorexia nervosa*, an avoidance of eating, as a symptom of depression in older girls. In addition he points out "hidden symptoms" that can mask childhood depression: extreme anxiety, nail biting, hair pulling or twirling, muscle tics, irritability, temper tantrums, sulkiness or moodiness, self-mutilation, and deliberately destructive behavior.

What about depression in teenagers? Dr. Hart writes,

> In determining whether an adolescent is depressed, we have to look at what changes have taken place. The following questions may help to clarify the state of the adolescent mind:
> - Has the once-outgoing child become withdrawn and antisocial as an adolescent?
> - Was the adolescent formerly a good student but is now failing or skipping classes?
> - Was the child happy-go-lucky but is now moping around for weeks or months?
> - Is the teenager inappropriately irritable, whereas once he or she was calm and longsuffering?
>
> If your answer is yes to any of these questions, it may indicate you need to get help for your teenager. In addition, if your youngster feels unable to cope, demoralized, or friendless, or is possibly suicidal, it's almost certain that he or she is depressed.[8]

If you have reason to believe your child's life is in danger, get him or her to a mental health professional right away. "God will honor your actions,"

Dr. Hart writes, "and completely understands why you need to act with speed and firmness."

THE GOLDEN KEY

Our world may be dark, dangerous, and desperate, but that's not the end of the story. There's light at the end of the tunnel, despite the bleak philosophy that dominates the culture in which our kids find themselves. Christ has provided them with a key to the dungeon and promised to stand beside them. That's a truth worth sharing with the pilgrims in our care.

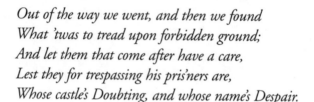

Out of the way we went, and then we found
What 'twas to tread upon forbidden ground;
And let them that come after have a care,
Lest they for trespassing his pris'ners are,
Whose castle's Doubting, and whose name's Despair.

Chapter 16

THE SPYGLASS
OF FAITH

*Helping Your Child Believe
in the Invisible*

Christian and Hopeful walked until they came to the Delectable Mountains, which belong to the Lord of that hill of which we have spoken before. They went up to see the gardens and orchards, the vineyards, and the fountains of water. There they drank and washed themselves, and freely ate from the vineyards.

On the tops of these mountains were four shepherds feeding their flocks, and they stood by the side of the highway. The pilgrims went to them, and leaning on their staffs (as is common with weary pilgrims when they stand to talk), they asked, "Whose Delectable Mountains are these? Who owns the sheep that feed on them?"

One of the shepherds, a burly fellow with a smile on his ruddy face, stepped up to answer. "These mountains are Emmanuel's land, and they are within sight of His city. The sheep also are His, and He laid down His life for them."

"Then this is the way to the Celestial City?" Christian asked.

"Exactly," said the shepherd.

Christian sighed, half from fatigue and half from relief. "How far is it from here?" he asked.

The shepherd chuckled. "Too far for everyone except those who will actually get there."

Christian, too tired to appreciate the man's wit, leaned more heavily on his staff. "Is the way safe or dangerous?"

"Safe for those for whom it is meant to be safe," the shepherd replied soberly. "But lawbreakers will fall along the way."

Sighing again, Christian gazed at the snow-capped peaks that surrounded them. "Is there in this place any relief for pilgrims who are exhausted?"

The shepherd's friendly grin widened. "The Lord of these mountains has told us not to forget to entertain strangers. So the good things of this place are yours."

The shepherds, introducing themselves as Knowledge, Experience, Watchful, and Sincere, took Christian and Hopeful to their tents and gave them food. "We would like you to stay here a while," said Knowledge, the ruddy one. "To be acquainted with us, and to rest in these Delectable Mountains."

"We are happy to stay," said Christian. So they went to bed, because it was very late.

The next day…the pilgrims and the shepherds wanted to go forward, so they walked together toward the end of the mountains. Then the shepherds said to one another, "Let us here show the pilgrims the gates of the Celestial City—if they have the skill to look through our spyglass, the 'eye of faith.'"

"By all means," said Christian. The shepherds took them to the top of a high hill, called Clear, and gave them the glass to look.

They tried to look.… They could not gaze steadily through the glass, yet they thought they saw something like the gate—and also some of the glory of the place.

After bidding farewell to the shepherds, Christian and Hopeful continued on their journey, singing:

"So by the shepherds secrets are revealed,
Which from all other men are kept concealed:
Come to the shepherds then, if you would view
Things deep, things hidden, and mysterious, too."

ON A CLEAR DAY YOU CAN SEE FOREVER

After Christian and Hopeful escaped the miserable dungeon at Doubting Castle, they couldn't wait to scurry back to the King's Highway. Returned to the right path, they would soon enter Emmanuel's Land.

That land was filled with spectacular mountains, lush gardens, orchards full of fruit, and a crystal-clear fountain of water. No wonder Bunyan calls these mountains "Delectable."

The pilgrims meet several shepherds. One of them, Knowledge, explains that from their vantage point, and with the right kind of spyglass, they can see the gleaming front gate of the Celestial City. Their goal is now in sight.

Knowledge urges them to look through a special telescope, the "eye of faith." For the first time Christian and Hopeful catch a glimpse of the majesty and glory of their destiny and hope.

Here Bunyan addresses one of the most profound questions of our earthly pilgrimage. It's a crucial question for our children, too. He asks, in effect, "What do you see as you behold your future? Have you gained a vision for your life by using the eyes of faith? Or do you only believe in what your naked eye can see?"

THREE ILL-CONCEIVED "ISMS"

Seers, philosophers, and "wise men" of every age have asked a similar question: How can we know truth? As the Greek philosopher Aristotle noted, wanting to know and understand the underlying principles of our world is an integral part of human nature.[1]

The field of philosophy has a name for this: *epistemology*. It's the study of how we know what we think we know.

Philosophy isn't on the minds of Christian and Hopeful at this point in the story. Like most of us, they simply want to reach their destination. But Knowledge, the shepherd, wants them to get their eyes off the stones in the road and to gain a broader view. He wants them to have a sense of vision as they travel—a "worldview" based on more than eyesight and human reason.

It's no accident that Bunyan names the shepherd Knowledge and gives him a spyglass called "faith." Bunyan is reminding us of the relationship between faith and knowledge. Faith is not merely a nightlight to keep the shadows from scaring us as we fall asleep. Faith is the way to gain knowledge.

That truth flies in the face of three "isms" that dominated the twentieth century—and continue to dominate the twenty-first. They are among the most aggressive opponents to the biblical, Christian worldview.

The first is *secular humanism*, which sees man as the "measure of all things." It categorically excludes the existence of God and the supernatural realm—or at least proclaims that we can never know whether they are real.[2] Secular humanism sees reason, and technological advances that spring from human ingenuity, as the only hope for mankind. It relies on human understanding as the only reliable source of knowledge.

The second "ism" is *relativism*. As we noted in Chapter 10, this view teaches that there are no universal, fixed absolutes regarding right or wrong. It claims that we can never know for sure what is the moral thing to do, because morality varies from person to person, culture to culture.

The third "ism" is *materialism*—the belief that only the physical world exists. To the materialist, notions of souls, heaven, and hell are figments of the imagination—which is itself a mere interaction of chemicals in brain tissue.

All of these "isms" reject the idea that faith leads to knowing any sort of objective truth. And they're joined by a fourth that will continue to challenge our children's worldviews in the coming decade.

Scientism: Reliance on Science

During the last 200 years, science has shaped the way we view the world. It's easy to understand why. Science has had a great track record, wowing us with everything from moon landings to gene mapping to artificial sweeteners.

Our love affair with the scientific method, however, can lead to absurd results. By the late 1800s, science was gaining a powerful hold over the world of ideas. Henry Adams, considered one of America's most brilliant intellectuals, was impressed with science's potential to answer life's questions. He proceeded to develop a "scientific" theory of history, using physics and mathematics. He postulated that historical epochs occur like phases of mechanical or electrical energy. Scholars now reject his ideas, calling them an embarrassing form of pseudo-science.[3]

There's nothing wrong with a *reasoned* reliance on science. After all, science proceeds on the assumption that there are certain fixed principles of nature, a certain uniformity about the way the universe operates. That premise is in line with the fact that the Creator made His universe a generally coherent place where things happen according to His uniform design.

What we're calling "scientism," however, is an unreasoning faith in the ability of science to answer life's most important questions—about morality, personal accountability, relationships, whether God exists, and if so, what He is like and what He expects from us.

Those who worship at the altar of science have failed to understand its limits. They see the world, in effect, as a chess game; science is the intellectual queen, kicking all other pieces off the board.

Blind faith in science has remade our culture during the last century. Because of technology's impressive accomplishments, it will be a particularly potent influence in the decade ahead.

THE EMINENCE OF EVOLUTION

One example of scientism's influence can be seen in the obsessive kinship many scientists and other thinkers feel with Darwin's theory of evolution. As a theory, it has come under a tidal wave of criticism and discrediting analysis. The fact that most scientists still revere Darwin's faulty hypothesis is evidence of scientism's greedy grip on modern thinking.[4]

The evolutionary perspective has invaded almost every discipline, whether it is the proper domain of science or not.

Science writer Robert Wright notes how "evolutionary psychology" has penetrated the moral question of right and wrong. The idea of a non-scientifically explainable "moral conscience" is less and less a matter of common belief. With the advent of DNA experimentation and advances in genetics, the tendency is to view how and why we act as mere exercises in biology.[5]

University professor Pascal Boyer has touted an evolutionary explanation for the existence of religion. According to him, we think about God and believe in religion not because those things are true, but because of a long process of natural selection. The God-talkers created a social advantage, thus causing religion to flourish—or so he concludes.[6] Dedicated to scientism, Boyer applies the false notion of Darwin's theory to everything, including our belief in God.

It will fall on our children to recognize the fallacy of scientism. Even more importantly, they'll need to understand what it means to base their worldview on their Christian faith.

STANDING UP TO SCIENTISM

How can we prepare our kids for the continuing onslaught of scientism? One way is to make sure they understand the concepts of science—including evolutionary theory.

Some Christian parents balk at this, thinking such knowledge might destroy their children's faith. Certainly our children must be spiritually grounded before being required to face the arguments of the "other side." But they can't avoid the wave of pro-evolutionary ideas that will mold the moral and spiritual discussions of the next decade. They need to be able apologists for their faith, which means understanding the opposition. They need to grasp the false theories and dismantle them with a biblical mindset.

When our oldest daughter, Sarah, was a freshman at a large public university, she took an evolutionary geology class. The final exam required her to explain the basics of an evolutionary view of the earth's creation.

Sarah explained the material so well that she got an A. At the end of her exam paper, however, she added a postscript describing why she believed in a God-created universe. In his written comments on her exam, the instructor praised her forthrightness about her religious beliefs—and her grasp of the course material.

Let's instill a proper respect for science in our children—and the truth that ultimate answers to ultimate questions are the province of what God has chosen to reveal to us in His Word.

THE RIGHT END OF THE TELESCOPE

Like Christian and Hopeful, our children need to gain a vision for their ultimate destination. They won't find that vision in the lenses of secular humanism, relativism, materialism, or scientism. They'll find it through the great telescope of faith.

As the Bible says, "Now faith is being sure of what we hope for and certain of what we do not see" (Hebrews 11:1). Because faith goes beyond senses and intellect, it gives us a vision of the future and how we fit into it.

Such was the message of Evangelist to Christian and Faithful earlier in our story:

They came to a field dotted with boulders, and Evangelist motioned for them to sit down on a broad, flat rock. "I am glad for my own sake and yours," he continued. "I have sown, and you have reaped. 'Let us not become weary in doing good, for at the proper time we will reap a harvest if we do not give up' (Galatians 6:9). The crown is before you, and it is an eternal one; so 'run in such a way as to get the prize' (1 Corinthians 9:24)."

He sat on the boulder next to them and stared down the road. "Some set out for this crown, but another comes in and takes it from them." He shook his head sadly, then brightened after a moment. "Let the kingdom be always before you, and believe steadfastly concerning the things that are invisible. Let nothing on this side of the other world get within you. And, above all, watch your own hearts; for they are 'deceitful above all things and beyond cure' (Jeremiah 17:9)."

He raised his fist in the air triumphantly. "Set your faces like a flint!" he declared. "You have all power in heaven and earth on your side."

FIRMING UP FAITH:
PRACTICAL PROGRESS FOR PARENTS AND KIDS

Have you noticed that children generally aren't born skeptical? Believing in God seems to come more naturally to them than it does to some adults. Psalm 8:2 says, "From the lips of children and infants you have ordained praise." We can feed and water that faith, helping it to grow strong enough to survive in the hostile environment of today and tomorrow.

Principle #1: Admit the Need for Faith

It's easy to assume, especially if we've grown up in the church, that any reasonable person would believe in Christianity if he just knew the facts. We can forget that it takes faith, too. As Hebrews 11:6 notes, "And without faith it is impossible to please God, because anyone who comes to him must believe that he exists and that he rewards those who earnestly seek him."

The shepherds knew it took a special spyglass to see the Celestial City's gate. They could have berated Christian and Hopeful, saying, "What's wrong with you? Why can't you see it? Try harder!" Instead, they offered the pilgrims the "eye of faith." We can do the same for our children.

Parental Action: Give Credit for Believing

Celebrate faith. If your child believes in God, don't take it for granted. Affirm it! Mention it occasionally in bedtime prayers with your younger child: "Thank You, God, that Shana believes in You and wants to follow You." With older children, write a letter when birthday or graduation time rolls around, expressing appreciation for the child's faith in God; if possible, point out examples of how that faith has improved your family's life.

Respect God's Spirit in them. If your child has received Christ as Savior, His Spirit lives in him or her. You can recognize and reinforce your child's faith by trusting the Holy Spirit to work in and through your child. In their book *Ignite the Fire*, Barry and Carol St. Clair write the following:

> Let's say you believe in Christ, as does your eighth-grade son. In that case…
> - Does the Holy Spirit live in you? (Yes.)
> - Does the Holy Spirit live in your eighth-grader? (We could debate if eighth-graders have souls! Just kidding. Yes.)
> - Then why do you play the role of Holy Spirit and tell your eighth-grader everything to do? What to wear? Who to have as friends? What to believe?
>
> Before you think we've gotten weird, stick with us. If the Holy Spirit lives in you…and your child, can't the same Holy Spirit speak to both of you? "He's not mature enough to hear," you protest. Tell that to Joseph, Samuel, David, and other young men in the Old Testament. Because "God is no respecter of persons," why can't you trust God to work in your child's life, as you expect Him to work in yours?[7]

Next time you and your child have a disagreement, encourage your child to pray about it and to tell you what he thinks God wants him to do. That may be a scary proposition, but it can go a long way in affirming your youngster's personal faith.

Parental Action: Allow Faith to Have Phases

Just as faith isn't automatic, it's not static. It can grow as we mature. And all of us, children included, trudge through times of doubt. As you cultivate your child's faith, don't panic when you see that faith ebb and flow.

Remember their age. Preschoolers can grasp the idea that God exists, that He created them, and that He loves them. They can begin to learn what it means to relate to God. Older children are ready to learn more about God's nature and how to maintain a relationship with Him. To discover how your child currently thinks and feels about God, ask questions like, "How is God like you? How is He different? What's one question you'd like to ask Him?"

See when they can't. Christian and Hopeful had a true "mountaintop experience" when they gazed through the spyglass of faith. At other times, though, their faith floundered. When that happens to your child—perhaps due to a seemingly unanswered prayer—gently remind him or her of times when God's reality has been clearer to your family. If nine-year-old Amber doubts God will help her adjust as her family moves to a new town, for instance, Mom can ask, "Remember your first day of second grade? You didn't know anybody on the bus, and we prayed that God would help you find a friend. Isn't that when you met Corinne?"

Principle #2: Keep Their Eyes on the Prize

As Evangelist exhorted the pilgrims, "Let the kingdom be always before you, and believe steadfastly concerning the things that are invisible." It's easy to lose sight of things you can't see! Still, we can help our children understand that our heavenly home is even more real than our earthly one—and well worth the journey.

Parental Action: Loosen the World's Hold

"Let nothing on this side of the other world get within you," Evangelist counseled the pilgrims. Use the following activities to get your child thinking about the temporary nature of the permanent-looking world around us.

See how they run (down). Take a walk through your neighborhood, or a field trip to another part of town. Challenge your kids to point out evidence that this world won't last forever. Some possibilities: a cemetery, a rusty car, decaying leaves, an old building being bulldozed, a funeral home, a fallen tree, dead flowers, a garbage truck, a junkyard. Ask, "If everything we see is going to fall apart, what can we count on? What part of you will last forever? How should that affect the way you live?"

Song drill. Borrow a couple of hymnals. Look through them for old favorites about how our true citizenship is in heaven, not on earth. Write down a few lines from each song. Divide the family into teams; as you call out lines from the songs you found, teams compete to find the hymns that contain them. Here are some examples; answers are in parentheses.

- "And the things of earth will grow strangely dim in the light of His glory and grace." ("Turn Your Eyes upon Jesus")
- "This world is not my home; I'm just a-passin' through." ("This World Is Not My Home")
- "I'm satisfied with just a cottage below; a little silver, and a little gold." ("Mansion over the Hilltop")
- "Lord, lift me up, and let me stand by faith on heaven's tableland." ("Higher Ground")
- "And, Lord, haste the day when the faith shall be sight." ("It Is Well with My Soul")
- "Someday my earthly house will fall—I cannot tell how soon 'twill be; But this I know—my All in All has now a place in heaven for me." ("Saved by Grace")

After a team finds a song lyric, the first team to explain its meaning gets an extra point. When the contest is done, ask, "In 10 words or less, what's the overall message of these songs?"

Parental Action: Envision the Goal

Does heaven seem vague or dull to your child? Here are two ways to sharpen the focus of your child's "eye of faith."

See the invisible. Gather as many of the following as you can: telescope, microscope, binoculars, magnifying glass. Spend some time with your child using these devices to examine things you can't see with the naked eye—the moon's craters, the fibers in a piece of cloth, a distant telephone pole, the colored dots that make up the comics in the Sunday newspaper. Ask, "Did these 'invisible' things exist before we could see them? How can we believe in 'invisible' things like heaven? If you could invent a device to help us see heaven, what would it be like? How is faith like that?"

Write a heavenly diary. What does your child think heaven will be like? Encourage her to write a diary entry about her first day in heaven. If your child can't write yet, let her tell you what to write. When the diary entry is complete, resist the urge to correct it. Simply talk about how your child envisions heaven, and point out as needed that the greatest thing about the place is that God is there.

Principle #3: Guard Against Faith-Stealers

How do people "lose" their faith? In some cases, a silver-tongued secularist may play a role. But other factors usually pave the way, as Christian explains in this exchange with Hopeful:

"Now that I have shown you why *people turn back,"* Hopeful said, *"tell me how* they *do it."*

"Gladly," said Christian. *He proceeded to relate the following list:*

1. They avoid thinking about God, death, and the judgment to come.

2. Then they give up—by degrees—private duties such as prayer, curbing their appetites, being watchful, and being sorry for their sins.

3. Then they shun the company of lively and warm Christians.

4. After that, they grow cold to public duties, such as listening to sound teaching and reading the Scriptures.

5. They then begin to pick holes, as it were, in the coats of the godly; they want to reject religion because of the weaknesses they have spied in some believers.

6. Then they begin to associate with those who are disobedient and who have no interest in spiritual matters.

7. Then they give way to rebellious, indulgent conversation in secret; they are glad if they can spot other believers doing this, as it gives them an excuse.

8. After this they begin to play with little sins openly.

9. Finally, being hardened, they show themselves as they are. Launched into the gulf of misery, they perish in their own deceit—unless a miracle of grace prevents it.

Preparing our children for philosophical debate is an important part of strengthening their faith. But so is guarding their hearts against apathy and rebellion. Let's be sure to do both.

Parental Action: Get the Facts

Discover intelligent design. Did life evolve randomly? Or is there a Creator behind it all? *Unlocking the Mystery of Life* is a riveting video making the case for intelligent design. Featuring sophisticated computer animation and interviews with scientists, this program reveals how the "irreducible complexity" of microscopic organisms and the information contained in DNA point convincingly to a Designer. Another video, *Icons of Evolution*, questions the integrity of several well-known evolutionary cornerstones. In addition, it tells the story of a biology teacher who dared to mention the weaknesses of Darwin's theory—and paid a heavy price. Both videos are appropriate for ages 12 and up, include discussion guides you can use at home, and are available from Focus on the Family (1-800-A-FAMILY).

Hit the books. Do any scientists believe in God? Of course! Older children can read about scientists who have placed their faith in Christ, as chronicled in *Scientists Who Believe* by Eric C. Barrett and David Fisher (Moody, 1984). This book tells the story of 21 such professionals. Older teens who face the challenge of college science courses may benefit from reading *Darwin on Trial* by Phillip E. Johnson (InterVarsity Press, 1993) and *The Creation Hypothesis: Scientific Evidence for an Intelligent Designer*, edited by J. P. Moreland (InterVarsity Press, 1994).

Parental Action: Guard the Heart

"And, above all," said Evangelist, "watch your own hearts; for they are 'deceitful above all things, and beyond cure' (Jeremiah 17:9)." As Christian also noted, it's the little things that corrode one's faith—slowly, a step at a time. Protect against subtle faith-stealers through activities like the following.

Give checkups. Many parents have a "don't ask, don't tell" policy when it comes to the state of their children's faith. You can do better—without being overly intrusive. One way is to give your child a chance to agree or disagree with the following statements at least once a year:

1. I like thinking about God.
2. I like to pray.
3. When I do something wrong, I feel sorry afterward.
4. I like to be around other Christians.
5. I like church.
6. I know some Christians who really practice what they preach.
7. I try not to let people who don't believe in God influence me to disobey Him.
8. I try to stay away from doing things I know are wrong, even if I think I might get away with them.
9. I want to follow Jesus, even if I don't always do it perfectly.

After getting responses, ask your child to elaborate if he can. Don't panic if he expresses doubts or dissatisfaction. Use the opportunity to find out how you can deal with them together before small shifts in attitude become hard-to-bridge chasms.

Engender excitement. Many young people find their faith "cooling off" not for intellectual reasons, but simply because Christianity seems boring and irrelevant. If your child's attitude toward church activities is one of listlessness or rebellion, or if he can't seem to find any Christian friends he really wants to spend time with, it may be time to find a different children's program or youth ministry that offers more variety and more kids. If that's not possible, consider supplementing your church's program with regional conferences, camps, and concerts. Ask yourself, too, whether your own attitude toward God and other believers might be less than enthusiastic—and whether it might be rubbing off on your kids. If so, talk with your pastor about how your whole family might connect with age-appropriate small groups or a one-on-one discipling program.

THROUGH A GLASS DARKLY

The Hubble Space Telescope, from its position beyond our atmosphere, has given us a glimpse into mysteries outside our solar system. Yet it can't hold a candle to the view our children get when they look with the eyes of faith.

Decades ago, a Russian cosmonaut commented sarcastically that he saw no signs of heaven in space. That's because he was looking through the wrong lens. When we use the lens of faith, we can see all the way to the gleaming front gate of our ultimate home.

That image should be ever before our children as they walk the pilgrim's path. It's only a hint of greater things beyond—where the Lord waits with a loving embrace and the desire to say those wonderful words: "Well done, good and *faithful* servant!"

Chapter 17

TRUE BELIEVERS AND FALSE RELIGION

Guarding Your Child Against Bogus Beliefs

꩜

Christian and Hopeful walked until they reached a fork in the road. They stopped, puzzled. Both forks looked identical, equally straight and narrow. Which should they take?

And as they were standing there, thinking, they heard a voice from behind: "Why do you stand there?"

Turning, they saw a man in a white robe. He smiled a peaceful smile.

"We are going to the Celestial City," Christian said. "But we don't know which of these ways to take."

The man made a little bow, then stepped in front of them, choosing the path on the right. "Follow me," he invited. "I, too, am bound for the Celestial City."

So they followed him. At first they did not notice, but the way the man had chosen began to turn, then turn some more. In time they were headed not toward, but away from their destination.

They continued to follow him, but eventually became uneasy. Christian slowed down, and Hopeful followed suit. "Something's wrong," said Christian. "The road has turned by degrees, and now we are so far from the city that our faces are turned away from it."

The man in the white robe frowned. "Just a little further," he said. A few steps later, the pilgrims found themselves suddenly surrounded by a net. Soon they were so entangled that they didn't know what to do.

They watched as the white robe fell from the stranger's back, revealing a much darker cloak beneath. With an evil laugh the man continued down the path and was gone.

Tears came to the pilgrims' eyes. "We are trapped, and cannot get ourselves out," Hopeful cried. For a long time they lay there, weeping.

FOLLOW THE LEADER?

Our two pilgrim friends are in trouble again, having relied on a "spiritual advisor" to tell them which way to go.

He looked and sounded like such a holy man; he even wore a white robe. Declaring that he was going to the same heavenly destination as the pilgrims, he called out, "Follow me," with a tone of authority and certainty. Today we might call him a take-charge guy who seemed to know exactly where he was headed.

But the decision of Christian and Hopeful to follow him ends in near disaster.

Before we fault the pilgrims too much, though, let's recognize that falling prey to spiritual deception is easier than we might imagine. Really effective false religion doesn't come at us looking clumsy or stupid; it sounds reasonable. It also aims at our most vulnerable spots, appearing self-assured to the insecure and biblical to the unstudied.

But deceptive spirituality doesn't score many points with the hardened humanist or the committed atheist. It succeeds with those who already accept a worldview that includes God. In fact, its easiest target is the person who is open to religious ideas but has neglected the biblical basics.

That brings us to a chilling truth: Raising our children in Christian homes doesn't guarantee that they'll never fall prey to false religious leaders or deceptive doctrines.

When Janet was in college, for example, she had a Christian roommate we'll call Betty. Soft-spoken and friendly, Betty joined Janet in a number of Christian activities on campus. But Betty wasn't grounded spiritually; she never really had a grasp of Scripture, or how it related to her life.

During semester break Janet received a long-distance call from an excited Betty, who said she had unbelievable news to share. "I've met the most wonderful group of people," Betty explained. "And they have given me a whole new outlook on God. They have changed my life!"

Janet started probing. What kind of group was it? What was its name? Where was it located? What did it teach? With each question, Betty's excitement faded; she grew more and more evasive.

After much prodding, Betty shared a little about the group. At the time, it was relatively unknown to us; today we know it as a mind-controlling cult.

The group was telling Betty to drop out of school and join its community. When Janet questioned this advice, Betty reacted strongly. She couldn't afford to talk to Janet again, she said—because her new beliefs would be corrupted.

Betty hung up. That was the last time we ever heard from her.

THE LURE OF CULTS

Some cults have grabbed headlines because their leaders led blinded followers into the jaws of self-destruction. In 1977 Jim Jones, leader of the People's Temple, convinced members to commit mass suicide. The rotting bodies of Jones and over 900 of his "sheep" were later discovered in the jungles of Guyana. Tragically, about a third were children and teens.

In 1997 another cult made instant news around the world. Members of Heaven's Gate followed their spiritual leader, Marshall Applewhite, into group suicide. These literate, well-educated, high-tech folks were duped into believing that after their deaths they would be "beamed up" to an orbiting spacecraft hiding behind the comet Hale-Bopp.

Heaven's Gate was a cult for our time, tailored to a culture saturated with *Star Trek* and fascinated with space travel. Media images featured smiling followers in androgynous haircuts and sexually ambiguous dress. One follower was a college student whose father would become a federal judge; another was the son of the president of Southern New England Telephone Company.[1]

Beneath the benign exterior, however, were classic signs of a dangerous cult. Applewhite demanded that members check in with him every 12 minutes. Those who questioned were sent to the "decontamination zone," a form of isolation. Followers were expected to completely detach from family and friends.[2]

Following the Heaven's Gate suicides, another doomsday cult garnered headlines. It was called Solar Temple, and it led 48 adherents to kill themselves in Switzerland.

Then, a year before the "new millennium," members of a group called Concerned Christians were arrested in Israel. They were suspected of planning a bloody confrontation which, according to their misunderstanding of Scripture, would hasten the second coming of Christ.[3]

Judging by the past decade, the one ahead will see a continued risk that our children may be approached by cults. Feeding off our natural desire for spiritual connection, these groups will continue to create a false sense of belonging. They will specialize in cookie-cutter answers that may sound biblical but actually reflect the speculations of power-hungry leaders.

Yet cults are only one form of religious deception that may say to our children, "Follow me." Others are often more subtle—and, for that reason, perhaps even more dangerous.

NEW SPIRITUALITY, OLD DECEPTION

Another wave of the present—and the foreseeable future—is a form of spirituality that uses some phrases that may strike Christians as warmly familiar. Its proponents often use a blend of pop psychology, scientific concepts, and Bible references. Its guiding principle, however, is a kind of inner mysticism that appeals to our highly individualistic, self-driven culture.

Ervin Laszlo, president of the Club of Budapest, head of the General Evolution Research Group, and advisor to the Director General of the United Nations Educational, Scientific, and Cultural Organization, is a good example. He speaks of the need for a new kind of religious consciousness, a grand synthesis between science and theology, a new spirituality for the twenty-first century.[4]

One high-profile model of this kind of synthesis is popular Eastern mystic and lecturer Deepak Chopra. Often seen on the Public Broadcasting System, Chopra uses terminology from advanced physics ("event horizon") to explain the relationship between our everyday lives and that place where, according to him, we can find God. Using Matthew 7:7 as his supposed frame of reference ("Ask and it will be given to you; seek and you will find...."), Chopra claims that the Christian "born again" experience is actually a form of "second attention." This mental peripheral vision, where we find God intuitively and inwardly, picks up God's clues as a mind reader might discover someone else's thoughts.[5]

Another proponent of this synthesis is Neale Donald Walsch, founder of ReCreation, a spirituality and "personal growth" foundation. Like Chopra, he douses his theories with biblical-sounding ideas. He refers to "Christ consciousness"—but clearly doesn't mean gaining the mind of Jesus Christ by personally receiving Him as Lord and Savior. Walsch is talking about a kind of super-consciousness, where our minds and emotions are "fully integrated," and we are "fully creative."[6]

CULTURAL SPIRITUALITY

Another trend that will affect our children might be called "cultural spirituality." This is the tendency to shape religion to fit the popular culture rather than vice versa.

The Bible tells us that instead of conforming to the world, Christians should be conformed to God's will by transforming our minds through a personal relationship with Christ (Romans 12:2). This includes measuring society by a biblical yardstick, not the other way around.

The coming decade, however, will see religion increasingly pressed into the world's mold. One example is the combination of feminism and Christianity. The resulting religious movement occasionally robes itself in traditional terminology, but actually marks a return to ancient paganism.

Feminism became an entrenched reality in the 1970s and 1980s; by the 1990s its influence on religion was clear. In 1993 an event called the Reimagining Conference was held in Minneapolis. It was attended by representatives of the Presbyterian Church USA and the United Methodist Church, as well as members of Lutheran, Roman Catholic, Baptist, and Episcopal churches.

News leaked out that attendees had danced and chanted to the image of Sophia, popular feminist goddess. They also had denounced traditional doctrines of Christianity as "patriarchal idolatry" and praised the "outing" of "Christian" lesbians.[7]

While the conference created a temporary controversy, the denominations represented took no formal action against the attendees. It's logical, therefore, to expect that this form of paganism will continue to spread. Even if such culture-born religion remains at the fringes of society, it will shift public perception of where the "center" of religious life is.

SYNCRETISM: RELIGIOUS GUMBO

The movement toward global "convergence" of beliefs will gain steam in the next decade, too. Our children will be encouraged to mix and match concepts from many different religions, picking the ones they like and rejecting those they don't. It's the "buffet style" approach to belief.

Syncretism is the word for this process. It means combining beliefs, even if they seem to conflict. The combinations are based not on truth but on personal preference.

George Barna has been watching this trend develop for more than a decade. He now speaks of syncretism as the official faith of choice in our culture.[8] As a result, we now have theologians advising Christians that there is much to learn from other world religions; Zen Buddhists, they say, can teach us how to let go of our ego-driven identity so we can live for Christ; Daoism can teach us how God seems to hide Himself from us, while still being real and present.[9]

What kinds of hybrid religions will be offered to our children in the "smorgasbord" of the near future? There seems to be no limit to the possible variations—and the harm these false faiths may do to the next generation.

SPRUNG FROM THE TRAP

When we last saw Christian and Hopeful, they were trapped in a net. They'd made the mistake of following a false religious leader.

Did they ever escape? And if so, how?

Bound up in the net, the pilgrims could barely move. Christian, who had been silent for some time, suddenly groaned. "Now I see my mistake," he said

to Hopeful. "Didn't the shepherds warn us to beware of the Flatterer? As the saying goes, 'Whoever flatters his neighbor is spreading a net for his feet' (Proverbs 29:5)."

Hopeful winced. "They also gave us a note with directions about the way, which we forgot to read. That's why we haven't avoided the Destroyer."

They continued to lie there, moaning about their plight. But at last they saw a Shining One coming toward them with a whip of small cords in his hand. "Where did you come from?" he asked them. "What are you doing here?"

Christian's reply was sheepish. "We are poor pilgrims going to Zion. But we were led astray by a man clothed in white, who invited us to follow him to the Celestial City."

The Shining One with the whip gave them a stern look. "It is Flatterer, a false apostle, who has transformed himself into an angel of light." Without another word, he stepped up to the net and ripped it in two. The two pilgrims, stiff and sore, slowly got to their feet.

"Follow me," the Shining One instructed, "so that I may set you on the right way again." So he led them back to the fork in the road at which they had begun to follow the Flatterer. Then he turned to face the pilgrims. "Tell me," he said, "where did you sleep last night?"

"With the shepherds in the Delectable Mountains," Christian answered.

"And didn't they give you a note with directions for your journey?"

"Yes," they admitted.

"And when you reached this fork in the road, didn't you take out your note and read it?"

"No," they answered guiltily.

"Why?"

Christian and Hopeful stared at the ground. "We forgot."

The Shining One looked exasperated. "And didn't the shepherds warn you about the Flatterer?"

"Yes," Christian said with a sigh. "But we did not imagine that this fine-spoken man had been he."

At that the Shining One, a sad expression on his face, commanded them to lie down. Then he took the whip and gave them several lashes to remind them to stay on the right path. Afterward he looked at them with compassion and said, "Those whom I love I rebuke and discipline. So be earnest, and *repent" (Revelation 3:19). "Now go on your way, and pay attention to the shepherds' other directions."*

Christian and Hopeful are released from the snare by "The Shining One"—probably a reference to Christ Himself. After saving our pilgrim friends, He poses some embarrassing questions. It turns out that Christian and Hopeful could have avoided this mishap if they'd heeded the warning of the shepherds and used the road map they'd been given.

In other words, they'd neglected the basics.

THREE THINGS TO REMEMBER

Let's help our children not to make the same mistake. Here are three things we need to teach them.

1. *The ultimate rules for faith and conduct are found in God's Word, not in the words of a single religious leader.*

This is the "map" Christian and Hopeful had neglected. Like the Berean believers who examined the Scriptures daily to make sure Paul was teaching the truth (Acts 17:11), our kids need to compare what they hear with what the Bible says.

This doesn't mean we should encourage disrespect for pastors, teachers, or other church leaders. But no godly pastor or Bible teacher will insist that his listeners blindly accept only his interpretation of the Bible.

2. *We can't judge the truth of an idea based on whether it sounds Christian, or on whether the person who presents it looks or acts like a Christian.*

Detecting false spirituality requires a sophisticated kind of "radar." Our children need well-honed discernment and wisdom. They can't afford to make sloppy assumptions about what "feels" spiritual or "seems" to be powered by God.

The next generation of Christians must be well acquainted with genuine, biblical teaching. Only then will it be able to spot counterfeits.

That's how our son Samuel was able to tell that his friend Frank had gotten involved with the wrong kind of group. A few months after Frank disappeared from college, Samuel got a letter from him. Frank said he was truly happy, because at long last he'd found God. He was heavily involved in a "Christian movement," he said, and invited Samuel to a meeting the group was planning in his area.

At first Samuel assumed Frank had received Christ. But a careful reading of the literature Frank sent revealed that the group's beliefs were a strange mixture of out-of-context Old Testament teachings and a smattering of the New—with no clear position on who Jesus Christ was. It turned out that the group was one of the most controversial and dangerous cults in America.

Samuel contacted Frank, declining the invitation to attend the meeting—but suggesting that he and Frank meet privately to discuss spiritual things. Frank never replied.

3. *To avoid getting "picked off" the fringes of Christian fellowship, stay in the thick of it.*

In Matthew 13, Jesus tells a parable about the sower and the seed. When the seed (the gospel) is scattered beside the road, Satan quickly swoops down like a hungry raven and picks it off before it has a chance to grow roots. Author and pastor Michael Youssef points out that shallow dirt lies at the edge of the road, while rich, deep fertile soil is in the middle of the field.[10] When our children stay at the fringes of Christian fellowship and church involvement, they're easy targets for the evil one.

We need to show our children the benefits of being involved with fellow pilgrims. That's one way to keep them from the wolves.

FENDING OFF FALSE FAITHS:
PRACTICAL PROGRESS FOR PARENTS AND KIDS

False teachers may be wily, but they aren't invulnerable. The weapons of truth, openness, and discernment are their undoing. As parents, we can help our kids wield those weapons in a world of increasingly bizarre beliefs.

Principle #1: Know the Basics

It's hard to tell truth from error if you're not sure what the truth is. For example, if 16-year-old Blair calls Jesus the "Son of God" but doesn't know why, she may be happy to join her boyfriend's church—where everybody is a "son of God" and Jesus is simply "showing us the way." Your child doesn't have to become a doctrinal expert to know where orthodoxy ends and heresy begins, but he does need to know a few fundamentals.

Parental Action: Name the Essentials

Create a creed. Collect the "statements of faith" of your church and several other Christian organizations you respect (you can usually find the latter in magazines or on Web sites sponsored by the organizations). Sit down with your son or daughter and compare the statements. What do they say about God, Jesus, the Holy Spirit, and the authority of the Bible? What else do they mention? How are they alike? How are they different? What do they tell you about the most important beliefs in Christendom? Can you confirm the statements, using the Bible?

Then, working together, come up with a statement of faith for your family by combining, adapting, and rephrasing the others. Post the result on your refrigerator, bulletin board, or in another prominent spot.

Find the address. A false doctrine may sound suspect to your child, but if he doesn't know where the Bible discusses the issue, he won't be able to confirm or refute the teaching. Show your preteen or teenager how to use a concordance to find verses on a particular topic. You might also help him memorize—or at least bookmark—passages like these:

- Jesus is God (John 10:30; 14:9)
- Jesus is the only way to heaven (John 14:6)
- Religious rituals can't save us (Ephesians 2:8-9)
- No one knows when Jesus will return (Matthew 24:36)

Parental Action: Contrast Truth and Falsehood

When 12-year-old Simon read about the suicidal Heaven's Gate cult, he shook his head and said, "I can't believe anybody would do that!" Knowing even a little about the strangest groups may be enough to keep your child away from them. But will "respectable" false religions have more appeal? Make sure your kids know the basics of what these groups really teach.

Share what they say. For an overview of several world religions, cults, and the New Age movement, see the "Resource H" section in the back of Joe White's book *Faith Training*. Teens can study this on their own; for preteens, paraphrase the information to share in several parent-child talks. As a model, here's a *Faith Training* devotional on the subject:

Whose Way?
(John 14:1-7)

America has over 1,800 active religious cults; each one has a leader who claims to be the way to God. These cults lower Jesus to less than He truly is and elevate their own leaders to more than they were intended to be. They all claim to have a special word from God, and each commits a drastic sin when they add to or replace Scripture with their own beliefs, supposedly obtained from "divine revelation."

Joseph Smith, founder of the Mormon Church, said, "All Christian denominations are wrong and their creeds are an abomination in God's sight." Church father Joseph Fielding Smith said, "There is no salvation without accepting Joseph Smith."

Shirley MacLaine, spokesperson for the New Age movement, said, "I know that I exist, therefore I AM. I know that the God-source exists, therefore IT IS. Since I am part of that force, then I Am that I AM."

Mary Baker Eddy, founder of the Church of Christian Science, said in her "Bible," *Science and Health*, "The material blood of Jesus was no more efficacious to cleanse from sin when it was shed upon 'the accursed tree,' than it was when it was flowing in His veins as He went daily about His Father's business."

The Watchtower Bible of the Jehovah's Witnesses teaches that Jesus was not God incarnate and the doctrine of the Trinity is false doctrine. (Jesus said, "I and My Father are one," and "If you have seen Me, you have seen the Father.")

These religions are all tragically mistaken, because Jesus stated simply and firmly about Himself, "I am the (only) Way, the (only) Truth, the (only) Life. No one gets to the Father except by Me." The first commandment also warns, "Thou shalt have no other gods before Me."

Questions

1. Why is Jesus the only way for sinful man to spend eternity with a holy God?

2. Why do people follow cult leaders?

3. What is wrong with cults and other world religions?

Lifeline

Many people who join cults are better followers of their faith than Christians are of theirs. How can we change that in our home?[11]

Make a chart. You'll need poster board, markers, and a ruler for this one. Help your child compare the teachings of Christianity and other groups by creating a chart that places answers to key questions side by side. Here are a few questions your chart might include:

- How do we learn what's true?
- Who is Jesus?
- What happens when we die?
- How does a person get to heaven?
- What kind of relationship does God want with us now?

For each religion's answers, check the nearest Christian bookstore for references like these:

- *The Challenge of the Cults and New Religions* by Ron Rhodes (Zondervan, 2001)
- *Charts of Cults, Sects, and Religious Movements* by H. Wayne House (Zondervan, 2000)
- *Handbook of Today's Religions* by Josh McDowell and Don Stewart (Thomas Nelson, 1992)

Principle #2: Learn to Discern

Remember the pilgrims' experience?

The Shining One looked exasperated. "And didn't the shepherds warn you about the Flatterer?"

"Yes," Christian said with a sigh. "But we did not imagine that this fine-spoken man had been he."

A large vocabulary is no indication of spirituality. Neither are a large donor list, a large headquarters, or a large hairdo. Christian and Hopeful should have known better, but they fell for a "holy" outfit and a confident manner. They learned discernment the hard way; you can help your child learn it less painfully.

Parental Action: Sound a Warning

Teach telltale signs. At a family meeting, announce that you've decided to start your own religion. The first members will be those in your household. Call this new religion anything you like (e.g., "The One True Church of Myron," "Pumpkinism," "Hamsterology"). Make up your own list of doctrines ("Eternity is really 200 years long," "Only those who do push-ups daily will go to heaven") and rules ("No talking before breakfast," "Pay Dad a dollar every time you drop something on the floor"). Declare that you will have final approval of the clothes each person wears every day, and that anyone who tries to leave your new religion will not be allowed to watch TV for a year.

Then ask family members what they think of your plan. Chances are they won't be too enthused.

Explain that many of the things family members don't like about your plan are things to watch out for in a real-life religious group. A controlling leader, arbitrary rules, and warnings not to leave the group are telltale signs of a cult.

Back off the buffet. Take your family to an all-you-can-eat buffet restaurant. After people have chosen their food, talk about their picks. Did they take only their favorites? Did they try for a balanced meal? Do they prefer a buffet to ordering from a menu? Why or why not? What would be the pros and cons of eating at a buffet all the time?

Then ask, "What if all the religions in the world were on a buffet, and you could pick just the parts you liked? What would you pick? Would your 'combination plate' contain 100 percent truth, or would it just 'taste good'? Why isn't that the best way to decide what to believe?" Point out that many people take the "mix and match" approach to religion, but they don't end up with the truth.

Parental Action: Encourage Questions

Want your child to develop a healthy skepticism about the claims of shady religious leaders? Start by sending the message that challenging authority figures is okay—even if it means challenging you.

Avoid autocracy. Do you run your home as if it were a cult? If you tend to demand unquestioning obedience from your child, consider these words from *Toxic Faith* by Stephen Arterburn and Jack Felton:

> As strange as it may seem, the child who grew up with a rigid parent (or parents) enters adulthood attracted to those who serve up any form of rigidity. One might think that, once freed from the rigidity, the adult child would avoid it. Instead the individual is often drawn to it, which makes the person highly susceptible to an addictive religious system or to follow a toxic-faith leader....
>
> One boy grew up in a very rigid family in which it was difficult for him to express who he was or what he wanted. His father communicated with directives, offering no reasons for his demands, just expecting compliance. The boy rebelled forcefully. He became a heavy drug user and at age eighteen quit school and moved in with several other drug addicts. Eventually his addiction put him out of work, and he found himself at the bottom with no hope.
>
> When a cult follower befriended him, he responded. He felt love and support and a genuine offer for help. Inside the cult he was confronted with a controlling leader who dictated every decision of the group. He had found home. He had come full circle, back to a variation of his original situation. He became a faithful follower, unwilling to question the validity of the group, its roles, or the demands it placed on him.[12]

Encourage openness in your home. Kids who grow up in freedom will be less likely to settle for the ask-no-questions atmosphere of a controlling cult.

Simulate boot camp. Some cults, after luring young people with promises of communal bliss, have broken down their intellectual resistance with an intense "boot camp" experience that borders on brainwashing. Try role-playing such an experience with your older child, taking turns as the cult leader and the prospective convert. But the "convert" should challenge what the cult leader says, using the Bible if possible. Your dialogue might go something like this:

LEADER: It's best to cut off all contact with those outside our group. They would only try to destroy your faith.

CONVERT: But didn't Jesus eat with "sinners"? And the Bible says to get along with people who disagree about little things, like which holidays to celebrate.

LEADER: This is not a little thing! The doctrine of holy hand-holding is central to my teaching!

CONVERT: But it's not even in the Bible.

LEADER: God revealed it to me in a vision!

CONVERT: How could He disagree with His own Book? The Bible says we can go to heaven because of what Jesus did on the cross—not because of anything we can do.

Don't worry if the "convert" doesn't clearly win the argument. The point is to encourage your child not to accept the claims of cults at face value, even under pressure.

Principle #3: Stay Connected

Christian and Hopeful had each other, but they could have used a bigger support group. Too bad they couldn't bring the shepherds along! Is your child deeply connected with other believers, and deeply involved in fulfilling a mission with them? "Alternative" religions won't appeal to a young person who's actively following Jesus as part of a supportive community.

Parental Action: Provide Closeness

Many young people have joined cults simply because those groups promised acceptance and belonging—a sense of family. Are your kids getting those things at home and at church? Satisfy your child's hunger for closeness now, and she won't need to seek it elsewhere.

Express love at home. Kids need to hear the words "I love you," even if they don't respond in kind. They also need to see demonstrations of your love. Here are some "ways to tell your child 'I love you' without saying the words," from Joe White's *Faith Training*:

- When your child is participating in an athletic event or musical performance, be there watching.
- Leave an "I love you" note in your child's school lunch box.

- Find a new way to trust your child by granting a new area of responsibility that he or she would both enjoy and benefit from.
- When your child is being punished, undergo the punishment with him or her (occasionally).
- Build a small animal or insect cage together; then go hunt together for something to put in it.
- Make up and tell stories with your kids as the heroes.
- Plant trees in your yard in honor of your kids (one for each kid).
- When you sense something is troubling your child, make a reason for a trip in the car alone together.
- With an Etch-a-Sketch™ toy, do a "silent partners" drawing together: Take turns adding a single line to the drawing, but don't tell one another what you're trying to draw. See what you come up with!
- Make it a special project one day to listen intently to every word your child says.
- Invite your child's friends over, build a mountain on a tray out of ice cream scoops and whipped cream (with all the toppings), and then eat it.[13]

Find community. Does your child feel a sense of belonging at your church? If you've been attending for a year or more, but your child can't name at least one or two good friends who go there, talk with a Sunday school teacher or youth worker about the problem. Are cliques excluding your child? Are there opportunities for kids to get to know each other? Are there other "left out" children your child might befriend?

Parental Action: Steer into Service
Many cult members are known for their diligence—selling flowers, ringing doorbells, offering books to strangers in airports. If only they could have found a sense of purpose in a Bible-believing church! Kids "on a mission" don't need to join cults in order to find something meaningful to do with their lives. You can help yours find that mission.

Let kids be the church. Kids aren't just the church of tomorrow—they're the church of today. Many children think they're supposed to wait until they grow up to get involved in ministry, but ministry will help them grow up—and keep them off the fringes of faith. Explain to your kids that they can be God's hands and feet on earth now, not just "someday." Here are some service opportunities to explore with them:

- Young children can participate in choirs, drama, and cleaning up after church events.
- Older kids can help with younger ones in children's church, the nursery, Vacation Bible School, and elsewhere.
- Teens can raise funds through car washes and meet physical and spiritual needs on missions trips.

Improve your family serve. In addition to keeping kids in the thick of things through "official" service projects, try creating your own ministry opportunities as a family. Here are some examples from *Steering Them Straight* by Stephen Arterburn and Jim Burns:

> The Rice family lives in San Diego. They save their money all year, and then, at Christmastime, they visit orphanages across the border in Mexico, open the back of their pickup truck, and pass out shoes to barefoot children. On a monthly basis, they return to play games with the children, build, paint, and serve any way they can. They are a close-knit family, and all the kids have a desire to serve God.
>
> The Rigery family weekly dishes up food at a local soup kitchen.
>
> The Johnsons visit a convalescent home once a month.
>
> The Culps have opened their home to drug babies, and the entire family gets involved.
>
> The Swantons have a volunteer workday at the church once a month.
>
> The Burkes have chosen to "adopt" several of the more elderly saints in their church who don't have family members in the area. They take meals, mow lawns, and visit at least weekly. Each child has a special chore.[14]

ON THE ROAD AGAIN

Cults, "new" religions, and customized cocktails of "spirituality" will continue to beckon your child in the years ahead. But by grounding your kids in the basics of Christianity, warning them about smooth-talking false prophets, and giving them a sense of belonging and purpose, you'll guard them from some painful mistakes:

The pilgrims thanked him for setting them on the right path. Then they took that path, singing:
"Come closer, you who walk along the way;
See what happens when you go astray:
You're caught in an entangling net,
'Cause you good counsel lightly did forget.
It's true, you may be rescued; but, you see,
You're chastised, too; let this your caution be."

Chapter 18

A MAN CALLED ATHEIST

Preparing Your Child to Face Secularism

❧

The pilgrims saw in the distance a man walking along the highway. Christian said to Hopeful, "He has his back toward Zion, and is coming to meet us."

"I see him," said Hopeful. "Let's be careful, in case he should prove to be a Flatterer, too."

The man drew nearer and nearer, and at last came up to them. He was a short, round fellow with a mischievous twinkle in his eye. His name was Atheist, he said, and asked them where they were going.

"To Mount Zion," Christian said.

At that, Atheist burst into laughter. He laughed so hard, in fact, that he bent double.

Christian was not amused. "What's the meaning of your laughter?" he asked.

Still cackling, Atheist straightened up and wiped a tear from his eye. "I laugh to see what ignorant persons you are—to undertake such a tedious journey, when you'll have nothing but travel to show for your pains!"

Christian frowned. "Why do you think we will not be received?"

"Received?" Atheist cried. "There is no such place as you dream of in all this world!"

"But there is in the world to come," Christian protested.

Atheist rolled his eyes. "When I was at home in my own country I heard the same story you're telling. I went out to see if I could find the Celestial City. I've been seeking it for twenty years, and I've found no more of it than I did the first day I set out!"

Christian pointed a thumb toward Hopeful. "We have both heard, and believe, that there is such a place to be found."

Atheist gave them a condescending smile. "I believed, too. If I hadn't, I wouldn't have come this far looking. But I found nothing—and I should have, if there were such a place, because I've gone further to seek it than you have! I'm going home, to enjoy the things I gave up when I hoped to find something that doesn't exist."

Christian glanced at Hopeful. "Is it true what this man has said?"

Hopeful bent close to Christian and whispered. "Look out! He is one of the Flatterers. Remember what it cost us once already for listening to this kind of fellow?"

Casting a disgusted look toward Atheist, Hopeful continued. "What, no Mount Zion? Didn't we see from the Delectable Mountains the gate of the city? And aren't we to walk by faith?"

Christian nodded, and his companion's whisper grew more urgent. "Let's go on, so that the Shining One with the whip won't overtake us again. I say, my brother, cease to hear him—and let's believe so that our souls may be saved!"

Christian patted Hopeful on the shoulder. "My brother, when I asked whether what this man said is true, it was not because I doubted the truth of our belief. I was testing you, to find out what is in your heart. As for this man, I know that he is blinded by the god of this world. Let's keep going, knowing that we believe in the truth—and no lie is of the truth."

Relieved, Hopeful smiled. "Now I rejoice in hope of the glory of God," he said.

So they turned away from the man. Still laughing at them, Atheist headed back toward the city of Destruction.

⟿

THE RUINS OF RELIGION

It's a little like walking through a ghost town.

When you visit Great Britain or Europe, there's no end to the magnificent cathedrals that loom into the sky, their spires towering. They're everywhere, even in picturesque little hamlets.

But then you notice something odd: They're empty. Tourists are greeted warmly enough, and sometimes guided tours are led for history buffs. But most of these buildings are almost tomblike in their emptiness, showing few signs of real spiritual activity.

The two of us attended a Sunday morning service in one of these ancient cathedrals during an overseas trip. Fewer than 20 people sat in the pews of that vast place. The average age appeared to be around 60 or 70.

Evangelical missions who work in Europe will tell you that the continent is, by and large, "spiritually dead." There are pockets of faithful believers and vibrant ministries, but most of Europe seems under a strange sleeping sickness—physically alive, going through the religious motions, but lacking any spiritual vitality.

What happened? Did Europe fall under an atheistic regime? Was Christianity condemned and outlawed?

Hardly. The explanation is less dramatic. The formalism of Christian worship continued; the cathedrals kept their magnificent stained glass windows and vaulted ceilings. But the heart and soul had become secularized. Today's Europe is a place in which Bunyan's Mr. Atheist would be all too comfortable.

ATHEISM, AMERICAN STYLE

What about the U.S.? According to polls, 90 to 95 percent of Americans express a belief in God. No more than 10 percent—perhaps much less—of the American public can be called atheists.

Yet John Bunyan's portrait of Mr. Atheist, and that character's aggressive ridicule of those who follow God, seem awfully familiar. The influence of this self-assured God-denier can be much greater than his small statistical representation might suggest.

A few years ago a series of congressional hearings were held regarding religious freedom in America. Janet covered the issues on her nationally syndicated radio show, *Janet Parshall's America;* Craig testified before the Subcommittee on the Constitution. The hearing chairman had lined up witnesses, pro and con, on the question of whether the Constitution should be amended to reinforce the idea of the "free exercise of religion."

American Atheists, Inc. presented written testimony. Not surprisingly, that group vehemently opposed any expansion of individual religious liberty. But it went further, suggesting that the notion of believing in God was nothing more than dependence "upon a fantasy world populated with imaginary beings."[1]

Audacity and persistence have been the hallmark of many activist atheists. Though their numbers are small, they've caused a major seismic shift in public policy regarding expressions of faith. Atheists have been the prime movers behind lawsuits that ended prayer in America's public schools, and that stripped religious symbols from public buildings.

The danger is not so much that our children will become atheists (convinced that God does not exist), or even agnostics (disbelieving that anyone can know for sure). Rather, in a secular society that permits personal faith but treats it with suspicion—and seeks to keep it out of the public arena—our kids will be pressured to practice it only in private.

Secular Spirituality

Looking into the next decade, we see two forces at work: First, the general hunger to connect with the "spiritual" probably will increase. According to the Gallup polling organization, 58 percent of those surveyed in 1994 felt the need for personal spiritual growth. By 1999 that figure had jumped to 78 percent.[2]

But there is a second and opposite trend at work. Our culture is becoming more secularized.

It's true that following the terrorist attacks of September 11, 2001, there was a national outpouring of prayer and other public expressions of faith, including the oft-heard "God Bless America." Even some hardened television journalists joined in. But that phenomenon gradually faded, and the question is where society will be in the years ahead.

The last 50 years of American history show that while Americans prize individual belief in God, the judiciary and many educational institutions have permitted the unchecked growth of hostility toward expressions of faith in the public square.

Combining these two forces—personal spirituality and public secularism—will mean that a kind of "spirituality" will flourish, but only in an individualistic form.

Three Unsettling Trends

If you doubt that your child will grow up in a culture whose public square is increasingly purged of Christian references, consider the direction taken by three leading U.S. institutions:

The Secular State. In 1947 the United States Supreme Court, in the case of *Everson v. Board of Education,* formally erected the "wall of separation" between church and state. That concept was read into the First Amendment, even though the writings of America's founding fathers, the context of the drafting of the Bill of Rights, the language of the First Amendment itself, and the religious practices of early America all contradicted that conclusion.

Since that case, courts around the nation have boxed faith into society's corners. Their decisions have:

- prohibited prayer in public classrooms;
- prohibited moments of silent prayer in public school;
- prohibited Bible reading in public school;
- prohibited public schools from inviting religious leaders to lead optional religious instruction;
- prohibited display of the Ten Commandments;
- prohibited teaching creation science as an alternate explanation for the origins of life;
- prohibited public schools from permitting a community representative to lead a prayer at a graduation ceremony.

The judicial system, while paying lip service to religious freedom, has increasingly confined the expression of faith to churches and homes. The implication is that public places are the exclusive domain of secularism.

The Secular School. Nearly 20 years ago we started noticing problems in the public schools some of our children attended. What started as everyday parental concern eventually led us to found a pro-family education organization, defend parents' rights and a pro-family perspective through legal cases, and for Janet to host a nationally syndicated radio talk show.

One of the most shocking trends we discovered was the outright hostility toward traditional Judeo-Christian values in many public schools.

Some of this came from the philosophies that undergirded newer curricula. Some came from school boards, attorneys, and administrators who took their lead from the courts. Whatever the cause, God has been treated as *persona non grata* in public school classrooms.

We've witnessed a seemingly endless parade of examples. One involved a high school junior we'll call Ted.

Ted was a Christian who regularly brought his Bible to the public school he attended. He would read it during study hall or at lunch. He was outspoken about his faith, but polite.

One day he carried his books into civics class, with his Bible on top of the stack. The teacher took a long, hard look at the Bible—and asked Ted to stay after class to talk.

When the rest of the students had left, the teacher explained that he had a problem with Ted bringing his Bible to class. "Other students are going to feel uncomfortable with that," the teacher said.

"What is it you want me to do?" Ted asked.

"You better cover up the Bible so other students don't have to see it."

Ted was thunderstruck, but tried to be reasonable. "Cover my Bible with what?"

The teacher paused for a moment, then answered. "Cover it with brown paper. That way no one can tell what it is."

Feeling he was compromising his beliefs, Ted relented—and covered his Bible with brown paper.

Next time Ted came into civics class, several students saw the paper-covered book and asked what it was. "My Bible," Ted said with a smile.

Again the teacher asked Ted to stay after class. The brown paper just wasn't going to work, the instructor said; it was drawing too much attention. "You're not going to be able to bring it into class, period," he declared.

That's when Ted called Craig, who dashed off a letter to the teacher, with a copy to the principal of the school—explaining that Ted's right to carry his Bible was protected by the First Amendment of the U.S. Constitution.

The good news is that the school administrator informed the teacher that Ted would be allowed to carry his Bible. The bad news is that the Constitution had to be explained, and a lawsuit threatened, before Ted's rights were protected.

Unfortunately, Ted's story is not unique. We've seen other cases, too:

- Children told not to share religious stories
- Elementary students forbidden from making religious figures during art class
- Students ordered not to distribute Christian tracts in the halls between classes
- Teachers told to remove crosses and Bible verses from their desks
- Christian T-shirts prohibited
- Bible clubs blocked
- A shop class ordered to dismantle a display of lights one December because it spelled out the word "Christmas"

Two generations, most of them schooled in public institutions, have been raised in this secularized atmosphere. The decade ahead will see more of the same.

The Secular Screen. For years there has been a growing body of evidence of anti-Christian bias in the news media. As we look to the future, though, it seems the entertainment industry—not the press—will play a much greater role in further secularizing our culture.

Jacques Attali is a former advisor to the president of France, an international consultant, and founding president of the European Bank for Reconstruction and Development. When asked to comment on one major influence in the newly birthed twenty-first century, he indicated that the most powerful influence over all of civilization in the near future will be the entertainment—movies in particular—that we enjoy.[3]

That's ominous, considering the fact that Hollywood has been notoriously hostile to conservative Christianity. Robert Duvall, one of the most accomplished actors in film, spoke candidly on this subject while promoting his movie *The Apostle*. In several television interviews he noted that the movie industry had not been fair or accurate in its portrayal of Bible-believing Christians.

Those who deny God are looking to the arts and popular entertainment to spread their values with even more gusto in the future. One self-declared humanist is urging others to generate a body of fiction and films that will propagate the "gospel" of nonbelief; he praised movies like Carl Sagan's *Contact*, as well as *The Contender* and *Chocolat*, as examples of successful humanistic entertainment.

Filling the Spiritual Void

Yet even though our public places, culture, and forms of entertainment are becoming more secularized, people's desire for spiritual meaning will continue. The unsaved human soul, as Pascal noted, has a God-shaped void.

This represents a challenge—and an exciting opportunity for our children. They will grow up surrounded by a huge demographic group that researcher George Barna calls "the unchurched." These folks have no formal connection to a congregation, no consistent Bible teaching, no discipleship, and no regular fellowship with believers. Of the nearly 100 million Americans who fit this category, only 14 percent are atheists. Most of the other 86 percent consider themselves "Christian," yet have little understanding of what that means.[4]

It will be up to our kids to introduce this vast group to Jesus Christ—despite the culture's warning that "religion" should be a quiet, private affair.

Grace That Amazes

When John Bunyan decided to write his "spiritual autobiography," he titled it *Grace Abounding to the Chief of Sinners*. Bunyan considered himself one of the least likely fellows to receive the love of God.

If our children are to reach their generation for Jesus, the grace of God will be the starting point. According to George Barna, understanding, practicing, and communicating God's grace will be a central factor in taking the gospel to unchurched people in our highly secularized culture.[5]

Legalistic rules and moral standards didn't save us. Nor will they bring our children or their peers into a personal relationship with Jesus Christ. That starts with God's infinite grace—His loving us even when we're unlovable.

Parents know—or should know—a lot about grace. We're always in the business of giving our children something they—at least technically—don't deserve. We give second (and third and fourth) chances; we give allowances even though that bed wasn't perfectly made; we let their noisy friends come to our house even though we planned on having a quiet night to ourselves. Without being preachy, you may want to describe one of those times to your child as a snapshot of what God's grace looks like—a loving parent giving a child a blessing when he or she really didn't deserve it.

If we model grace to our kids, they'll be better able to communicate it. The spiritual future of a secularized generation may depend on our doing just that.

Surviving Secularism: Practical Progress for Parents and Kids

How can you prepare your child to live in an increasingly "God-free" society? The first step is to strengthen her faith, knowing it will be challenged by our culture's opinion-makers. The second step is to keep her from being silenced by those who would banish believers from the public square. The third step is to help her truly understand grace and impart it to others—a message sorely needed in a world that's lost touch with a loving heavenly Father.

Principle #1: Build up Belief

Mr. Atheist was so self-assured, so experienced. Yet Christian and Hopeful remained steadfast in their faith. Their travels had prepared them to withstand this sophisticated unbeliever's arguments. You can do the same for your child.

Parental Action: Reinforce the Reasons

Our secular society sends kids a message: "It's normal *not* to believe in God. If it makes you feel better to believe, go ahead. Just don't try to convince the rest of us." When atheism and agnosticism are the "default" mode, children need to be reminded that faith in God makes sense.

Act natural. Why should anyone believe in God? "The Bible tells me so" won't impress your child's secularized peers. While knowing Scripture is a must, your child will also benefit from knowing other arguments for God's existence. One such argument is based on the natural world. With younger children, take a nature hike and point out the large and small wonders—ants marching in single file, crystals in a rock. Ask, "Could all of this just happen by itself? Who do you think made the world?"

With older children and teens, the "natural" argument can be summarized as follows, loosely based on points made by Dr. Charles Ryrie in his book *Basic Theology*:

1. The universe around us is an effect that must have had a cause. Either it came from nothing, or it came from something that must be eternal.
2. To say that the universe came from nothing means it created itself. That's not logical, since it would have to exist and not exist at the same time.
3. If the universe didn't create itself, then something eternal must have caused it. Practically all scientists hold that the universe had a beginning, however long ago it may have been.
4. One option is chance. But mathematics show that random chance couldn't have produced the universe we see today.
5. The other option is that the eternal Being who caused the universe is God. The universe doesn't reveal all the details of what that Being is like, but it does mean that there is a living, powerful, intelligent One who caused the universe. Living, because nonlife can't produce life. Powerful, because of what was formed. Intelligent, because of the order and arrangement of the universe, things that chance couldn't create.[6]

Look into lives. With your older child, use an encyclopedia or the Internet to research the lives of some famous unbelievers. Were they happy? How did their lives turn out? Do their experiences suggest that it's better to be an atheist than a Christian? Here are a few examples:

- Alexandre Dumas, French author of *The Three Musketeers* and other novels, said, "If God were suddenly condemned to live the life which He has inflicted upon men, He would kill Himself." Dumas gave expensive gifts to a series of mistresses, which put him deeply in debt. After cranking out a succession of inferior books that were mostly rejected by the public, he died in relative obscurity and poverty in 1870.
- Friedrich Nietzsche, German philosopher, said, "I cannot believe in a God who wants to be praised all the time." He died a slow death from syphilis; 11 years before dying, he lost his mind and began sending people strange letters signed, "Dionysus—the Crucified."
- Marie Henri Beyle, a French author who used the name Stendhal, said, "The only excuse for God is that He doesn't exist." Beyle, whose

mother died when he was seven and who disliked his father, grew up hating authority and masking his hurt with cynicism. He wrote a book called *On Love*, which sold only 17 copies during his lifetime. He dedicated another of his books "To the Happy Few."

Parental Action: Test Faith

"Is it true what this man has said?" Those were Christian's words to Hopeful after Mr. Atheist had made his case. Later Christian revealed that his question was a test of Hopeful's faith. We, too, can challenge our kids to think through their faith—*before* they have to face a secularized society without us.

Put on a Pilgrim Play. As a family, act out the following adaptation of the conversation involving Christian, Hopeful, and Mr. Atheist:

CHRISTIAN: Look! There's a man walking along the highway, coming to meet us. But he's walking *away* from the Celestial City.

HOPEFUL: I see him. Let's be careful.

ATHEIST: Hello, friends! My name is Atheist. Where are you going?

CHRISTIAN: To the Celestial City.

ATHEIST: Ha, ha! Oh, that's a good one!

CHRISTIAN: Why are you laughing?

ATHEIST: Oh, hee hee! I'm laughing because you're so ignorant! Here you are, on a long and dangerous journey. And when you're done, you'll have nothing but sore feet to show for your hard work!

CHRISTIAN: Why do you think we won't be allowed into the Celestial City?

ATHEIST: Allowed? There's no such *place* as the Celestial City!

CHRISTIAN: There is in the next world.

ATHEIST: Oh, brother! I used to believe that story too. I went out to see if I could find the Celestial City. I've been looking for 20 years, and I still haven't found it!

CHRISTIAN: Hopeful and I believe there is such a place to be found.

ATHEIST: I believed too. If I hadn't, I wouldn't have come this far looking. But I found nothing—and I should have, if there were such a place, because I've gone further to seek it than you have! I'm going home, to enjoy the things I gave up when I hoped to find something that doesn't exist.

CHRISTIAN: What do you think, Hopeful? Is it true what this man has said?

After acting out the scene, pose the question to your family: "Is it true what this man has said?" Follow up with questions like these: "If Mr. Atheist didn't find heaven, does that mean it doesn't exist? How do you know? How would you answer someone who says that since she can't see God, He doesn't exist?"

Stage a debate. Divide the family into two fairly equally-matched teams. Team A will take the position that there is no God; Team B will argue for His existence. Give teams a week to line up all the arguments they can for their stances. Then stage your "great debate." Team A gets three minutes to make its case, followed by Team B's one-minute response. Team B then defends its position for three minutes, followed by Team A's one-minute reply. Each team then gets two minutes for a closing statement. Then talk about the strongest and weakest arguments made by both sides.

Principle #2: Ignore Intimidation

The pressure to keep faith "a private matter" comes in many forms. It may sound like Mr. Atheist's smug laughter; it may even take the shape of a legal battle. Just as Christian and Hopeful withstood the pressure to abandon their "foolish" faith, our children need help to ignore the threats of those who would keep believers out of the public square.

Parental Action: Consider the Source

Do atheists outnumber believers? Are secularists smarter and more sophisticated than anyone else? Are their arguments always objective, never emotional? No, but it's easy to get that idea from many media outlets and educational institutions. To keep your kids from assuming that secularism is an unstoppable, intellectually superior force, try the following activities.

Share statistics. As your child grows up in a culture that's erasing God from public life, does she have the impression that most people don't believe in Him? Ask her the following questions:

- Do most of the characters you see on TV believe in God? (Probably not; at least they don't talk about it.)
- Do most of the teachers at school believe in God? (If your child attends public school, this will be hard to answer—since discussion of the subject is usually off-limits there.)

Then ask the following (answers are from research cited earlier in this chapter):

- Of every 10 Americans, how many believe in God? (At least nine.)
- Of every 10 Americans who don't go to church, how many believe in God? (At least eight.)

Explain that it's easy to get the idea from TV and public schools that "most people" don't believe in God. But the fact is that most people do.

Listen for feelings. Watching a debate between a Christian spokesman and an agnostic attorney who wanted to ban religion from public discourse, one father couldn't help wondering how the lawyer had developed such negative attitudes toward believers. Listening carefully, he realized that the man feared the power of a church that had persecuted his Jewish forebears. That fear had shaped the man's view of God as well as his opinion of Christians. After the debate, the father vowed to try to understand the fears, hurts, and disappointments of those who seemed to be "enemies" of Christianity—and to encourage his children to do the same.

Kids need to know that unbelief often stems not from superior intellect, but from anger or disillusionment. To help your older child understand that, watch and discuss the Ken Burns documentary *Mark Twain* (PBS Home Video). The great satirist and skeptic suffered many painful experiences, including the deaths of family members and financial reversals—and grew increasingly bitter about religion toward the end of his life. Ask, "How might the death of his brother have affected Mark Twain's attitude toward God? What kinds of experiences might lead a person to stop believing in God? How could we help someone who feels that way?"

Parental Action: Help Them Speak Up

Should anyone "afflicted" by religious belief be banned from holding elective office? From publicly discussing issues of right and wrong that affect everyone? Some people think so, but your child doesn't have to be one of them. Build his confidence as a believer by helping him to make his opinions known.

Express yourself. Does your child feel strongly about something she's seen in the news, or an issue you've discussed at the dinner table? Help her explore what the Bible might have to say on the subject. Then encourage her to write a letter to your local newspaper, respond to an online poll, or call a TV station's telephone survey line to express her opinion.

Enter the public square. Do you and your children know why and how believers can speak up in a secularized society? Here are some resources to help your family understand a Christian's rights and responsibilities:

- *Why You Can't Stay Silent* by Tom Minnery (Tyndale, 2001). This book makes the case for shaping our culture, citing stories of Christians compelled by God's love to change the course of history.
- *The Rutherford Institute.* This non-profit legal organization offers a Web site (*www.rutherford.org*) and e-newsletter with news and commentary about civil liberties issues including religious freedom. A booklet, "Students' Rights in Public Education," is also available from the group. For more information, call (434) 978-3888 or write P.O. Box 7482, Charlottesville, VA 22906-7482.
- *Focus on the Family. Citizen* magazine, the "CitizenLink" Web site (*www.citizenlink.org*), and a daily, complimentary e-mail news service (*www.family.org/linkmail*) keep you up to date on public policy issues with which Christians need to be involved. To subscribe to *Citizen* magazine, visit *www.family.org* or call 1-800-A-FAMILY (in Canada, 1-800-661-9800).

Principle #3: Grow in Grace

A world that denies God can offer many things—but it can't offer God's grace. Most people know they've sinned, whether or not they'd use that word to describe their transgressions. Where will they find real forgiveness? Your child can answer that question—if he's found grace in your home.

Parental Action: Understand the Undeserved

Does your child know what grace is? Here are two activities that can help kids of all ages grasp this vital concept.

Stamp it out. Give each family member a sheet of paper and some markers or crayons. Explain that the task at hand is to design a new postage stamp—one that illustrates the idea of "grace." First ask whether anyone knows what grace is. One possible definition: the forgiveness God offers even though we don't deserve it. Here are some ideas to get you started:

- A big hand reaching from above, and a small, muddy hand reaching up from below.
- The words "Free Postage."
- A jail cell door swinging open.

Have family members work on their designs (pair very young children with older ones or parents). Then show and discuss the results—and post them on the refrigerator.

Invent Graceland. With your child, have fun coming up with ideas for a new theme park—Graceland. Rather than paying tribute to Elvis Presley, however, you'll be illustrating the concept of God's grace. After explaining what grace is, ask, "In a theme park where the theme is grace, what would be the ticket price? What would the rides be like? The food? How would employees act?" Here are a few possibilities:

- You could get in even if you'd forgotten to bring your money.
- If you broke the rule about no flash photography, they'd give you a second chance before ejecting you from the park.
- If the roller coaster was going too fast for you, they'd slow it down.
- The ice cream stand would be called "Unmerited Flavor."
- If you were too short to go on a ride, the management would make up the difference.

If your child likes to draw, map out your version of Graceland together on a large sheet of poster board or newsprint.

Parental Action: Model Mercy

Teaching the *fact* of grace is one thing; creating a grace-filled atmosphere that will shape your child's idea of relating to God is quite another. Realizing your importance as a role model in this process can be daunting, but ideas like the following can help.

Tear up the bill. Announce that for one week, you'll be keeping track of your children's misbehavior. Post a chart on the refrigerator or bulletin board, assessing a dollar for each instance of wrongdoing. At the end of the week, tally up the results. Chances are that your kids will be too deep in debt to pay for their offenses. Ask, "How is this like the debt we owe God for the wrong things we've done? Could we ever pay it? How can it be paid?" Explain that because God is merciful, He paid that debt through His Son's death on a cross. To illustrate mercy at work, tear up the chart and forgive your kids for the week's offenses. Then ask, "Since God has been merciful to us, how can we show mercy to each other this week? How can we tell people who don't know Him about His forgiveness?"

Suspend a rule. When your kids least expect it, declare that you're going to suspend one of your "house rules" for the next hour. If you have a ban on eating in front of the TV, for instance, you might break out some snacks and let everyone watch a show while chowing down. Or if your child is supposed to clean his room every Saturday morning, let him skip a week. You could call these "Grace Attacks." Keep the timing a surprise, so that kids don't come to expect them—and feel entitled to them. If you like, explain that you're doing this "just because I love you" or "because it reminds me of how God gives us good things we don't deserve." Encourage family members to grant each other moments of mercy, too—for instance, helping a sibling with homework or forgiving him for borrowing a toy without permission.

The Ultimate Weapon

It's scary, sending your child to do "battle" in a secularized culture. It may even seem unfair to burden him with the mission of sharing his faith under fire.

But you have a secret, spiritual weapon.

What is it? A story shared by Ravi Zacharias illustrates the point.[7]

During the Korean War, an American soldier huddled in a bunker under intense enemy fire. His commanding officer ordered him to head toward enemy lines to rescue wounded comrades.

After the officer left, the soldier didn't get up; he simply checked his watch. Another soldier reminded him of his orders, but again, he did not move. Finally, after looking repeatedly at his watch, he jumped up and raced toward the deadly guns in order to complete his mission.

Later, when the fighting had subsided, the soldier safely returned. His buddy in the bunker asked why he'd kept looking at his watch instead of immediately obeying the commanding officer's order.

The soldier, choking back tears, explained that his mother had promised to pray for his safety at a specific time each hour of the day. He didn't want to face the possibility of death until he knew he had the protection of his mother's prayers.

The task before our children is a daunting one—to live their faith in a society increasingly opposed to open expressions of that faith. Let them know that as they wade into the line of fire, they won't be alone. You'll be lifting them up before God's throne of grace in loving, continual prayer.

Chapter 19

CROSSING OVER

Teaching Your Child
About Death and Heaven

When Christian and Hopeful awoke, they got ready to go up to the Celestial City. But the sun's reflection on the city—which was made of pure gold—was so gloriously bright that they couldn't look at it directly. They could only behold it through a lens made for that purpose.

As they hiked toward the city, they were met by two men in clothes that glistened like gold, and whose faces shone like the light.

These men asked the pilgrims where they had come from, where they had lodged, and about the difficulties and dangers and comforts and pleasures they had encountered on the way. Christian and Hopeful told their story; the Shining Ones responded by saying, "You have only two more difficulties to meet with, and then you are in the City."

"Will you go along with us?" asked the pilgrims.

"Yes," said the Shining Ones. "But you must get there by your own faith." So the four of them walked together until they were in sight of the gate.

Christian and Hopeful were stunned by what they saw next. Between them and the gate was a river; but there was no bridge to go over, and the water was very deep.

"You must go through," said the Shining Ones, "or you cannot reach the gate."

"Is there no other way to the gate?" Christian asked faintly.

The Shining Ones looked at each other. Then one said. "Yes. But only two—Enoch and Elijah—have been permitted to tread that path since the foundation of the world, and no others will until the last trumpet sounds."

Christian and Hopeful looked this way and that, desperate to find a way to escape the river. But there was none.

"Is the water the same depth everywhere?" Christian asked.

"No," said one of the Shining Ones. "But we cannot help you with that. We can tell you this: You will find it deeper or shallower depending on the depth of your faith in the King of this place."

Christian gulped. Hopeful took a deep breath, then exhaled shakily. After a glance at each other, they approached the edge of the river.

As soon as Christian entered the water, he slipped and lost his footing. His heart hammered and his arms flailed wildly. "Hopeful!" he cried. "I'm sinking! The billows go over my head; the waves go over me!"

"Be of good cheer, my brother!" shouted Hopeful. "I feel the bottom, and it is good!"

But the current was strong, and Christian continued to panic. "The sorrows of death have surrounded me," he called. "I will not see the land that flows with milk and honey." A great darkness and horror fell upon him, clouding his vision and blotting out all memory of the times he had been rescued during his pilgrimage.

"I will die in the river," he panted, "and never enter the gate." He began to recall the sins he had committed, both before and since he had become a pilgrim. His mind swirled with apparitions of evil spirits, multiplying his terror.

Hopeful swam to his side and tried to keep his brother's head above water. Christian thrashed, went under, then bobbed to the surface, half drowned.

THE FINAL CHALLENGE

Of all of the difficulties experienced by our pilgrim friend, this is perhaps the most poignant.

John Bunyan is very plain—even a bit brutal—in his portrait of Christian's confrontation with death. There are no soft, cushy illusions. Bunyan knew that even for the faithful pilgrim, dealing with dying is one of life's biggest challenges. That's why Christian doesn't hop across a sparkling little stream; he thrashes, panicking, in a deep, cold, dark river.

C. S. Lewis noted that death does not appear as a dark power because it inclines us to doubt God's existence. Just the opposite: It forces us to confront things about Him that seem unanswerable—perhaps even dreadful.[1]

For example, why does God permit suffering? Why must we go through the process of dying before entering His heavenly kingdom? Why didn't He pick an easier way for us weak, frail humans to leave one world and enter the next?

Coping with death has been a critical life lesson for every generation. How will the next one handle the challenge? Looking ahead, we see two trends in the way our children and their peers will struggle with their own mortality.

Trend #1: Prolonging the Journey

As the science of genetics flourishes, and as researchers probe the mysteries of DNA and map the human genome, there is talk of prolonged life and enhanced health that would have sounded like science fiction just a few decades ago.

Futurists have predicted the eradication of entire groups of diseases. Some have estimated that by the year 2025, some 4,000 genetic ailments will be eliminated by blocking or removing harmful genes and replacing them with healthy ones. Dozens of cancers, according to some predictions, will become extinct.

Optimism abounds on the subject of lengthening our lives. We are, one national magazine announced, entering a new epoch in which the human race will start "to take control of its biological destiny."[2] It's unlikely that during our children's lifetimes society will have the audacity to pronounce that it has "killed death." Yet an increasing atmosphere of optimism will pervade the culture, at least superficially, regarding death and disease.

That's not surprising, since most of us look for reasons not to dwell on the grave anyway. Denial of death is common, and will be reinforced by the mirage of immortality that technology will help to create. Medical science will lead the media to make bolder and bolder promises, suggesting we're on the verge of reversing the aging process and mastering mortality. Future citizens will feel they deserve longer and healthier lives, and ought to expect that death can eventually be defeated.

In our children's world, death will be viewed as a fixable "glitch" in the system—rather than a spiritual and physical consequence of human sin, something each of us must deal with personally.

Trend #2: Dulling the Pain

All this unmerited optimism can survive only at a superficial level. Down deep, most people will still carry the burden of anxiety and despair about death. Those promises of immortality will be impossible to honor, and the reality of death will inevitably sink in for everyone. Like chattering guests at a funeral, the next generation will eventually find itself unable to ignore the casket at the other end of the room.

Death's inevitability is one of life's constants. We need to address this reality lovingly and carefully with our young pilgrims. If we don't, our culture will—and its explanations won't reflect a biblical perspective.

We've read several elementary-level curricula, for instance, that attempt to teach children about death. The problem is that, since public education has become a thoroughly secular enterprise, anything it has to say about death is mostly beside the point.

One lesson plan told the story of a grandpa bunny rabbit who died. The mother bunny was explaining the idea of death to her tearful bunny youngster. Death was just a normal part of the life cycle, she said. It was sad that Grandpa bunny had to leave—but wonderful to realize that he was now part of the ecosystem, helping to fertilize the ground.

The lesson plan advised the teacher to have children share recent losses—and urge them to see the positive side of their loved ones being part of the earth's ecosystem!

Another popular view of the dying process is that it's a horror to be avoided at all costs—especially if you're young. A survey by the American Association of Retired Persons and *Modern Maturity* magazine revealed that the younger the interviewees, the more they expressed fears about aging and death.[3]

This is understandable in a culture where comfort and pleasure are the highest values. Dying is a nightmare scenario for those who shudder at the thought of losing bladder control, suffering constant pain, or feeling their bodies fall apart.

So how will the next generation deal with this horror? It will shift the focus from the *fact* of death to the *process of dying*. Our culture will become increasingly preoccupied with making the process of dying more comfortable, more hospitable, more "consumer-friendly."

Make no mistake; we believe in the "hospice" movement. Janet's mother, a nurse, was a leader in setting up hospice units in several large hospitals around the U.S., seeking to remove dying patients from the cold sterility of the hospital whenever possible and allowing them to spend their final days surrounded by family and friends. This has been a welcome development for terminally ill patients.

But social engineers, counteracting modern angst, have sought any means to dull the pain and blur the reality of death itself. One of the logical outcomes has been the euthanasia movement.

Billionaire George Soros, having super-funded many of his radical ideas about social restructuring and global unity, has taken on death. The Open Society, a foundation created by Mr. Soros, donated $15 million to The Project on Death in America (PDIA) in an effort to shape public policy on death and dying. After the Supreme Court struck down physician-assisted suicide, a PDIA board member announced that it was time to recognize the constitutional right to seek a physician's aid in ending one's life.[4] Soros himself has publicly endorsed euthanasia and physician-assisted suicide.

There is a lesson here about the importance of family in shaping beliefs about death. George Soros has explained that his approach to the "right to die" grew from his mother's membership in the Hemlock Society, one of the first modern groups to support the "right" to suicide.[5]

What messages should *we* deliver to our children about death? Softening the pain and fear of dying can only go so far. It will not satisfy one's spiritual hunger for hope beyond the grave. Our challenge is to show our kids what that hope really looks like.

TEACHING CHILDREN ABOUT DEATH

When our children were young, we began talking about death as most parents probably do—when the subject arose naturally. This happened when a pet died, for instance, or when we attended funerals.

That doesn't mean, of course, that all of our teaching on this subject was interpreted correctly.

Joseph, our youngest, was in elementary school when his great-grand-father died. At the funeral, all six members of our family passed by Grandpa's open coffin and said good-bye. It was then that Joseph whispered, "Are his bones in there too?"

Baffled by the question, we nevertheless chalked it up to childhood curiosity. "Yes," we answered, "Grandpa's body still has the bones in it."

It wasn't until years later that we realized why Joseph had asked the question. We had told our children that the body was just an "empty shell," and when we die our spirits—our true selves—go to heaven to be with God. To illustrate, we'd pointed out the way a snake sheds its skin. Joseph's question was perfectly logical; he was really asking, "Is that just the skin 'shell' left in the coffin? If so, did Grandpa take his bones with him to heaven?"

Talking to our children about death may risk misunderstandings, but *not* doing so risks even more. Our kids need to understand three key truths about the end of this life—and the beginning of the next.

Truth #1: Eternity Is a Relationship

As parents, we often emphasize the physical aspects of death when talking with our children. But death and heaven aren't just about our bodies. The most important factor is *relational.*

While it's not clear exactly what our "spiritual bodies" will be like in heaven (1 Corinthians 15:44), one thing is very clear: The focus of heaven and God's future kingdom is our family relationship with Him.

Our children need to know that after death, if they have received Christ by faith, they will continue *perfectly* the relationship with their heavenly Father that they began *imperfectly* in this life. Christians are "going home" not just to a place, but to an eternal relationship of love, harmony, and joy with the One who loves them beyond measure. They can look forward to walking in God's palaces as beloved, intimate members of His royal family.

Truth #2: We Have a Hope to Share

As their peers place vain hopes in medical technology and "dying with dignity," our children can be poised to share the truth about death, heaven, and eternity.

Our world provides plenty of opportunities to bring up those subjects.

The terrorist attacks of September 11, 2001, for example, rattled our culture's complacency about eternal things. The fragility of life became utterly palpable as the truth of Scripture rang out like a bell: "Why, you do not even know what will happen tomorrow. What is your life? You are a mist that appears for a little while and then vanishes" (James 4:14).

At such times, sharing our hope should begin with empathy. All of us grieve the loss of loved ones; Jesus Himself wept at the tomb of His friend Lazarus. Our children must understand the reality of grief and fear that comes with the end of life.

But as Hopeful reminded Christian when the latter struggled through the river of death, "Be of good cheer, my brother! I feel the bottom, and it is good!" For believers in Christ, death is not an endless abyss, as it is for one who has no hope:

"Brother," Hopeful said, "I see the gate! There are men standing by to receive us!"

"It is you they wait for," Christian moaned. "For you have been hopeful ever since I met you."

"And so have you," his friend said softly.

Christian swallowed a mouthful of water, then coughed it out. "Surely if I were right," he managed, "the Lord would now arise to help me; but because of my sins He has brought me into this snare, and left me."

"My brother," said Hopeful, "you have forgotten where, in your book, it is said of the wicked, 'They have no struggles; their bodies are healthy and strong. They are free from the burdens common to man; they are not plagued by human ills' (Psalm 73:4-5). These troubles and distresses you go through in these waters are no sign that God has forsaken you. They are sent to test you, to see whether you will remember His past goodness to you and depend on Him now."

Christian kept fighting the river's flow, but fell silent, thinking.

"Be of good cheer," Hopeful added. "Jesus Christ makes you whole."

All at once Christian's eyes widened. "I see Him again!" he shouted. "He tells me, 'When you pass through the waters, I will be with you; and when you pass through the rivers, they will not sweep over you' (Isaiah 43:2)."

Then they both took courage. After that the enemy who had been tormenting Christian's thoughts was as still as a stone. Soon his feet touched the riverbed, and he stood. The rest of the river was shallow, and they finally crossed it.

Christian's fears were resolved when he came to rest on the promises of God. The person without Christ can gain this same hope; salvation is available to everyone. Our children can bring this amazing promise to an aching world that tries to deny death.

Truth #3: God Is in Control

The Bible tells us that death resulted from mankind's fall in the Garden of Eden. It's real because of the rule of God, not because we lack the technology to eradicate it.

Likewise, only God can banish death—and someday He will:

> He will wipe every tear from their eyes. There will be no more death or mourning or crying or pain, for the old order of things has passed away. (Revelation 21:4)

Until then, we—and our children—must count on the fact that God is in control.

That truth was brought home to Dr. Howard Hendricks, longtime professor at Dallas Theological Seminary, as he and his wife sat in the lobby of a medical center. They were waiting for a diagnosis of Dr. Hendricks's condition. Finally his physician walked in and gave him the kind of news that would make most people's knees quiver. It was cancer, and the prognosis was foreboding.

Despite the grim diagnosis, Dr. Hendricks was able to sleep peacefully that night. Why? Because he recognized two great facts about God: He is perfectly sovereign, and perfectly good.[6] His sovereignty means that nothing, including the length of our days, escapes His divine supervision. His goodness guarantees that He wants the best for us and that His grace will be sufficient for us on the day that we need it most.

We can prepare our children for the reality of death. We can teach them that death is only the short path between our earthly pilgrimage and our "family reunion" in heaven. We can help them understand that God is in charge and that He is good. And we can demonstrate the assurance that the grave has no power over a follower of Jesus Christ—by confidently living out our days, even the last of them.

LIVING WITH DYING:
PRACTICAL PROGRESS FOR PARENTS AND KIDS

Discussing death with a child isn't easy for any parent; each stage of childhood presents its own challenges. Preschoolers find it hard to grasp the permanence of death, often thinking that a deceased relative will return as if from vacation. Older children, especially boys, may be fascinated with the "creepiness" of death, but can't relate to the ethereal nature of the afterlife. Teens usually think themselves invulnerable, and shrug off the subject of death as irrelevant.

As if those hurdles weren't enough, you'll also want to avoid being morbid or frightening as you approach the topic. Your goal is to counter the culture's denial of death and to offer assurance of everlasting life—a positive message your child can absorb over time and eventually share with others.

Principle #1: Prepare for the Passage

When Christian and Hopeful saw that the only way to the Celestial City was through a rushing river, they were stunned. Hadn't they suffered enough? Why couldn't they just walk through the gates? Fortunately, Hopeful had learned Psalm 73:4-5 and concluded, "These troubles and distresses you go through in these waters are no sign that God has forsaken you. They are sent to test you, to see whether you will remember His past goodness to you and depend on Him now."

Our children need not be shocked to find that getting into heaven usually requires a painful transition. Let's tell them the truth—that the "valley of the shadow" is ahead, and that God will be with them every step of the way.

Parental Action: Dispel Denial

When a family pet dies, when a memorial service is held for a loved one, or when natural or man-made disaster strikes, the opportunity to talk about death's reality is obvious. But what about the rest of the time? You can create your own "teachable moments" with activities like the following.

Observe obituaries. With your older child, turn to the obituary section of the newspaper. Look together at the brief chronicles of people's lives. Ask, "How does it feel to read these? How old were the people who died? Why doesn't the newspaper have any stories about people who have lived, say, 150 years? Why do you suppose these death notices aren't on the front page? Do you think most people read these every day? Why or why not?" Then talk about some things each of you would like included in your own obituaries. Ask, "If we know our earthly lives will end someday, how should it affect the way we live?"

Trace your tree. Ever charted your family roots? If not, interview relatives and search the Internet to find out who your ancestors are. Keep the project fun; unless you're really into genealogy, gather information on just a few generations. As you do, note the life spans of family members and how they died. Without belaboring the point, make sure your child notices that they *did* die. Ask, "How many of our ancestors have died? Do you think when they were growing up they realized that this would happen? How long do you hope to live on earth? What would you like to ask some of our ancestors if you see them in heaven?"

Parental Action: Deal with Fears

Will dying hurt? Will I be alone? If Mom and Dad die, who'll take care of me? Kids, like adults, find death a scary subject. You can address your child's fears by listening carefully and responding with actions like these.

Visit the valley. Read Psalm 23 with your child, paying special attention to verse 4:

> Even though I walk through the valley of the shadow of death, I will fear no evil, for you are with me; your rod and your staff, they comfort me.

Ask, "What do you think this means?" Depending on the maturity level of the child, you may need to explain that this verse describes times when a person could be close to dying. Some kids will have trouble connecting "rod and staff" to "comfort," since these may sound like tools of punishment.

To aid understanding, try creating a symbolic "valley of the shadow." If your child is very young or fearful, blindfold yourself and have her guide you through a couple of rooms in your home. If your child is older, let him wear the blindfold as you guide him. Then ask, "When you can't see where you're going, what are you afraid might happen? How does it 'comfort' you to have a guide who can see?" Explain that the "rod and staff" in Psalm 23:4 are used to guide sheep away from danger, not punish them. Point out that when a Christian dies, he isn't alone. God is there like a loving shepherd, guiding the person to his heavenly home. If your child hasn't already memorized the verse, help him do so.

Introduce guardians. Steve and Kacie were surprised one evening when their nine-year-old son Brandon ran into their bedroom and tearfully flopped on the bed.

"What's wrong?" Kacie asked.

"I just realized," Brandon said, "that someday you and Dad are going to die."

There was silence for a few moments as Steve and Kacie tried to figure out what to say. Finally they wrapped their arms around their sobbing son and reassured him that they probably weren't going to die anytime soon. They also explained that if something happened to them, another couple Brandon knew had agreed to take care of the children. And no matter what happened, God would watch over Brandon and his two brothers.

Like Brandon, many children need assurance that they'll be cared for if their parents are gone. If you've named legal guardians, tell your children about the arrangement. Visit the guardians when possible, to help your kids grow more comfortable with them.

If you haven't named legal guardians, consult an attorney about the process. Your child deserves to know that trustworthy people who share your values will be there even if you aren't.

Principle #2: Share the Hope

Hopeful lived up to his name as Christian despaired in the river. "Be of good cheer," Hopeful told his companion. "Jesus Christ makes you whole."

That's our message—to our children, and to a hopeless world. Christ has defeated death. No wonder Bunyan adds, "After that the enemy...was as still as a stone."

Parental Action: Emphasize the Relationship

Do your children understand that they already have a Friend in heaven? Do they realize that eternal life starts now, and that they can begin building an everlasting relationship with the One who's preparing a place for them? Use the following activities to remind them that, for Christians, death is the doorway to a very happy family reunion.

Celebrate Father's Day. Try observing "Heavenly Father's Day." Encourage family members to make cards honoring their heavenly Father, and to bring presents He'd be pleased with (an offering for your church, a coupon promising to help a sibling with chores, etc.). Serve refreshments; leave one chair at the table empty to remind family members of the Guest of honor. Ask, "How does it feel to pay tribute to a Person we can't see? If we could see our heavenly Father right now, how might it change our celebration? What do you think it will be like when we get to heaven and can celebrate in His presence?"

Get homesick. You can try this activity anytime, but it may be most effective when it's dark, cold, and rainy—or oppressively hot. With your child, take a walk (or drive) away from the comforts of home. Sit on a bench or in the car and talk about the things and people you miss—the TV, air conditioning, a pet, a parent. Ask, "Have you ever been homesick? How did it feel to get back home? What would you like to do when we get back?" Explain that going to heaven is like going home. Ask, "Who would you like to see when you get to heaven? How do you think it will feel to finally be with the One who made you and knows you better than anyone else does?"

Parental Action: Teach God's Sovereignty and Goodness

If you were in charge of the universe, would you put an end to death? God will—but has chosen not to do it yet. In the meantime, it's easy to forget that this suffering world hasn't spun out of His control, and that He really cares. Teach your kids both of these concepts with activities like the following.

Examine expiration dates. With your elementary-age child, remove from your refrigerator every item that has an expiration date on it; put the items on the kitchen table. As needed, explain that an expiration date indicates when the food has outlived its usefulness. Ask, "What seems to be the oldest thing here? Has anything expired? What has the longest 'life' ahead of it?" Note that "expiration" is also a way of saying "death." Ask, "What if we had 'expiration dates' to tell us when our earthly lives will end? Would you want to know that date? Why or why not?" Explain that we don't know our own "expiration dates," but God does. As the One in charge, He knows when even a sparrow falls—and will see to it that we go to be with Him on the date of His choosing.

Meet Chris and Hope. Check the nearest Christian bookstore for *Christian's Journey* (Chariot Victor Publishing, 1998), a picture book retelling *Pilgrim's Progress* for today's kids. Adapted by Karl Schaller, Lee Hough, and Liz Duckworth, *Christian's Journey* tells the story of Chris, a boy struggling over the death of his grandfather. Joined by his friend Hope, Chris finds himself on a trek that ends at the Celestial City—where he sees that God has provided a wonderful home for Grandpa. Read the book aloud to children ages 4-7; ages 8 and up can read it for themselves.

HOME AT LAST

In 2001 we lost a dear friend—Brandt Gustafson, Christian radio pioneer and president of the National Religious Broadcasters. From the diagnosis of his cancer to his death, he had only a few meager months.

Before his death, Brandt talked with Bill Bright, founder of Campus Crusade for Christ—who also suffered from serious health problems. The two of them, Brandt noted, had spent their lives encouraging Christians on how to live; now it was their turn to show believers how to die.

In his final hours, according to those who were with him, Brandt left no doubt that he was entering a land so glorious, and into the presence of a God so loving, that words could not describe them.

When we pour our lives into our children, cheering them on as they navigate the pilgrim's path, we not only show them how to live; we show them how to cross a chilly river to that indescribable place where God will welcome them home.

Breathing heavily, Christian and Hopeful climbed the bank of the river. Before them waited the two shining men.

"We are ministering spirits," said the Shining Ones, "sent to aid those who

will inherit salvation." Joining the pilgrims, they walked toward the gate to the Celestial City.

The city stood on a mighty hill; but the pilgrims went up that hill with ease, because the two Shining Ones led them up by the arms. There were no mortal garments to hinder them, either, since the pilgrims had left those behind in the river.

Ascending with much agility and speed, they saw that the foundation of the city was framed higher than the clouds. They seemed to float through the air, conversing in wonderment as they went, comforted because they had safely gotten through the river—and because they had such glorious companions to attend them.

Chapter 20

CONCLUSION

Strength for the Road Ahead

⤚◦

Open the curtains, look within my veil,
Turn up my metaphors, and do not fail.
There, if you seek them, such things you'll find
As will be helpful to an honest mind.

⤚◦

Christian has completed his bold, dangerous, exhilarating journey. He's risked everything for the promise of the Celestial City—and reached it.

What an adventure!

And what an adventure awaits us parents as we guide our children in Christian's footsteps.

READY FOR THE ROAD

At the beginning of this book, we described the Bible as God's perfect map for the Christian life. *Pilgrim's Progress* has been our travel guide.

Scripture calls all of us Christian parents to model the same eternal principles and instill them in our children. But along the way, the picnic spots and potholes will be unique to our own families.

Fortunately, John Bunyan has taught us about more than potholes. We trust that his tale has also given you hope—hope that the same infinite resources available to Christian will sustain you as you protect and direct your children in the decade ahead.

When God calls us to be parents, after all, He also equips us. He does that in two ways—through His Word and through His Spirit.

Remember the book Christian was given at the beginning of the story? Reading it aided him in his journey, lifting his heart and sharpening his eye for the road ahead. That's the main method God uses to prepare each of us for the awesome privilege of raising, training, and loving the little ones He gives us.

In 2 Timothy 3:16-17, Paul instructs,

> All Scripture is God-breathed and is useful for teaching, rebuking,
> correcting and training in righteousness, so that the man of God
> may be thoroughly equipped for every good work.

When we read, believe, and apply the Bible to our parenting, we'll be "equipped for every good work." And raising children who serve and honor Him is truly a good work.

The second way in which God equips parents is through His Holy Spirit. In the words of Hebrews 13:20-21, "May the God of peace…equip you with everything good for doing his will, and may he work in us what is pleasing to him."

How amazing that God is able to equip us with the same power that raised Jesus from the dead! That's like having the cord for our living room lamp connected to the nuclear power of the sun.

There's one other way in which we can be equipped for the job of guiding our young pilgrims. But this one depends on us—on our willingness to be spiritually cleansed:

> In a large house there are articles not only of gold and silver, but also
> of wood and clay; some are for noble purposes and some for ignoble.
> If a man cleanses himself from the latter, he will be an instrument
> for noble purposes, made holy, useful to the Master and prepared to
> do any good work. (2 Timothy 2:20-21)

How can we tell whether we've been cleansed? The lives we lead at home are a pretty good test. We can put on a wonderful spiritual show at work or at church, but it's hard to fake it around our children. That's just as well, since they need us to model authentic Christian living—the kind that will help them faithfully finish the final stretch of the pilgrim's path.

DON'T BE DISCOURAGED

It's easy to see our failures as parents. It's tempting to dwell on our mistakes.

Christian in *Pilgrim's Progress* could have done that, and almost did. Instead, he kept getting up, brushing himself off, and returning to the straight and narrow path God had prepared before the worlds were formed. We can do the same.

Condemnation and self-doubt don't come from God. Once we confess our sins, the Bible promises that "[God] is faithful and just and will forgive us our sins and purify us from all unrighteousness" (1 John 1:9). It's the devil, not the Lord, who forever whispers in our ears about our inadequacies as moms and dads.

God has chosen us Christian parents—imperfect though we are—to be the most important moral compasses in our children's lives. We all need to read, then reread, Deuteronomy 6:6-9 and Proverbs 6:20-22. Go ahead, look them up! You'll find that we parents have been assigned as trainers for our children's treks down the road to the Celestial City.

THE FINISH LINE

Someday, when you look back on these years of training your children, what will you see? There will be regrets—but there will be satisfaction, too.

That was our experience recently after our oldest child, Sarah, went to her 10-year high school class reunion. The story she shared with us was the kind that makes a mother weep with joy, and puts a lump in a father's throat.

Back in high school, Sarah and sister Rebekah had lots of friends. Our approach had always been, at least in theory, to turn our home into a combination recreation center, philosophy class, and coffee house for pals of the

Parshall kids. That way we could get to know them and perhaps be a positive influence.

It didn't always work that smoothly, of course. Friends would appear at all hours—sometimes colliding with family plans, sometimes just when Mom and Dad were hoping and praying for a little peace and quiet.

We didn't know the results of our efforts—until Sarah's report on her reunion. Excited, she updated us on a boy we'd known well. It turned out that he'd accepted Christ as Savior, married a Christian girl, and was "on fire" for the Lord. He told Sarah how he'd been affected by his visits to the Parshall Home for Wandering Teenagers; the seeds of the gospel had been planted during our late-night chats.

Later, when we told our son Samuel the story, he said, "Oh, I remember that! I remember the two of you talking about Christ with him in the living room, along with Sarah and Rebekah, while I was sitting and listening on the staircase." After a pause, he added, "You guys were always doing that kind of stuff with all of our friends. You were really great that way."

For a parent, there is no golden trophy, no Olympic medal, that could match the reward that comes in that kind of moment.

Like all parents, we're tempted to dwell on the things we wish we hadn't done when our kids were growing up—and the things we should have done, but didn't. In fact, we were in one of those moods when Sarah told us her story.

But that story, like John Bunyan's, gives us hope.

When we look at the world our children will face in the coming decade, with its physical dangers and cultural traps, it would be easy to let fear overpower us. Instead, God calls all of us pilgrims to be grounded in faith. He will guide us, and our children, as we make this most important of journeys.

When we follow Christ and guide our precious kids to do the same, our story will end at no less a place than the glittering streets of heaven.

Like *Pilgrim's Progress*, that's one adventure that can truly conclude with these time-honored words: "And they all lived happily ever after."

Notes

Chapter 2

1. George Barna, *Real Teens: A Contemporary Snapshot of Youth Culture* (Ventura, Calif.: Regal Books, 2001), p. 121.
2. Ibid., pp. 85-86.
3. Ibid., p. 123.
4. Barna Research Group, news release, November 15, 1999, p. 1.
5. Rick Osborne and Marnie Wooding, *God's Great News for Children* (Wheaton, Ill.: Tyndale House Publishers, 2002), p. 5.
6. *Focus on the Family Parents' Guide to the Spiritual Growth of Children*, John Trent, Rick Osborne, and Kurt Bruner, eds. (Wheaton, Ill.: Tyndale House Publishers, 2000), p. 302.
7. Osborne and Wooding, *God's Great News for Children*, pp. 5-6.
8. Ibid., p. 17.
9. Ibid., pp. 17-18.
10. Ibid., p. 108.

Chapter 3

1. Stan Campbell and Randy Southern, *Mind over Media* (Wheaton, Ill.: Tyndale House Publishers, 2001), pp. 18, 74.
2. *Mind over Media* video (Wheaton, Ill.: Tyndale House Publishers, 2001), interview with Lucas Salmon.
3. "Teens Opt for Virtual Reality Without Insects, Study Finds," *Washington Times*, February 5, 2001, p. A-2.
4. James Dobson, *Parenting Isn't for Cowards* (Dallas, Tex.: Word Publishing, 1987), pp. 228-229.

Chapter 4

1. Barna Research Group, news release, October 23, 2000, p. 2.

2. Josh McDowell and Bob Hostetler, *Right from Wrong* (Dallas, Tex.: Word Publishing, 1994), p. 306.

3. Norman Geisler and Ron Brooks, *When Skeptics Ask: A Handbook of Christian Evidences* (Grand Rapids, Mich.: Baker Book House, 1995).

Chapter 5

1. *George Washington: Writings* (New York: Literary Classics of the United States, Inc., 1997), p. 971.

Chapter 7

1. Tom W. Smith, *The Emerging 21st Century American Family,* National Opinion Research Center, University of Chicago (November 24, 1999), table 17.

2. Larry Bumpass and Hsien-Hen Lu, "Cohabitation: How the Families of U.S. Children Are Changing," University of Wisconsin-Madison, Institute for Research on Poverty, *Focus,* vol. 21, no. 1 (spring 2000), pp. 5-6.

3. Smith, *The Emerging 21st Century American Family,* table 10.

Chapter 8

1. Thomas Hine, *The Rise and Fall of the American Teenager* (New York: Avon Books, 1999), p. 277.

2. John Duckworth and Mike Yaconelli, *Going Against the Flow* (Elgin, Ill.: David C. Cook Publishing Co., 1994), p. 9.

3. Ibid., p. 54.

Chapter 9

1. *New International Dictionary of New Testament Theology,* vol. I, Colin Brown, ed. (Grand Rapids, Mich.: Zondervan Publishing House, 1981), p. 458.

2. William J. Bennett, *The Index of Cultural Indicators* (New York: Broadway Books, 1999), p. 87.

3. *The Trends Journal,* vol. X, no. 1 (winter 2001), p. 4.

4. Saul Alinsky, *Rules for Radicals* (New York: Vintage Books, 1971), title page.

5. Stephen Carter, *Civility: Manners, Morals, and the Etiquette of Democracy* (New York: Basic Books, 1998).

Chapter 10

1. Josh McDowell and Bob Hostetler, *Right from Wrong: What You Need to Know to Help Youth Make Right Choices* (Dallas, Tex.: Word Publishing, 1994), p. 265.
2. Barna Research Group, news release, December 12, 2000.
3. McDowell and Hostetler, *Right from Wrong*, p. 20.
4. Francis A. Schaeffer, *The God Who Is There* (Chicago: InterVarsity Press, 1968), p. 143.
5. Randy Petersen, *My Truth, Your Truth, Whose Truth?* (Wheaton, Ill.: Tyndale House Publishers, 2000), pp. 43-44.
6. Ibid., pp. 141-143.
7. Ibid., pp. 82-83.
8. Ibid., pp. 145-146.
9. Ibid., pp. 136-137.

Chapter 11

1. Neelesh Misra, "Missionary Mourned in India," Associated Press, January 24, 1999.
2. Jeff Taylor, "Christian Remains Jailed in Brunei," *Compass Direct*, April 20, 2001, p. 19.
3. Paul Davenport, "Martyrdom of Liu Haitao Confirmed in China," *Compass Direct*, April 20, 2001, pp. 20-22.

Chapter 12

1. Pacific Justice Institute, Newsletter, May 31, 2001.
2. Emily Rahe, "Hymns for Her? Methodist Supplement's Feminist Lyrics Rapped," *Washington Times*, July 24, 2001, p. A2.
3. Josh McDowell and Bob Hostetler, *The New Tolerance: How a Cultural Movement Threatens to Destroy You, Your Faith, and Your Children* (Wheaton, Ill.: Tyndale House Publishers, 1998), pp. 15-19.
4. Petersen, *My Truth, Your Truth, Whose Truth?*, pp. 148-149.
5. Ibid., pp. 135-136.
6. Ibid., pp. 128-129.

Chapter 13

1. Jonathan Eig, "Edible Entertainment: Food Companies Grab Kids by Fancifully Packaging Products as Toys, Games," *Wall Street Journal*, October 24, 2001, p. B1.
2. Christine Dugas, "Teens Need Some Training Wheels," USAToday.com, August 18, 2000.
3. "Maxed Out!" *Newsweek*, August 27, 2001, pp. 34-36.

Chapter 14

1. Daniel Okrent, "Raising Kids Online: What Can Parents Do?" *Time*, May 10, 1999, p. 41.
2. Barbara Kantrowitz and Pat Wingert, "How Well Do You Know Your Kid?" *Newsweek*, May 10, 1999, p. 39.
3. Robert Kraut and Vicki Lundmark, Michael Patterson and Sara Kiesler, Tridas Mukopadhyay, and William Scherlis, "Internet Paradox: A Social Technology that Reduces Social Involvement and Psychological Well-Being?" *Quality of Life 2000: The New Politics of Work, Family, and Community* (New York: Demos, 2000), p. 145.
4. George Barna and Mark Hatch, *Boiling Point: It Only Takes One Degree: Monitoring Cultural Shifts in the 21st Century* (Ventura, Calif.: Regal, 2001), p. 114.
5. Barna Research Online, "Practical Outcomes Replace Biblical Principles as the Moral Standard," news release, September 10, 2001.
6. John Naisbitt, Nana Naisbitt, and Douglas Philips, *High Tech, High Touch* (New York: Broadway Books, 1999), p. 5.
7. McDowell and Hostetler, *Right from Wrong*, pp. 19-20.
8. Miles J. Stanford, *Principles of Spiritual Growth* (Lincoln, Neb.: Back to the Bible Publications, 1966), p. 14.
9. Kantrowitz and Wingert, "How Well Do You Know Your Kid?", p. 39.
10. Charles R. Swindoll, *Growing Wise in Family Life* (Portland, Ore.: Multnomah Press, 1988), p. 63.

Chapter 15

1. James Dobson, *Bringing Up Boys* (Wheaton, Ill.: Tyndale House Publishers, 2001), p. 40.

2. "Suicide and Suicide Attempts in Adolescents," *Pediatrics*, vol. 105, no. 4 (April, 2000), pp. 871-874.
3. Kantrowitz and Wingert, "How Well Do You Know Your Kid?" p. 40.
4. Archibald Hart, *Dark Clouds, Silver Linings* (Colorado Springs, Colo.: Focus on the Family Publishing, 1993), pp. 2-3.
5. Ibid., p. 19.
6. Ibid., p. 75.
7. Ibid., p. 60.
8. Ibid., pp. 67-68.

Chapter 16

1. Aristotle, Metaphysics, Book I. *The Pocket Aristotle*, Justin Kaplan, ed. (New York: Washington Square Press, 1970), pp. 108-110.
2. For an introduction to secular humanism, see: David A. Noebel, *Understanding the Times: The Religious Worldviews of Our Day and the Search for Truth* (Eugene, Ore.: Harvest House Publishers, 1991), pp. 51-65.
3. B. G. Brander, *Staring into Chaos: Explorations in the Decline of Western Civilization* (Dallas, Tex.: Spence Publishing, 1998), pp. 45-46.
4. There is an extensive body of literature that soundly refutes Darwin's theory. A sample includes: Michael J. Behe's *Darwin's Black Box: The Biochemical Challenge to Evolution* (New York: Touchstone Books, 1998); and *The Face That Demonstrates the Farce of Evolution*, by Hank Hanegraaff (Dallas, Tex.: Word Publishing, 2001).
5. Robert Wright, *The Moral Animal: The New Science of Evolutionary Psychology* (New York: Vintage Books, 1994), pp. 348-352.
6. Pascal Boyer, *Religion Explained: The Evolutionary Origins of Religious Thought* (New York: Basic Books, 2001), pp. 326-328.
7. Barry St. Clair and Carol St. Clair, *Ignite the Fire* (Colorado Springs, Colo.: Victor, 1999), p. 74.

Chapter 17

1. Jerry Adler, "Far from Home," *Newsweek*, April 7, 1997, pp. 38-39.
2. Ibid., p. 32.
3. Tom Kenworthy, "Relatives Left in Dark about Kin Who Joined Christian Cult Leader," *Washington Post*, January 8, 1999, p. A3.

4. Stanislav Grof, Ervin Laszlo, and Peter Russell, *The Consciousness Revolution* (Boston: Element Books, 1999), pp. 29, 35.

5. Deepak Chopra, *How to Know God* (New York: Harmony Books, 2001), pp. 267-297.

6. Neale Donald Walsch, *Friendship with God: An Uncommon Dialogue* (New York: G. P. Putnam's Sons, 1999), pp. 115-116.

7. Philip G. Davis, *Goddess Unmasked: The Rise of Neopagan Feminist Spirituality* (Dallas, Tex.: Spence Publishing, 1998), p. 28.

8. George Barna and Mark Hatch, *Boiling Point: It Only Takes One Degree* (Ventura, Calif.: Regal Books, 2001), p. 187.

9. Gerald R. McDermott, *Can Evangelicals Learn from World Religions?* (Downers Grove, Ill.: InterVarsity Press, 2000), pp. 153, 159.

10. Michael Youssef, *Know Your Real Enemy* (Nashville: Thomas Nelson Publishers, 1997), p. 104.

11. Joe White, *FaithTraining* (Wheaton, Ill.: Tyndale House Publishers, 1994), pp. 212-213.

12. Stephen Arterburn and Jack Felton, *Toxic Faith* (Wheaton, Ill.: Harold Shaw Publishers, 2001), pp. 20-21.

13. White, *FaithTraining*, pp. 111-129.

14. Stephen Arterburn and Jim Burns, *Steering Them Straight* (Colorado Springs, Colo.: Focus on the Family Publishing, 1995), pp. 194-195.

Chapter 18

1. American Atheists, Inc., "A Statement of Principles, Re: Proposed Religious Freedom Amendment (H.J. RES. 78) to the Constitution of the United States," as submitted to the Committee on the Judiciary, U.S. House of Representatives, July 22, 1997.

2. Marc Gunther, "God & Business," *Fortune*, July 16, 2001, p. 61.

3. Jacques Attali, "How Hollywood Rules," *Civilization* (February/March 2000), p. 64.

4. George Barna, *Re-Churching the Unchurched* (Ventura, Calif: Issachar Resources, 2000), pp. 68-69.

5. Ibid., p. 74.

6. Charles C. Ryrie, *Basic Theology* (Wheaton, Ill.: Victor Books, 1986), p. 29.

7. Ravi Zacharias, *Deliver Us from Evil: Restoring the Soul in a Disintegrating Culture* (Dallas, Tex.: Word Publishing, 1996), p. 159.

Chapter 19

1. C. S. Lewis, *A Grief Observed* (New York: Bantam Books, 1961), p. 5.
2. Thomas Hyden, "The Year We Control Our Destiny," *Newsweek*, December 1999–February 2000 (Special Edition), p. 90.
3. Found online at www.aarp.org/mmaturity/sept-oct00/finalanswers.html.
4. The Project on Death in America, press release, May 27, 1998.
5. George Soros, "Reflections on Death in America," a speech delivered on November 30, 1994, for the Alexander Ming Fisher Lecture Series at Columbia Presbyterian Medical Center; found online at www.soros.org/death.
6. *Veritas*, Dallas Theological Seminary, vol. I, no. 1 (July 2001), page 6; interview with Dr. Howard Hendricks.

FOCUS ON THE FAMILY®

Welcome to the Family!

Whether you received this book as a gift, borrowed it, or purchased it yourself, we're glad you read it. It's just one of the many helpful, insightful, and encouraging resources produced by Focus on the Family.

In fact, that's what Focus on the Family is all about—providing inspiration, information, and biblically based advice to people in all stages of life.

It began in 1977 with the vision of one man, Dr. James Dobson, a licensed psychologist and author of 18 best-selling books on marriage, parenting, and family. Alarmed by the societal, political, and economic pressures that were threatening the existence of the American family, Dr. Dobson founded Focus on the Family with one employee and a once-a-week radio broadcast aired on only 36 stations.

Now an international organization, the ministry is dedicated to preserving Judeo-Christian values and strengthening and encouraging families through the life-changing message of Jesus Christ. Focus ministries reach families worldwide through 10 separate radio broadcasts, two television news features, 13 publications, 18 Web sites, and a steady series of books and award-winning films and videos for people of all ages and interests.

•   •   •

For more information about the ministry, or if we can be of help to your family, simply write to Focus on the Family, Colorado Springs, CO 80995 or call 1-800-A-FAMILY (1-800-232-6459). Friends in Canada may write Focus on the Family, PO Box 9800, Stn Terminal, Vancouver, BC V6B 4G3 or call 1-800-661-9800. Visit our Web site—www.family.org—to learn more about Focus on the Family or to find out if there is an associate office in your country.

We'd love to hear from you!

Powerful, Positive Resources to Keep Your Family Strong

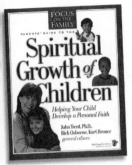

Parents' Guide to the Spiritual Growth of Children
Passing on a foundation of faith to your children is an awesome responsibility. Now, the job is easier–thanks to this guide from Heritage Builders. Co-edited by best-selling author John Trent, Rick Osborne and Kurt Bruner, it's a simple, practical and comprehensive tool for developing your child's Christian values from birth to age 12. Softcover.

The Mom You're Meant to Be
Motherhood is meant to be a blessing, not a burden. So why do so many moms seem exhausted and frustrated? The author encourages moms to forget the formulas and rely on God for the wisdom they need. Her message gets to the essence of the role God has called moms to, and will reawaken them to the miraculous gift they've been given. Hardcover.

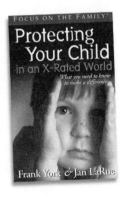

Protecting Your Child in an X-Rated World
Pornography is invading homes, libraries and schools—and your children are in its path. But you can take protective measures! Learn what and where the threats are, practical tips for prevention and intervention and discussion points to use with your kids. Yes, pornography is a serious challenge–but with the valuable information in this book, you'll be ready to do all you can to protect your children's minds, hearts and souls. Paperback.